WALTER GROPIUS

WALTER GROPIUS

Sigfried Giedion

DOVER PUBLICATIONS, INC.
New York

This Dover edition, first published in 1992, is an unabridged and unaltered republica-
tion of the work originally published under the title *Walter Gropius: Work and Teamwork* by
the Reinhold Publishing Corporation, New York, 1954. The English-language version is a
translation of the work published in the same year by Max E. Neuenschwander, Switzerland, and sponsored by the Andrea & Virginia Matarazzo Foundation, São Paulo, Brazil.

Manufactured in the United States of America
Dover Publications, Inc., 31 East 2nd Street, Mineola, N.Y. 11501

Library of Congress Cataloging-in-Publication Data

Giedion, S. (Sigfried), 1888–1968.
   [Walter Gropius, work and teamwork]
   Walter Gropius / Sigfried Giedion.
         p.   cm.
   Originally published: Walter Gropius, work and teamwork. New York : Reinhold Pub.
Co., 1954.
   Includes bibliographical references and index.
   ISBN 0-486-27118-8 (pbk.)
   1. Gropius, Walter, 1883–1969—Criticism and interpretation.   I. Title.
NA1088.G85G52   1992
700′.89′96073—dc20   91-41978
                                                                              CIP

PREFACE

São Paulo, November, 1951. After a morning's work in the First Biennial Exhibition, the three foreign members of the Judging Committee – Mario Pani (Mexico), Sakkakura (Japan) and myself – had lunch in the hospitable home of Mr. and Mrs. Francisco Matarazzo. While we were talking of our work on the jury, the suggestion came up that it would be a good idea if there could be a sort of Nobel Prize for architecture, because at present the general public certainly does not see architecture in the same light as painting, sculpture or literature. Next day Mr. Matarazzo told me: "I have been thinking over that suggestion. We should set up a *Grand Prix d'Architecture de São Paulo.*" The final task of the Judging Committee, which included two Brazilians, Kneese de Mello and Francisco Beck, was to draw up proposals for the Second International Exhibition. These were later incorporated almost unaltered into the regulations for the Second *Bienale.* To awaken interest in the work of the younger generation of architects, we proposed that another prize should be allotted for the work of an architect under 35; and to get some insight into the comparative standards of the teaching of architecture, we proposed yet another prize for the school or university that produced the best work on a set theme: in this case a small town center.

The *Grand Prix d'Architecture* was quite distinct from all the other prizes, being independently endowed and administered. At our request, Prof. Paulo E. de Berrêdo Carneiro, the Brazilian delegate to UNESCO, provided the following more detailed description of it:

"The Andréa and Virginia Matarazzo Foundation, created in São Paulo, in 1949, has established a 300,000 cruzeiros international prize for architecture, to be awarded every two years to the architect whose work may be considered to have played a highly important role in the development of contemporary architecture.

"Under the name of" *São Paulo Prize*' this award will be granted for the first time in January 1954. The jury – including the architects Alvar Aalto, José Luis Sert, Le Corbusier, Ernesto Rogers, Max Bill, Alfonso Eduardo Reidy, G. Warchavchik and a representative of the Council of the Andréa and Virginia Matarazzo Foundation – has selected the great architect Walter Gropius.

"The Andréa and Virginia Matarazzo Foundation has invited all the foreign members of the jury to visit São Paulo in January 1954, so that they may be present at the official presentation of the prize to Mr. Walter Gropius. This ceremony will be held under the auspices of the Commission of the 4th Centenary of the City of São Paulo.

"An exhibition of the complete works of Walter Gropius will be displayed on this occasion."

In February 1953, Prof. de Carneiro asked me in Paris whether I could not use this opportunity to write a book on Walter Gropius. The proposal took me by surprise. I was in the midst of a study in quite a different field, which I could only interrupt with great difficulty. But, after a few days of reflection, I consented, and some weeks later I flew to the United States to go through the material with Walter Gropius himself at Lincoln. Outside the windows fluttered the birds of New England; inside the floor was soon littered with a flock of white papers. There, together, we decided on the first layout of the book, though I had complete freedom in the selection of material. Without the help of Ise and Walter Gropius, who prepared the biographical data, list of works, bibliography and many of the captions, the book could certainly not have been prepared so quickly.

This book is in many ways incomplete. It pretends to be no more than an account by a contemporary of the beginning of modern architecture in Germany, but it provides an opportunity to recall that many things nowadays taken for granted were only brought to birth with great difficulty and by deep personal devotion after defeats, suspicion and threats.

I am deeply indebted to Jaqueline Tyrwhitt for the English equivalent of the original text, and, finally, I would like to express my thanks to Max E. Neuenschwander, whose untiring perseverance has made it possible to bring this book out simultaneously in several languages and not to forget the careful handling of the different editions by the printer the Buchdruckerei Union AG., Solothurn.

ZÜRICH, DOLDERTAL,   S. GIEDION
January 1954.

CONTENTS

1883	Born, Berlin, May 18th.
1903–07	Student of Architecture, Berlin Hochschule and Munich Hochschule.
1907–10	Chief Assistant to Peter Behrens, Berlin.
1910	Set up architectural practice in Berlin.
1918	Director of School of Arts & Crafts and Academy of Arts, Weimar. Amalgamated the two under the name "*Staatliches Bauhaus*" (State Building Institute), Weimar.
1926	Continued as Director to the same school after its move to Dessau (Anhalt), now under the name "Bauhaus, Dessau". Appointed Professor by the Anhalt Authorities.
1928	Moved to Berlin. Resumed private practice.
1929	Honorary Doctor of the Technical Hochschule Hannover.
	Member of the Expert Committee of the Government Research Institute for the Building Industry.
	Vice-President of the International Congresses for Modern Architecture (CIAM).
1934–37	London. Partnership with Maxwell Fry, F.R.I.B.A.
1937	Professor of Architecture at the Graduate School of Design, Harvard University, Mass., USA.
1937	Honorary Member of the Royal Institute of British Architects.
	Vice-President of the Institute of Sociology, London.
1938	Chairman of the Department of Architecture, Graduate School of Design, Harvard University.
	Member of the American Institute of Architects.
1942	Honorary M.A., Harvard University.
	Honorary Member of Phi Beta Kappa (Harvard Chapter).
1944	Fellow, American Academy of Arts & Sciences.
1945	Consultant Architect to the Container Corporation of America.
	Consultant Architect to the Michael Reese Hospital, Chicago.
1946	Founder and Member of "The Architects' Collaborative" (TAC).
1947	Awarded honorary title "Royal Designer for Industry" (RDI) by the Royal Society of Arts, London.
	Member at large of the National Education Commission of the American Institute of Architects.
1949	Honorary Fellow of the Society of Industrial Artists, London.
1951	Honorary Doctor of Science, Western Reserve University, Cleveland, Ohio.
	Foreign Corresponding Member Institut d'Esthétique Industrielle, Paris.
	Gold Medal of Honor, The Architectural League of New York.
1952	Professor Emeritus, Harvard University.
	Honorary Member, Cercle d'Etudes Architecturales, Paris.
1953	Member of the Visiting Committee, School of Architecture & Town Planning, Massachusetts Institute of Technology.
	Honorary Doctor of Architecture, North Carolina State College.
	Honorary Doctor of Art, Harvard University.
1954	"Grand Prix d'Architecture", São Paulo, Brazil.
	Honorary Professor, Escuela Nacional de Ingenieros, Lima, Peru.
	Fellow, American Institute of Architects.

BACKGROUND

The achievements of a creative man reach out far beyond the bounds of his national background and environment. They soar like mountain peaks above the narrow confines of his immediate setting and become part of a world panorama. The scale changes.

This is as true of the work of a scientist as of the work of an artist. As soon as it leaves the world of the not-yet-known for the world of the unknown, it departs from the country of its origin and enters into a wider sphere – the realm of human wisdom.

Nevertheless such work cannot exist in a void. Its specific nature, its scope and its limitations are all to a large extent determined by its immediate environment.

This book, therefore, which deals with the work of a pioneer of contemporary architecture, must first touch on his national *background*, his *heritage* and family circle before embarking upon a discussion of his creative work.

The history of every country consists of a sequence of disasters and achievements interspersed with periods of lethargy. But there are differences in the time-scale of these changes. Only in the East are there civilizations still existing whose roots reach back into pre-history. European civilizations seem to have a shorter breathing span than those of Asia, and hardly any European country has been subject to so rapid a sequence of disasters and successes as Germany – wedged in as it is between East and West.

Germany's high culture of the late medieval period was followed by a slow decline. In the seventeenth century the Thirty Years' War wrecked her material and political potential for more than a century. In the late eighteenth century, during a period of political impotence, classic German literature was produced in the small princely courts. In the early nineteenth century, a thin layer of highly cultivated individuals began to produce Romantic music and poetry, at a time when Germany as a whole was pervaded by a depressing political reaction which expressed itself in bitter opposition to economic freedom in the development of commerce and industry.

Germany in the Nineteenth Century

In France freedom of enterprise in manufacturing had been instituted at the time of the Revolution, 1798; but in Prussia it was not permitted until 1846, and in Baden, Würtemberg and Bayern not until 1862. By the early nineteenth century England was already in the throes of an industrial crisis caused by the sudden change-over from small cottage industries to factory production; and by 1840 the handloom weaving industry in France

5

was reported to be in a final flicker of agony[1]. But in Germany the period between 1816 and 1843, which saw the flowering of its Romantic music and literature, also witnessed an ever-increasing proportion of the population engaged in handicrafts[2]. Not only this, but the number of employers increased in proportion to employees: a clear indication of a growing number of smaller businesses. The expanding population of Germany was finding its outlet in cottage industry rather than in factory employment. This situation only began to alter in 1860[3], but even in 1865 the textile industry of the German Zollverein (all the German States that had linked themselves together in a common customs union) had only some 219 thousand spindles as against 600 thousand in France and 1781 thousand in Great Britain[4]. The position was similar in other fields, including shipbuilding and railways which, as W. Sombart puts it, "entered upon the crutches of English industry".

The victory of 1870 precipitated a flood of industrialization: Germany changed overnight into a highly industrialized country and in a few decades rivaled France and even England. A new period of prosperity was ushered in, such as she had not known since the heyday of her late medieval cities.

Fig. 28 ff.
This was the period of Walter Gropius' youth. He came from a family of state officials and nothing stood in the way of a successful start in life. When but 28 years old he was able to build the Fagus factory – a *coup de génie* of the new architectural movement.

HERITAGE

Nature pays no respect to race, rank or family. She distributes the qualities that go to make up a creative personality quite irrationally. All of a sudden she endows an individual with powers that far surpass anything possessed by his forbears.

The qualities of the creative individual are, of course, colored by the personalities and walks of life of his parents and grandparents. Indeed some features can only be well understood after a study of his immediate environment. This influences, in part at least, his strength and weakness, his behavior and even his moral attitude.

In the case of Walter Gropius, the influence of his social environment and family background can certainly not be disregarded. This is reflected in the character of his work and also in that friendliness of personality which has contributed greatly to his work and significance.

---

[1] E. Buret, *De la Misère des Classes Laborieuses*, Paris, 1840.
[2] G. Schmoller, *Zur Geschichte der deutschen Kleingewerbe im 19. Jahrhundert*, Halle, 1870, p. 65.
[3] Schmoller, *op. cit.* p. 465.
[4] Schmoller, *op. cit.* p. 468.

His widespread family, which originated in the neighborhood of Braunschweig, possesses records that go back to the 17th century. These depict a pattern of craftsmen and clergy, with ever recurring *"praeceptores"*, teachers. In the generations of the 19th century a strong artistic tendency became evident. There were painters and architects and sometimes, as in the case of Walter Gropius' father, these were combined with an official position; others were connected with industrial enterprise, in which case they showed a marked inclination for experimentation. All in all the family tree includes the mosaic of professions that built up the Germany of the 19th century. At the same time contact with the countryside was never fully severed. This makes it easy to understand how the first commissioned

1. *The parents of Walter Gropius.*

project prepared by the twenty-three-year-old Gropius was for cottages for agricultural workers. Artist, public servant and experimenter are all mingled and reflected in the personality of Walter Gropius. *Fig. 19, 20*

This same combination is apparent in the figure of Carl Wilhelm Gropius (1793–1870). By inclination and temperament he was a painter and, as early as 1822, a member of the Academy, but he was also at the same time a businessman. In the *"Allgemeine Deutsche Biographie"* (vol. 9, 1879), the art historian Dohme states that: "his friendly jokes and quick wit were a feature of the pre-revolutionary Berlin (before 1848) and a large part of the illustrated broadsheets, popular anecdotes and caricatures distributed at that time were based on his sayings." **Carl Wilhelm Gropius**

Carl Wilhelm Gropius was a close friend of Karl Friedrich Schinkel (1781–1841). Schinkel, the finest German architect of the period, brought a new sense of exhilaration into architecture as was admitted by the French art-pontiff Quatremère de Quincy and even by the English. More than any other architect of his time he imbued his buildings with Romantic Classicism, that strange mingling of classical forms with the romantic spirit that was to pervade the whole of the 19th century[1].

---

[1] S. Giedion, *"Spätbarocker und romantischer Klassizismus"*, Munich, 1922.

Schinkel drew and painted passionately, whether at home or on his travels. Like Le Corbusier, painting was a necessary part of his personal fulfilment. And everywhere his basic romanticism breaks through; in his watercolors, his studies for the frescoes of the old Museum of Berlin (his finest building), his brush sketches of architectural fantasies, his lavish decorations for the Berlin Theater and his studies for the colossal paintings of Gropius' diorama.

The Diorama, 1827 The diorama (transparent three-dimensional picture) was a curious phenomenon which without question, arose from the spirit of late Romanticism. Its chief intent was to transplant the observer as dramatically as possible into remote landscapes or remote periods of time. Mont Blanc at sunrise or afterglow, a cathedral shrouded in mist or burning in flames could be conjured up, while the spectator stood in darkness upon a revolving turntable which presented him with each view in turn. An invisible beam of light from a circular aperture high above his head was directly reflected from the transparent screen. All manner of screening devices and color filters were employed.

It was no accident that the first diorama was made by Daguerre (1789–1851), the painter and chemist who also invented photography. He erected this first diorama in Paris in 1822 in a circular hall whose turntable could accommodate 350 viewers. Gropius saw it when on a visit to Paris and, it is said, made some improvements upon it when he built his own diorama in Berlin in 1827, which "was for a long time a center of the artistic life of Berlin"[2]. Even as late as 1870, the *Larousse du XIX* siècle records that the effect of the diorama was magical and arresting. This is not surprising. The aim of the diorama was to enable the romantic public of the period to participate in an actual experience. The effect was similar, though achieved with somewhat primitive means, to that accomplished over 100 years later (1952) by the Cinerama with its complicated methods of pro-

Fig. 141 ff. jection upon a curved screen. The "total theater" of Walter Gropius (designed in 1926 but never built) was based on the same intention.

The architecture of the second half of the 19th century still awaits the winnowing and screening that will sift its really vital creations out from the great mass of its production. When this has been done, several buil-

Martin Gropius dings designed by Martin Gropius (1824–1880), the great–uncle of Walter Gropius, will certainly remain in the select category, such as for instance the Museum of Arts and Crafts, Berlin. Martin Gropius' father was a manufacturer of damask tapestry who had exhibited at the first International Exhibition (London, 1851), and the house was a rendezvous of the Berlin art world. Among the most frequent visitors was K. F. Schinkel. He strongly influenced Martin Gropius who carried his tradition through to the middle of the 19th century. Martin Gropius was closely connected with the Arts and Crafts Reform Movement. In the seventies, following the example of Henry Cole's circle in London, he published a collection of selected decorative patterns *(Archiv für ornamentale Kunst)*. In 1867 he became Principal of the Arts and Crafts School in Berlin and Director of art education for the whole of Prussia. This gave him an opportunity to raise the standard of design, at least as far as this was understood

---

[2] Thieme-Becker, *Allg. Lexikon der Bildenden Künstler*, Vol. XV, 1922.

8

at that period. As is apparent in a cartoon published in a Berlin paper around 1850[3], Martin Gropius had some of the same delight in experimenting with new materials that later came out so strongly in Walter Gropius.

The quiet and introspective father of Walter Gropius was also an architect, who rose to a high position as a state official. He greatly preferred to live in the country where his wife's family had many connections. The childhood of Walter Gropius, therefore, oscillated between a gaslit apartment in Berlin and close contact with his native soil.

PERSONALITY

It is not difficult to find traces of his heritage in the development of Walter Gropius himself: the educators and preachers and, in the latter part of the 19th century, the pull towards industry and the fondness for experiment. Among them had been many who did not confine their activity to one profession but who also struck out into other fields. Carl Wilhelm Gropius combined work on his diorama, 1827, with his interest in art publications and, around the two activities, formed one of the social gathering places of Berlin. Martin Gropius, the architect, was at the same time interested in art education, over which he exerted a decisive influence. The public servant, always represented somewhere within the family, is also reflected again in Walter Gropius.

This mosaic of professions was only of secondary importance; for it is a sign of all true talent that it must shake itself free from its environment and – in a way that defies explanation – make a metaphysical leap into the unknown.

In this case there was also something else: in contrast to the middle-class stability which enveloped the lives of the former generations, the generation of Walter Gropius was at least twice whirled around in the dance of Fate without losing its power to fight back.

A brilliant boyhood, a brilliant start in life: the road lay clear ahead, the future seemed within his grasp. Then suddenly came four years of war, in which Gropius played his part. As an officer he invented a special signaling system. He was not stationed behind the front lines, but he does not speak of his experiences. Only once, after a party at which a well-known painter had been giving colorful descriptions of his adventures in a French internment camp, Gropius mentioned casually when leaving that he had been shot down when an observer in a plane. It afterwards came out that the pilot next to him had been killed.

1914–1918

---

[3] Cf., " *Mechanization Takes Command* ", Oxford University Press, New York, 1948, p. 381, fig. 226.

Fig. 76, 82–93

1919 and the building up of a new existence: years fully occupied with the Bauhaus and with battling against an increasingly aggressive nationalistic movement. In the midst of his struggle to develop a new method of artistic education and to hold it against attack, he built the Bauhaus at Dessau, 1925–26, his second stroke of genius. In 1928 Gropius and his closest friends resigned. Immediately afterwards came a first visit of several months to the United States, which left a deep impression. On his way home he wrote (21st June, 1928) that he could not attend the meeting at La Sarraz to found the International Congresses of Modern Architecture (CIAM = Congrès Internationaux d'Architecture Moderne) as "I must first go back to Berlin and find a new field of work". Berlin, 1928–34, was the period of his most

2. *Walter Gropius*
at the Bauhaus.

intensive activity in urban planning, intermixed with struggles against the rising tide of Nazidom. Despite undoubted successes many schemes remained on paper. It was time to leave for England.

England, 1934–37

A few year's break in England and then it might be possible to return. John Pritchard invited Gropius to stay in the newly completed Lawn Road Flats, the first modern block of apartments in London, designed by Wells Coates. While in England Gropius worked in friendly partnership with Maxwell Fry. They built several private houses, but by far the most important building

Fig. 94–98

of his English period was a school, Impington College, 1936, which both in its program and architectonic development set a new standard. There were other plans, such as for Christ's College, Cambridge, and for some apartment

Fig. 261–263

blocks in an old park near Windsor, that were never carried out. England at that time was undecided in her attitude towards modern architecture. This was not surprising for, during the time that Holland, Germany and France had been in the forefront of the modern architecture movement in Europe, Great Britain had lain wrapped in slumber.

In 1937 Gropius decided to go to America and, at his farewell dinner presided over by H. G. Wells, it became clear that those who led the cultural life of the country had realized whom they had among them. This was expressed when Herbert Read said: "Gropius belongs to the whole world."

Harvard
1937–1953

Joseph Hudnut, Dean of the School of Architecture, Harvard University and, soon afterwards, James B. Conant, President of the University, had come over to England to meet Gropius face to face. They were about to make a most responsible move. Architectural education at Harvard, as in other American universities, had lain under the spell of the *Ecole des Beaux Arts*. Now suddenly it had been decided to leap the intervening steps and to entrust it to really creative hands. On contact with the President mutual confidence was immediately established.

This was the start of an unusually productive period in which Gropius was able to develop to the full as an architectural educator. The situation was entirely different from two decades earlier in Dessau. He was no longer perpetually harassed by problems of the financial support of the school nor was he continually threatened by ill will from outside. At last he could teach in peace. On the other hand, as in all large institutions, it was not possible suddenly to change everything from top to bottom, nor to engage a new staff at will. As with any Chairman of a School of Architecture, his hands were sometimes tied. His inspiring activity spread wide over Harvard University, changing many standards. It is not that his teaching gave rise to a number of imitators. His innate quality of deep respect for the viewpoint of others and his great patience in assisting their development stood in the way of this. No teacher can prevent those who have no backbone of their own from becoming mere copyists, but no one with spirit has ever had his wings singed by Walter Gropius. The architectural development of Paul Rudolph[1] and I. Ming Pei, to name but two, can bear witness to this. The theme of his teaching has ever been "*In an age of specialization, method is more important than information*".

Theme of his
Teaching

The influence of his teaching is described by one of his former students in a special number of *Architecture d'Aujourd'hui*: "*Walter Gropius et son Ecole*", February, 1950, as follows: "Gropius was the first man who interpreted the industrial revolution to us in terms of architecture, in terms of design, in terms of community planning. He constantly investigated the great potentialities of industrial society and showed us how to assimilate them to our ever-changing needs ... looking back over the last twelve years, we, who have been Gropius' students, can say gratefully that he has shown us a place in society; that he has taught us that mechanization and individual freedom are not incompatible; that he has explained to us the possibilities and values of communal action and... I shall always doubt that a lesser human being could have given us that new faith in our world."

Contact with other
Disciplines

In his first small program for the Bauhaus, 1919, Gropius had set forth the need for teamwork between architect, painter and sculptor. This he reinterpreted at Harvard by an integration of the teaching of architecture, town planning and landscape architecture, and from that to a close contact with other disciplines. The purpose was to widen the outlook of the students from the beginning and to develop their ability to work later together with specialists from other faculties as members of the same team.

---

[1] São Paulo Prize 1954 for an architect old less than 35 years.

Obviously one of the first considerations in this respect was to make sure that the different years of student life did not exist entirely independently from one another, as is so often the case. In the summer term of 1950, when I was working at the Massachusetts Institute of Technology, I was invited to act as critic for a Museum project undertaken by one of the lower years at Harvard. This program had been based on the project for a Civic Center carried out by the Master's Class in the previous year.

The future requires an inter-penetration of the teaching of disciplines. Those who try to practise this at present run up against the dominating isolationist mentality of the specialist. This Gropius also found.

As a University Professor, Gropius had to work rather differently from when in the Bauhaus to bring out the desire for integration that lies dormant in so many of us. But the present structure of Universities cannot be altered at the first assault, and a patience is needed that exceeds the active life of one man. Gropius' successor, J. L. Sert, who also holds the post of Dean of the School of Architecture, must now tackle the next step...

Building in the U.S.A.

Fig. 103–105

Fig. 297–303

Gropius had first to overcome a strong American prejudice against 'school teachers'. So he began by building his own house. Many other houses followed. The fine project that he developed with Breuer for the Wheaton College Art Center, 1937, was too early and could not be carried through. In 1941 he received his first official job, the housing scheme for New Kensington. In 1945 he went into partnership with a group of the youngest generation of architects. His name however did not appear; it was hidden behind the title of the firm "The Architects' Collaborative". Housing projects and schools began to go up. Large schemes came forward for Chicago, Washington and, in 1953, the plan for Boston Center. At seventy his plans are more far-reaching than ever, and the world looks kindly upon him.

At a Christmas dinner in San Francisco, 1953, F. L. Wright stated "Youth is a quality, not a matter of circumstances". This is certainly true of Walter Gropius, as well as others of his generation.

Intellectual Structure

Personality

There is a curious intermingling in the personality of Walter Gropius. On one hand he is governed by sternly disciplined rational thinking, on the other he has an instinct for the line of future development that far transcends the logic of the moment. His actions repeatedly reflect his firmly held conviction that people can be persuaded by reason to adopt solutions that have not yet been accepted by their inner feelings.

In the course of this book it will become evident how again and again Gropius laboriously works out problems, whose solution he has instinctively perceived in advance, by means of painfully exact calculations.

His work is grounded upon the philosophy of a universal approach to the world. It is natural to him to set all problems in their wider context. This leads him to penetrate to the roots of many matters far removed from architecture. The humanist basis of his teaching is no veneer but an integral

12

part of his being. Gropius is one of the few architects who reads widely, thus continually enriching his mind by contact with other spheres of thought. All this gives him a measure of natural authority and emanating power possessed by very few.

The distinctive quality of his work is its instinctive and cogitative relation to forthcoming development. This is always apparent in his approach to any problem.

When a young man, in 1909, long before any realization was thinkable, Gropius was busying himself with the two-edged problem of the prefabricated house; and he realized even then that the mass production of entire houses could never be satisfactorily solved. Only the standardization of component parts could "satisfy the public desire for a home with an individual appearance" (Walter Gropius, 1909).

Gropius was the first to grasp the significance of transparency in contemporary architecture; which was given its first architectonic expression in his Fagus factory, 1911.

In the Bauhaus, 1925–26, he developed the organization of large volumes in space.

The formulation of the slab apartment block, meticulously calculated in 1928–29, heralded the appearance of a new type of dwelling. This was tied up with the coming development of the neighborhood unit, the habitat in which the individual dwelling is not an isolated cell but part of a complex whole oriented towards the development of collective activity and social life.

The plastic possibilities of the high-rise apartment slab enter into the formulation of the looser structure of the new city. This new image of the city grew ever clearer during the Harvard years and was given expression in the fine studies made by the Harvard students, 1942, for a city of 30,000 inhabitants.

During this period general development has been rapidly catching up with the forerunners. The main stream has now broadened. This is nowhere more evident that in the cooperative scheme for Boston Center, 1953, which would have been impossible of realization a few years ago: the reservation of a pedestrian area in the heart of the city, from which all cars are banned, just for the undisturbed enjoyment of the people.

Teamwork

The idea of *teamwork* is part of Gropius' very nature as well as of his actions. His faith in the value of teamwork – of human cooperative effort – has stood unshaken throughout his life. It means much more to him than a simple addition of human forces, it means a way towards a higher level of performance.

On the cover page of the four-page program that he published in 1919 as Director of the Bauhaus is a woodcut by Lyonel Feininger: a cathedral over *Fig. 12* whose three towers hover three stars. Their rays become stronger as they interpenetrate one another. On the following page stands the slogan: "Together we Desire, we Design and we Create the New Building in which Architecture, Painting and Sculpture are One Complete Unity..."

Under the name of "The Architects Collaborative" his own name has become absorbed within the team. Like almost all architects, Gropius has done much of his work with partners and associates. The first was Adolph Meyer with whom he worked until he moved to Dessau; in England he worked in partnership with Maxwell Fry and in America with Marcel Breuer. All the same one cannot forget that on such an important building as the Bauhaus and on most of his urban studies around 1928 Gropius worked alone.

Regard for Fellow Creatures Walter Gropius' attitude towards teamwork springs from his attitude towards his fellow men. He possesses a gift rarely owned by creative people: he is not enclosed within his own productive life as within a block of ice. He can give ungrudging recognition to the work of others. He is sincerely interested in the achievements of his fellows and spares neither time nor effort to stand up for them and their work.

The UNESCO Building A recent event will illustrate this: his Chairmanship of the Consulting Committee for the UNESCO Building. In this position he tried by all means in his power to persuade the official authorities to obtain a better site for the new UNESCO building than the one originally contemplated, and for which a preliminary project had already been prepared. As a result of his efforts a magnificent site was procured on the fringe of the Bois de Boulogne, and for this the first official building project was prepared. The reasons why this site was afterwards rejected do not concern us here.

Walter Gropius and CIAM Le Corbusier once expressed the principles of CIAM in a few words: "In CIAM we do only what the individual can't do alone." Though organized in Groups, CIAM (Congrès Internationaux d'Architecture Moderne) is an association of individualists who share a common aim. An association of this kind is only possible when the participants also share a common vocabulary. By use of the comparative method CIAM has been able to establish the principles of the trends of development. This is perhaps most clearly expressed in the 'Charte d'Athènes' 1933, which gave a framework for the next phase of urban development.

It is obvious that this *teamwork of individuals* in the service of an idea is very much akin to Gropius' objective. He has actually taken part in relatively few of the Congresses. He was not even able to be present at the founding of CIAM at the Swiss Château of La Sarraz in 1928, because – despite an urgent invitation – his conscience obliged him to hasten back to Berlin after his first visit to America. However, whenever he has had to be absent we have always felt the lack of his human approach and his rare combination of friendliness and radical decision. An authoritative quietness combined with uncompromising courage won him our immediate confidence. Gropius has no enemies within CIAM. In a group that by no means consists of 'yes men' he has always known how to coordinate the different streams of thought.

Teamwork in Architectural Education The secret of the extent of his influence as a teacher lies in his personal interest in his fellow creatures. This is immediately perceived by students, who have an instinctive appreciation for the qualities of a teacher. The con-

14

fidence they have reposed in him has come from the instinctive perception of these young men that here is someone who doesn't merely transfer knowledge and experience, but who takes some sort of personal responsibility for each student. A sense of responsibility is something other than a sense of duty. It penetrates far more deeply into *human* nature and is – not for Gropius alone – the only basis for a fruitful cooperation between the teacher and the taught.

In July, 1949, at the 7th CIAM Congress at Bergamo, Italy, Gropius presented twelve points as a basis for discussion on " *The Search for a Better Architectural Education*". One of them said: "The students should be trained to work in teams – also with students of related techniques – in order to learn methods of collaboration with others. This will prepare them for their vital task of becoming coordinators of the many individuals involved in the conception and execution of planning and building tasks in later practice. The nature of teamwork will lead the students to good 'anonymous' architecture rather than to flashy 'stunt' design."

Another of these twelve points gives the key to his own teaching methods: "The HOW is far more important than the WHAT! In an age of specialization, method is more important than information. The training of an architect should be whole rather than sectional. In essence it should be all-inclusive throughout its duration, gaining in certainty of approach – that is, in clearness of thought and in the know-how of its realization. It should aim at teaching the student that it is through a creative attitude and independence of conception that he will arrive at basic convictions, not by accepting ready-made formulas."

To apply these general directives to a specific instance – the teaching of statics to students of Architecture – means that the architectural student would cease to be taught to become a semi-structural engineer. Instead he would acquire a sufficient understanding of statics to enable him, later on, to know what he can ask from the structural engineer. It is far less important for the architectural student to know how to carry out the detailed calculations for a space-frame construction than to know what it is possible to construct and what not. The great structural engineer, P.L. Nervi, once complained in conversation that he had repeatedly to handle designs which showed that many architects had no real sense for statics.

The concept behind the statement that "in an age of specialization training in method is more important than information" reaches far beyond the bounds of education in architecture. It will be concurred with by all who are opposed to the specialist hemmed between his blinkers. Precise research and the ever growing ramifications of the field of knowledge must remain. But the isolation of the specialist, the failure to set his subject in a meaningful context, without which no culture can arise; this must come to an end.

Teamwork in its Wider Significance

A demand for synthesis is expressed to-day by all creative spirits. Two-dimensional specialization must be put at the service of the three-dimensional setting of our new civilization.

When Walter Gropius sets knowledge of methodology above knowledge of detailed facts, he does this because we are not so much concerned to-day with creating 'beautiful architecture' as with creating a new way of life. It is one of the hopeful signs of our times that, even in the exact sciences such as physics, questions have been raised regarding the moral responsibility of the scientist for the effect of his discoveries. In our terminology this means that the specialist is becoming aware of the need to see his work in its human context.

Similar questions are arising in almost all disciplines. To enable them to give any period its three-dimensional setting, the architect needs to have some understanding of sociological development and the historian some methodological insight into almost all aspects of human knowledge. But the curricula of the universities to-day are still far away from teamwork or from the establishment of bridges between the different disciplines.

ON WALTER GROPIUS

Mies van der Rohe

During a large Chicago luncheon in honor of Gropius on his 70th birthday, May 18, 1953, the ever-silent Mies van der Rohe unexpectedly rose to his feet and said:

"I don't know if Gropius remembers that forty-three years ago to-day, we, the office of Peter Behrens, the great German architect, had a birthday party for him. This party was in the back room of a very cheap restaurant in a suburb of Berlin. I remember this party very well. We had a very good time. I have never seen Gropius so happy. I think Gropius had the best time in his life. Then he had no idea he would carry this awful burden of fame.

"Gropius, a few years older than most of us, left the office of Peter Behrens and started on his own. He built a factory constructed of steel, glass and brick. You can see that it is still going on. But this building was so excellent that he became, with one stroke, one of the leading architects in Europe.

"A few years later, he built, for the exhibition in Cologne, a complex of several buildings, office buildings and machinery halls. This building was still more radical than his first one, though he proved there that the first one was not an accident.

"After that, the first world war stopped all work for four long years. After the war, Gropius took over the Academy of Weimar. It was headed before the war by van de Velde, the great Belgian architect. Now it is always very difficult to succeed a great man, but Gropius did. He took over this academy and changed it from top to bottom and called it the Bauhaus.

"The Bauhaus was not an institution with a clear program – it was an idea, and Gropius formulated this idea with great precision. He said, 'Art and technology – the new unity'. He wanted to have painting, sculpture, theater and even ballet on the one hand, and on the other, weaving, photography, furniture – everything from the coffee cup to city planning.

"For art, he asked the Russian Kandinsky, the German Klee, and the American Feininger to work with him – at that time, very radical artists. To-day, everyone knows them as some of the great masters of our time.

"In 1923, Gropius wanted to show some of his work and to demonstrate his idea: the Bauhaus. There was a Bauhaus week in Weimar, and during this time, people from all over Europe came to look at his work and pay him tribute for what he did.

"I said before, it was an idea. The fact that it was an idea, I think, is the cause of this enormous influence the Bauhaus had on any progressive school around the globe. You cannot do that with organization, you cannot do that with propaganda. Only an idea spreads so far.

"By 1926, when Gropius moved the Bauhaus to Dessau and built his own school buildings there, Gropius was interested in industrialization. He saw the necessity of standardization and of prefabrication. I am glad that I had once the possibility in Stuttgart to give Gropius a hand so that he could demonstrate his ideas on industrialization and standardization and on prefabrication. He built two houses there which were the most interesting houses in the exhibition.

"But later on, Gropius became interested in the social importance of housing – that was when he left the Bauhaus. He was the most important member of the board of the Federal Housing Research Institute in Germany. He built large housing developments in several parts of Germany. He was one of the most important members, with Corbusier, of the International Congress of Modern Architecture with its chapters in nearly every country.

"When the Nazis came, Gropius went to England, worked there with friends together for a few years and then he was called to Harvard. I think most of you know his work from here on. He trained and educated a great number of students. A lot of them are in leading positions to-day in our large architectural offices, from the east to the west. I do not have to tell you that Gropius is one of the great architects of our time, as well as the greatest educator in our field, you know that, too. But what I want to say, and what you may not know, is that he was always a gallant fighter in the never-ending battle for new ideas."

Le Corbusier

To speak of Walter Gropius is to speak of a friend, of a friendship founded upon dignity, loyalty and generosity, upon his warm heart, his intelligence and his talent.

This bouquet of fine qualities has come into flower through the course of a long and difficult life (not unassociated with the equally long and difficult life of the writer). Always taking the long view, always putting one's faith in the positive values of life and never succumbing to its negative aspects: this puts one in the position of being, quite justly, thrown through the door by a society bent entirely upon material profits. A terrible existence? Far from it! It only demands that instead of merely studying philosophy, one must become a philosopher – the close friend of wisdom.

This action has its reward. A partial recompense may even be acquired during one's own life-time. Until now it has usually been necessary to wait patiently half a century after one's death. But to-day, thanks to photography, printing and transport, things move faster and even sanctification can arrive while a man is still living. (Thanks to progress!)

Gropius has radiated his qualities upon students from all quarters of the earth. It has been the good fortune of America to provide both the place and the budget, but the name of Gropius is pronounced with reverence over the entire world.

This reverence is in effect the pure gold distilled in the crucible of his entire life span.

Paris, October 3rd, 1953

EARLY WORK

The Cultural Setting of Gropius' Early Work

Conflicting Trends in Germany

The period of Gropius' early work – from the turn of the century to 1914 – saw Germany rise to the forefront of the European scene in the fields of economics, politics and military might: a matter for both concern and fear. As is not infrequent in the lives of nations, there were two conflicting trends, dangerously at loggerheads with one another. One was personified by the military and the public officials, who at that time constituted almost a separate caste. The other was represented by a cross section of intellectuals, who wanted to charge the stupendous upsurge of industrialization with some spiritual content. The great industrialist, Emil Rathenau, who took Peter Behrens into his employ, was not an isolated phenomenon in the Germany of that time.

Craftsmen and Artists from abroad welcomed in Germany

In no other country could foreign craftsmen then obtain positions of such prestige nor foreign artists so generous a welcome. It is enough to instance the case of the director of the Berlin National Gallery, Hugo von Tschudi. From the first year of his appointment, in 1896, he began to amass a collection of the works of the French impressionists such as did not exist anywhere at that time, least of all in their native country. This action naturally brought him into direct conflict both with the expressed will of the Kaiser and with the ruling taste. It was a foregone conclusion that such an attack upon the ruling powers and the ruling taste could end only in Tschudi's downfall, but the strength of the intellectual undercurrent is shown by the fact that it was possible to assemble the collection at all.

Van de Velde, Dresden, 1897

The great Belgian architect, Henry van de Velde, did his finest work in Germany, before the outbreak of the first World War in 1914. Indeed it is probable that it was the exhibition of van de Velde's furniture in Dresden, 1897, that gave the final impetus to the formation of the Arts and Crafts Reform Movement. At any rate it set it in motion. The objects on show here were, in many cases, identical with those displayed in Paris the previous year by the art dealer, S. Bing. There they had given rise to public protest, but in Germany van de Velde became famous overnight.

The German Craftman's Workshops (Werkstätte)

Around this time, 1898, Karl Schmidt started a joinery workshop in Dresden with a couple of workmen[1]. By 1907 this had become " The Dresden Crafts Center" employing some 300 workers. Its products were all designed by contemporary artists. The rise of such craft centers provided unmis-

---

[1] Josef August Lux, author of the most important source book for this period, gives a long list of examples establishing that the official birth of the Modern Movement in Germany took place in 1898: see J. A. Lux, "*Das neue Kunstgewerbe in Deutschland*", Leipzig, 1908, p. 21.

takable proof that the German Arts and Crafts Movement was not confined to a limited circle. The Dresden Crafts Center got in touch with others in Munich and together they built up sales outlets in all the main cities of Germany. At Hellerau, just outside Dresden, Karl Schmidt built a garden city beside his factory with the help of an accomplished architect, Heinrich Tessenow. In the center of the town he placed a theater for the Genevese musician and educationist, Jaques-Dalcroze, to expound his theories of rhythmic dancing.

Around the turn of the century a drive for reform had become evident in many different places, notably in the small principalities and the centers of industrial activity. In 1899 Ernst Ludwig von Hessen commissioned the Austrian Josef Olbrich, Peter Behrens and other artists to build some houses for themselves and an exhibition building. The result was a new type of exhibition containing houses in which every detail, down to the coffee spoons, was designed by the artist.

Uprisings in Darmstadt, Weimar, Hagen and Berlin

In 1902 the Grand Duke of Sachsen-Weimar requested Henry van de Velde, who was already working in Berlin, to found a new School for Arts and Crafts at Weimar.

In the same year, Karl Ernst Osthaus, patron of the arts and an art historian, founded a collection of the most modern art in the Folkwang Museum at Hagen, a town in the heart of industrial Rhineland. He entrusted the erection of his own house, near to the museum, to Henry van de Velde. Like the theater in Hellerau, this museum formed the center of a well-planned garden city.

In 1907 Emil Rathenau, President of the General Electric Company of Berlin (A.E.G.) appointed Peter Behrens as art director. It became his task to infuse art into all products of the industry, from the firm's trademark and standardized electric light fittings to the famous buildings of the new A.E.G. factory. This appointment signalized, at long last, a recognition of the rightful position of the architect alongside the engineer. This was an event of outstanding importance.

At the time of the founding of the *German Werkbund* in Munich, also in 1907, all these activities were in full swing. The main function of the Werkbund was to coordinate all the various movements and also at times itself to sponsor large-scale cooperative enterprises. It further undertook to promote and to watch over the interests of creative personalities. The most important paragraph of its constitution, 1908, reads: "The aim of the League is to raise the standard of manufactured products by the joint efforts of art, industry and craftsmanship." Its great achievements include the Cologne Exhibition, 1914 (which was cut short by the outbreak of war), the Weissenhof Housing Project in Stuttgart, 1927, directed by Mies van der Rohe, and the Paris Exhibition, 1930, directed by Walter Gropius, of which there will be more to say[2].

Foundation of the German Werkbund, 1907

Fig. 64–68

---

[2] The most reliable information about the Arts and Crafts Movement before 1908 can be found in the work of a sociologist, Heinrich Waentig, "*Wirtschaft und Kunst*", a study of the aims and history of the contemporary arts and crafts movement, Jena, 1909. This is an indispensable and most carefully compiled reference book that traces the movement back to Henry Cole, Ruskin and William Morris. For his account of the movement in Germany and Austria see pp. 226–297.

An effervescent optimism, energy and goodwill pervaded the air. An era of unbounded prosperity seemed to lie just ahead. No one could imagine otherwise. The yearbooks of the German Werkbund, especially those between 1912 and 1915, convey the prevailing cultural optimism.

One of the yearbooks bore the title "*Art in Industry and Trade*" (1913) and displayed pictures of the American grain silos and factories, which up till then no one had considered anything other than mere containers of grain or places of work. Walter Gropius was the first to acclaim their "unacknowledged majesty", far superior to anything of the kind in Germany[3]. For a whole year he wrote to Canada and the United States for material which, in the 1913 yearbook, he presented together with an article on "The development of modern industrial architecture" where he openly stated that the "monumental power" of the grain silos of North America "can stand comparison with the constructions of ancient Egypt".

After this he started to collect examples of pure form for the 1914 yearbook on "Transport" wherever they could be found in "automobile and railroad car, steamship and sailing vessel, airship and airplane". It was the same program that Le Corbusier was later to proclaim, almost in the form of a manifesto, in the famous first chapter "*Les yeux qui ne voient pas*" of "*Vers une Architecture*", Paris, 1923. In the first number of "*L'Esprit Nouveau*", 1920, a journal produced by Le Corbusier and his friends, several of the same silos to which Gropius had drawn attention are displayed as the first of the "Admonitions to Architects" *(Rappels à MM. les Architectes)*. This is the article that ends with the proclamation "*Les ingénieurs américains écrasent de leurs calculs l'architecture agonisante*".

In the yearbooks of the German Werkbund such matters were splendidly presented, served up as it were upon a silver platter. In the hands of Le Corbusier they receive less deferential treatment and are employed to support two definite themes: "ferroconcrete frame construction" and the "space conception of modern painting". In Germany at the start of the Arts and Crafts Movement both these were quite unheard of. For this reason the German movement, which was saddled with a preoccupation with the wealthy middle classes, was never able to move on from an "arts and crafts" attitude of mind. The painters whom they employed were for the most part merely skilful decorators and were used as such. But the "De Stijl" movement in Holland as well as Le Corbusier could draw upon the new conception of space developed by Cubism.

It was not only the war that brought the Arts and Crafts Movement in Germany to a close: it was without a future. It lacked the inspiration of an inherent conception of architecture.

This was the atmosphere surrounding the young architect, Walter Gropius. Though his furniture may have been more severe than that of others in the details of its design, there was little difference in its spirit[4]. In his simple designs for single pieces of furniture one can sense a leaning towards a standardization of pure form.

---

[3] "*Die Kunst in Industrie und Handel*", p. 21.
[4] Vestibule of the section for interior decoration with a sculptured frieze by G. Marcks and glass windows by Cesar Klein in *Jahrbuch des Deutschen Werkbundes*, 1915, fig. 49.

When it came to tackling problems which required the utmost technical precision and economy of space utilization – such as railroad cars and sleeping cars – he was by no means alone.[5] His most interesting experiment in this field was the result of close collaboration between architect and engineer. This was the benzol locomotive, 1913 (Diesel railway car), which anticipated the principle of the Diesel truck that came into general use much later. The certainty with which the problem of air resistance was resolved is remarkable. This, which as "streamlining" was later to become so greatly overemphasized, was basic to this design.

Fig. 24

Fig. 26, 27

The Fagus Factory

All this would have little importance if one of Gropius' early works had not given immediate and convincing proof of a mind that stood in direct opposition to the hot-house cult of the Arts and Crafts Movement. In Germany at that time such a demonstration could not of course have taken the form of a house; it had to be a factory[6].

Fig. 18, 28–31

The Fagus works, a shoe-last factory near Alfeld, North Germany, was the first large building commissioned from the twenty-eight-year-old architect. Impeled by his desire for self-realization, Gropius ransacked periodicals and papers for announcements of projected buildings. He then offered his services and, as might be expected, usually received no reply. The only person attracted by his proposals was the industrialist, Karl Benscheid. It is to his courage in placing himself in the hands of a young unknown architect that we owe the Fagus factory.

Importance of the Fagus Factory, 1911

This building presents a new architectural vocabulary, as spontaneous as it is unexpected. While Gropius was working with Peter Behrens in Berlin the erection of the A.E.G. factory was in progress. The same problem there and the same problem here were however quite differently handled. The great glass walls of Behrens' famous hall of turbines are tied in right and left by monumental masonry. In Gropius' design this has disappeared. He has discovered the art form of the steel framed structure. His walls show clearly that they no longer carry and support the building, but that they simply depend from it – mere shields against inclement weather, or, as Gropius said: "The role of the walls becomes restricted to that of mere screens stretched between the upright columns of the framework to keep out rain, cold and noise[7]."

Gropius transmutes this into an art form. He hangs the wall on the supporting columns which stand behind it, as can be seen in the ground plan. At one corner of the building the glass walls butt directly up against one another with no intervening column. This presented an unusual spectacle to eyes accustomed to the supporting wall. The architect justified his column-less corner to the builder by explaining that it saved the cost of a support. A more important point is that here for the first time the trend

Fig. 28, 29

---

[5] See *Jahrbuch des Deutschen Werkbundes*, 1915, fig. 133–137.
[6] Information on the projects of this early period is incomplete owing to the inadvertent destruction of records when the Bauhaus was being cleaned out.
[7] Walter Gropius, "*The New Architecture and the Bauhaus*", London, 1937, p. 22–23.

towards transparency and absence of weight found undeniable architectural expression.

It was just this that struck Gropius' contemporaries as somehow uncanny. The Fagus factory is illustrated in the 1913 Yearbook of the German Werkbund, plates 18–20, but it is barely recognizable. The glass walls and the corner at which they meet are thrust into the far distance and the views have been so selected that the building appears as much dominated by walls of masonry as do all the other examples shown.

The Fagus factory is one of the building types in which glass and steel are married together. The first construction of this type was demonstrated by Gustav Eiffel in the glass walls of the main Paris Exhibition building, 1878, but here no close relationship was expressed between architecture and construction technique[8]. In the Fagus factory this duality between architecture and construction techniques, which had persisted throughout the nineteenth century, is at last resolved. These two streams that had for so long been flowing in different directions here again merge into one another. Architectural and construction media have been given a mutually satisfactory expression.

Fig. 32–40 Gropius' buildings for the 1941 Werkbund Exhibition in Cologne mark the termination of Gropius' early period. The chief points of the Fagus factory were audaciously advanced in these buildings which are discussed in the chapter on "Exhibitions and Life". Even the Bauhaus is, architecturally speaking, a further development of ideas first expressed in the Fagus factory.

---

[8] "*Space, Time and Architecture*", 10th printing, Harvard University Press, USA., 1954, p. 263.

THE ARCHITECT AND INDUSTRIAL PRODUCTION

Walter Gropius has always been deeply conscious of the gulf between the forms of artistic expression and the forms produced by the machine. This sundering of industrial production from artistic insight has gaped like an open wound ever since mechanization first began to penetrate man's intimate environment.

The dire effects of the misuse of materials together with the closely related devaluation of meaningful forms was first recognized by the English group of reformers around Henry Cole, the real initiator of the first Great International Exhibition, 1851, in the Crystal Palace at Hyde Park[1].

In the nineties, nearly half a century later, Henry van de Velde was extolling the possibilities of the machine and inveighing against the prevailing taste for imitative forms. By his efforts he awakened the conscience of his contemporaries. There was Adolph Loos. There was Peter Behrens who, through a kindly industrialist, was for the first time in history given the opportunity of bringing direct artistic influence to bear upon all the products of a large manufacturing concern. There was the German Werkbund. There was the early work of Walter Gropius – a varied output which included designs for wall hangings, metal furniture for a battleship, interior decoration schemes, mass-produced modular furniture, designs for a Diesel engine (1913) and for a car (1930).

Fig. 25
Fig. 26, 27, 42–47

The bridging of this gulf between artistic form and industrial production was one of the chief motives of the Bauhaus. It aimed to educate a new generation capable of producing models and prototypes conceived by a conjunction of the spirit of pure form with the spirit of the machine. Contact with industrialization began in the school itself. The student had to go through the whole process of developing his first rough model into a smooth finished product perfectly detailed for mass production. There is no difference in the process whether one is designing lamps, chairs, fabrics or dishes.

For more than a hundred years the machine has been penetrating ever more deeply into our everyday life, affecting not only the form of the objects we use but also the foodstuffs we eat. The deterioration of bread in the U.S.A. through ever more rapid mechanical processing is a vivid example of the dangers we encounter in the misuse of the machine; and what has happened to bread now menaces the entire house. No blame attaches to the machine which is by its nature devoid of aim or purpose. It is man who is at fault. Here more than anywhere else, it is important that

---

[1] Cf. *"Mechanization Takes Command"*, fig. 347–360.

the keenest control be exercized over the human spirit, that guiding lines be very clearly defined; for industrial production left to itself inevitably follows the line of least resistance. The prefabricated house of to-day is just as apt to look like a pseudo-handmade product as the bric-a-brac of a hundred years ago. Assembly-line methods have resulted in houses as like to each other as mass-produced cooking pots, except that their exterior façades still try to imitate the work of individual craftsmen. By this fake the speculator plays upon the sentimental dreams of the buyers.

The chapter on the Prefabricated House deals in greater detail with the ways in which mechanization can be employed in the home. One way leads to a deadly uniformity, opposed to all the ideals of contemporary town planning; another, to the possibility of satisfying each individual's tastes and preferences. Walter Gropius had this in mind when he delivered a stern address to the American architects in 1952. It was up to them to do all in their power to handle the dangerous intrusion of the uncontrolled might of the machine into the domain of the architect. Unless they themselves took drastic steps, they and all that they stood for – a sensitive understanding of form and of the human scale – would be swept into limbo.

The violent repercussions caused by this speech showed that the most responsible elements among architects were already well aware of the results to be expected from the mass production of uncoordinated building parts, parts which themselves dictate the form of the whole: whereas the alternative method would permit such a degree of interchangeability that each whole could be composed according to the individual needs and pleasures of the owner.

WALTER GROPIUS AND THE BAUHAUS

The fate of the Bauhaus is involved in a tragic contradistinction. Nowhere else would the director of a state organization have been permitted the freedom, given to Walter Gropius from the outset, to carry through such an uncompromising project and to call in the best talents from wherever they might be. On the other hand probably nowhere else would this have given rise to such violent opposition.

It was sheer madness to jeopardize one's reputation and position by the appointment of artists such as Klee, Kandinsky, Feininger, Schlemmer and Moholy-Nagy as government servants in a state institution: artists whose significance was appreciated only by a very small circle and whose work and outlook excited the strongest expressions of outrage, abuse and detestation throughout Germany and even beyond its borders. With this group of derided outcasts Walter Gropius then proceeded to establish what one might call an "educational party line" in regard to the rights of contemporary man to a way of life able to satisfy both his material and his spiritual needs.

The desire to attempt the impossible and to persist, despite both official and surreptitious opposition, is one of the few positive attributes of human nature. One of the clearest expositions of the secret of the Bauhaus was given by that taciturn authority, Mies van der Rohe, when he rose to speak after a dinner in honor of Gropius at the Blackstone Hotel in Chicago on May 18, 1953.

"The Bauhaus", he said, "was not an institution with a clear program – it was an idea, and Gropius formulated this idea with great precision... As I said before, it was an idea. The fact that it was an idea, I think, is the cause of this enormous influence the Bauhaus had on every progressive school around the globe. You cannot do that with organization, you cannot do that with propaganda. Only an idea spreads so far..."

Sources of information on the Bauhaus

This is neither the time nor the place to discuss in detail the work of the Bauhaus. Here we can only deal with its general significance and its intimate connection with the personality of its director. There follow, therefore, some general references to publications on the Bauhaus; a report of the "Bauhaus Week" of 1923 that I published at the time, and a few personal notes on Gropius' final evening at the Bauhaus in 1928.

The worldwide recognition ultimately given to the work of the Bauhaus has given rise to a number of publications and others are still in course of preparation[1].

Publications issued during the actual period of the Bauhaus' struggle for existence have long been out of print and are now book collectors' pieces. The most important were:

1919: *Programm des Staatlichen Bauhauses, Weimar* (Syllabus of the State School of Building, Weimar) a first, four-page, manifesto.

3. *The Bauhaus staff, 1925: on the roof of the Students' quarters (Prellerhaus). From left: Joseph Albers, Hinnerk Scheper, George Muche, Ladislaus Moholy-Nagy, Herbert Bayer, Joost Schmidt, Walter Gropius, Marcel Breuer, Wassily Kandinsky, Paul Klee, Lyonel Feininger, Gunta Stoelzl, Oscar Schlemmer. When the school was opened in Weimar in 1919 Gropius started with Johannes Itten, Lyonel Feininger and Gerhard Marcks (who also taught at the Bauhaus); in 1920 the painter George Muche joined the staff, in 1921 Paul Klee and Oscar Schlemmer, in 1922 Wassily Kandinsky, and in 1923 Ladislaus Moholy-Nagy.*

1922: *Satzungen, Staatliches Bauhaus in Weimar*
(Constitution of the State School of Building, Weimar)
1923: *Staatliches Bauhaus, 1919–1923, Weimar-Munich*
(The State School of Building, Weimar-Munich, 1919–1923)

---

[1] The art historian Ludwig Grote, who was in close contact with the work of the Bauhaus throughout the notable Dessau period, is writing a "*History of the Bauhaus*". Dr. Grote, who was at that time director of the Dessau Art Gallery, conducted the preliminary negotiations with the Mayor of Dessau, Dr. Fritz Hesse, for the establishment of the Bauhaus. He later supported the Mayor in his successful efforts to raise funds from the city council, during a difficult period, for the building and upkeep of the enterprise. Other books on the Bauhaus that are still in preparation include one by A. Dorner.
A considerable amount of Walter Gropius' own material on the Bauhaus is now in the Germanic Museum in Harvard. Dr. Grote has also established a Bauhaus collection in the German National Museum at Nuremberg of which he is now director.

This last publication was brought out in the middle of the inflation period with twenty colored plates, a cover designed by Herbert Bayer and typography by Moholy-Nagy. It contains valuable contributions from members of the Bauhaus teaching staff and a democratic juxtaposition of the work of masters and students. Even now it remains the most magnificent publication on the Bauhaus and gives an historic insight into the workings of the school during its first period. It was issued in connection with the "Bauhaus Week" held in the summer of 1923, which is described later.

4. L. MOHOLY-NAGY:
Cover for No. 7 of the Bauhaus Books.

In the same year Walter Gropius published his " *Idee und Aufbau des Staatlichen Bauhauses, Weimar*" (The Aim and Organization of the State School of Building, Weimar). In these twelve pages he crystallizes the Bauhaus program as it had developed during the four years between 1919 and 1923. 1925–1930: The fourteen volumes of the "*Bauhausbücher*" (Bauhaus Books), edited jointly by Walter Gropius and L. Moholy-Nagy, not only give insight into the workings of the school during its second period but also cover a much wider field.

They began with a frequently reprinted booklet by Walter Gropius entitled " *Internationale Architektur*" (International Architecture) and ended with L. Moholy-Nagy's "*Von Material zu Architektur*" which was later translated into English[2] as "The New Vision, from Material to Architecture".

---

[2] Moholy-Nagy, " *The New Vision, from Material to Architecture*", New York, 1938.

Other volumes included Paul Klee's *Pädagogisches Skizzenbuch* (A Teacher's Sketchbook) which has been published in several English translations, and W. Kandinsky's *Punkt und Linie zu Fläche, Beitrag zur Analyse der malerischen Elemente* (From Point and Line to Plane, an Essay on the Analysis of Pictorial Elements). These showed how masters of their art are able to go beyond the normal limits of a school program and to establish new levels of perception.

Information on the practical achievements of the Bauhaus up to 1923 is contained in *Ein Versuchshaus des Bauhauses* (An Experimental House of the Bauhaus). This describes the "House on the Horn" at Weimar which was built for the occasion of the "Bauhaus Week" in 1923 and for which almost every article of equipment, down to the cannisters for spices in the kitchen, were designed by Marcel Breuer, then at the Bauhaus. It is typical of Walter

Fig. 266 Gropius that, though he designed both the master plan for the housing settlement and procured the building funds, he then stood back and left the actual design of the prototype House on the Horn (the only one of the settlement houses to get built) to the painter Muche, who was also then on the Bauhaus staff.

Die Bühne im Bauhaus (The Theater at the Bauhaus) by Oskar Schlemmer is an account of the headway in stage design he was able to make at the

Fig. 5 ⌐ Bauhaus. His use of the new conceptions of space and form put these designs among one of the most imaginative achievements of the Bauhaus. Most of this work was done during the Weimar period, though some of it is earlier.

L. Moholy-Nagy's *Malerei, Photographie, Film* (Painting, Photography, Film) is based on the fact that painting with light is common to all the three. The book is a lesson in optics, showing how the new media of the camera and light-sensitive materials could serve the new vision.

Neue Arbeiten der Bauhauswerkstätten (New Designs from the Bauhaus Workshops) leads up to and connects with the Dessau period. Its description of the individual projects, shows the ever-strengthening emphasis laid upon industrial production and the realities of everyday life. Unfortunately, circumstances prevented the publication of another volume containing the work of the last three years of the Bauhaus under Gropius' leadership. The achievements of these years of "teamwork" (to use Gropius' favorite expression) can be found in exhibitions such as the Paris exhibition of the

Fig. 64–68 German Werkbund in 1930, even though by then the Bauhaus team itself had been broken up.

Bauhausbauten in Dessau (The Bauhaus Buildings in Dessau) which is by far the largest volume in the series, was written by Walter Gropius and published in 1930. In it his architectural achievements are illustrated by a series of excellent photographs, taken with rare perception and clarity by Lucia Moholy. This book also gives some insight into the work produced during the Dessau period and shows how an experiment, in less than a decade, succeeded in breaking through to a new way of life which could be expressed in all its detailed forms – from the first tubular steel chairs of the

Fig. 58 *Aula*, designed by Marcel Breuer in 1926, to the details of a dressing table.

From 1923, L. Moholy-Nagy stood beside Walter Gropius, as his closest collaborator. This connection carried over to America where, in his Institute of Design in Chicago, Moholy further developed the theories and teaching methods of the Bauhaus from 1938 until his untimely death in 1946. Moholy, the painter, could always see things in terms of the whole and could recognize that the many art "isms", that caused so much misunderstanding at the time, would form part of a later synthesis. He was mainly responsible for the publication of the series of Bauhaus books by representatives of the different movements: *Kubismus* (Cubism) by Albert Gleizes, *Neue Gestaltung* (New Design) by Piet Mondrian, *Grundbegriffe der neuen gestaltenden Kunst* (Basic Conceptions of a New Plastic Art) by Theo van Doesburg, *Die gegenstandslose Welt* (The Non-Objective World) by Kasimir Malevitsch, the earliest Russian abstract painter. Again, circumstances prevented the publication of further volumes in this series. Even so, these few small books often still present the only easily comprehensible insight into the various art movements, and are passed from hand to hand. New editions are urgently needed.

In 1938, a year after Walter Gropius and his closest friends, L. Moholy-Nagy, Marcel Breuer and Herbert Bayer, had been invited to America, they introduced themselves to the American public through a retrospective exhibition prepared at the request of the Museum of Modern Art, New York. The exhibition itself was designed by Herbert Bayer and the publication which was based upon it: "*Bauhaus 1919–1928*"[3] is at present the only easily accessible source of information on the work of the Bauhaus.

The Bauhaus Week, 1923

The peak of the Weimar period of the Bauhaus was reached during the "Bauhaus Week" of August, 1923. The ultimate aim of the enormous efforts put forth on this occasion was to appeal to the world, to come, to see and to save, all that could be saved, from the threatening uncertainty of the immediate situation. Everyone who was present during this festival will remember it for the rest of his life. There were exhibitions of the work of the staff and students of the Bauhaus, theatrical performances and concerts, including one of the first performances of Stravinsky's "*L'Histoire du Soldat*" conducted by Hermann Scherchen in the Weimar Theater. The spectator was plunged into a new world emerging in all its freshness and directness.

It was on this occasion that I was granted my first insight into the universe of contemporary art and I was strongly moved to write down an account of it. The resultant article "*Bauhaus und Bauhauswoche zu Weimar*" (The Bauhaus and the Bauhaus Week at Weimar) appeared in the Swiss Periodical *Das Werk*. Though hesitant and uncertain on many points, some extracts may give an eye-witness account of the events:

"After three and a half years of life, the State School of Building in Weimar **Report from 1923** makes an appeal to the contemporary world, to accept the justification of its existence on the basis of its aims and its accomplishments. It is in any case entitled to respect for its unswerving pursuit of its objectives in spite

---

[3] Cf. "*Bauhaus, 1919–1928*", edited by Herbert Bayer, Walter Gropius and Ise Gropius, The Museum of Modern Art, New York, 1938; new edition, Boston, 1952. In the following pages reference to this book will be made whenever possible.

of the present situation in Germany, which makes her the slave of immediate necessity; in spite of paltry funds; in spite of cheap ridicule; in spite of malicious attacks from reactionaries and, not least, in spite of internal difficulties. These objectives are to discover the new principles of form which are essential if the creative forces of the individual are to be reconciled with industrial production. We are plagued by an unhappy duality which can be traced back to the beginning of the last century. If we truly desire to arrive at an independent way of life we can no longer repudiate the machine and remain wrapped in nostalgic dreams. The aim of the Bauhaus is to grapple

5. OSCAR SCHLEMMER:
Dancers for his Triadic Ballet.

with this dilemma and to resolve it by training those with creative talents to find a place for themselves in the world, instead of clipping their wings and confining them in an ideological glass cage, which will inevitably become shattered by the scoffs and buffets of active life.

"The Bauhaus intends to encompass a wide range of creative activities, from typography, weaving and ceramics to stage design, painting, sculpture and architecture. It demands that every student should learn to use his hands at some craft and that he should pass the same open examinations as the ordinary trade apprentice. The aim of the Bauhaus is not, however, to educate craftsmen but to train talent and it insists that the creative man can only make full use of his talents if he first learns as a craftsman how to handle material.

"Instead of learning various individual conceptions of form, the student will study the basic principles that underlie the relationships of colors to one another and the shapes of simple hard objects. This is very clearly presented in the exhibition, where the evolution of form is handled by Klee and the examination of color-values by Kandinsky. In the search for new basic principles it was essential to go back to the beginning and wrest the laws of matter from its very substance. These new principles provide the basis for new creative designs. At the Bauhaus, the freed and activated imagination is continually exploring further into new fields...

"In the theater Schlemmer's *Triadic Ballet* was being shown which opens up entirely new dramatic possibilities for the dance. The human body has become moulded into clear-cut forms; in the dancing very definite lines are insisted upon. Here the work of the Bauhaus approached perfection. A maenad no longer fled to and fro across the stage, like a will-o'-the-wisp, trailing fluttering garments, until forced by shortness of breath to come to a halt. The curtain rose upon a motionless figure before a chrome yellow plane. It wore a many-colored wooden skirt shaped like a top, surmounted by a breastplate of varnished leather; arms and feet were also lacquered and the head was covered by a transparent helmet crowned by a jaunty wooden knob. When the music started, the figure responded with strong rhythmic movements. While the armor-like clothing restricted the range of possible movements and gestures, it at the same time gave added emphasis to every tiny motion – like the action of a pendulum. Every caper, every shake of the head, every movement of the arms became exaggerated and intensified. Further fantasy was in store. Dancers appeared with great balls instead of hands or with heads enclosed within gleaming brazen masks and invisible arms, like an Archipenko sculpture. Their bodies were confined within the rigid spirals of their costume and only their feet retained freedom of movement. It is conceivable that the effect of this strictly disciplined movement, which is in such striking contrast to our customary lack of control, may be to revive in a new way the human dignity that we have lost so utterly[4].

"However strongly the machine may have influenced the shapes of the figures and the precision of the movements in this ballet, the machine alone can never produce creative results.

"For the past ten years all the arts have been dependent upon painting, for architecture and craftsmanship have remained at a standstill since their spurt of activity at the turn of the century... The creative work of the Bauhaus is similarly based upon the principles of contemporary painting. But this does not imply a simple transference by skilful imitators. The Bauhaus did not engage a single craftsman-designer but only pure artists; in other words, the greatest masters of abstract art available in Germany... Methods of handling material were to be derived directly from artistic principles, and at once it becomes evident that Cubism is not simply a destroyer of form, as many would like to maintain. In the history of artistic development it has an entirely new task... Cubism seeks to make us aware of the realm of the amorphic and the formless. The Bauhaus endeavors to explore the world of matter and to reveal hidden life in amorphic and inanimate objects. These, by being seen from all sides, disclose their new meaning and take on new forms. The underlying rhythm of things can again be sensed.

Oscar Schlemmer's
Triadic Ballet

Fig. 5

The Situation
of Painting
and Sculpture
in 1923

---

[4] Cf. "*Bauhaus 1919–1928*", p. 62; also an excellent monograph "*Oskar Schlemmer*" by Hans Hildebrand, Stuttgart, 1952, which gives information on the artistic background of Schlemmer's art.

6. The original photograph.

(Fig. 7–11) Variations by the artists at the Bauhaus upon a newspaper photograph (Fig. 6) at the suggestion of Moholy-Nagy. They were mounted together as a birthday gift for Walter Gropius.

7. Lyonel Feininger: Water color and indian ink, 1924.

8. Moholy-Nagy: Pencil and wash, 1924.

9. Wassily Kandinsky: Water color and indian ink, 1924.

10. Paul Klee: Gouache, 1924.

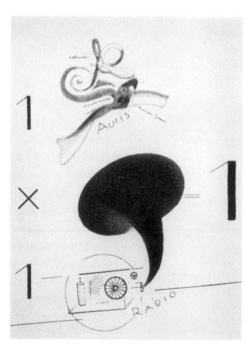

11. Oscar Schlemmer: Red and black ink, 1924.

"Probably the nearest direct similarity to abstract painting can be seen in the horizontal and vertical warp and weft of textile designs; also there is no difficulty in deciphering it in the play of light through glass windows – Klee is here the teacher. In the City Theater, Jena, which Gropius has renovated and transformed, a remarkable experiment has been made of presenting a ballet of completely abstract forms. The dancers are invisible behind great blue, red and yellow panels which move about in time to the music. The result is not without charm, as when, for instance, towards the end of this 'Mechanical Ballet', two red and a blue squares pass to and fro before a black backcloth and then, in the final movement, stand on their corners and slip sideways into the wings[5]."

Fig. 136–140

The report continued with tentative questions regarding the nature of the new architecture which, in 1923, was just beginning to appear, though in a somewhat fragmentary form. Gropius had collected together all that was then available into the first exhibition of contemporary architecture[6], and the report closed with the following somewhat critical remarks:

First Exhibition of Modern Architecture

"We cannot end without at least recording that no Swiss name appears in the exhibition of architecture." (That the pseudonym Le Corbusier, which appeared on several houses, concealed the Swiss Charles Edouard Jeanneret was not then known.) "This cannot be excused on account of the smallness of the country. We have only to recall that Holland has produced more than half a dozen figures – from Cuypers through Berlage to Oud – whose names will always be recorded in the history of modern architecture. The fault does not lie entirely at the door of the architectural profession, but mainly with those responsible for commissioning the buildings."

This article was followed by a "reply" from someone who, in the words of the editor, was "the man best qualified to speak from the point of view of Swiss lovers of art[7]."

Effect on the Outside Public

It appeared that, to this reader, the "Report on the Bauhaus and the Bauhaus Week in Weimar" had sounded like "the dismal wail of a siren or the spurting 'pfiff' of a fireman's hose... The report on the Bauhaus at Weimar presents an astounding medley of new possibilities... a chaotic jumble of truth and falsehood, of good and bad, of nostalgia and delirium... We will quietly push the accusations of philistinism and reaction into our trouser pockets, where indeed the hands of the good-natured Swiss citizens remain most of the time, so long as we are not too strongly provoked.

"In a country where money has sunk to one fifty-millionth of its former value, not only economic standards but all other values have been cast aside. Since, there, everything that is old or repaired has been thrown away as junk and every day yet more things are seen to decay, it is only too easy to understand why the people hanker after new fashions and new experiences. However, let us not reproach our neighbors for this, but show them the sympathy due to anyone who has fallen on evil days... Not only political and economic circles but also artistic and above all intel-

---

[5] Cf. "*Bauhaus 1919–1928*", p. 62.
[6] The exhibition of the Dutch "De Stijl" group in Paris, with buildings by van Doesburg, Van Eesteren and Rietveldt showed the rapidity of architectural development at that time.
[7] Cf. "*Das Werk*", Vol. X, 1923, p. 259–260.

lectual circles are caught up in a mad frenzy of revolution. This feverish dance is at times both staged and promoted with an uncanny intelligence and sense of opportunism that is unquestionably largely induced and fostered by alien elements."

Not satisfied with this, the writer, who was at that time President of the Swiss Werkbund, asked the editor of *Das Werk* to insert the following *correction* in the next number of the journal[8].

"In the article 'A Swiss Rejoinder' by E.R.B. the end of the penultimate sentence should read "that is unquestionably largely induced and fostered by Jewish influences"".

This is the tune which, ten years later, rang throughout Germany and which enabled Göring in 1933 to have the Bauhaus closed down by the police as "an incubator of cultural bolshevism".

It goes without saying that these gibes in a remote Swiss journal had no direct influence upon the actual fate of the Bauhaus, but they are all too representative of the way in which the public first reacts to new artistic manifestations. There was little difference between this Swiss reaction and the local attacks on the Bauhaus such as were, for example, expressed in a pamphlet written at the same time by Arno Müller, a Weimar locksmith, who demanded "the firmest rejection of these artistic abortions" which make "insufferable demands on the patience, clear thinking and nerves of the beholder[9]."

Why this Assault? To-day when there is general recognition of the absence of insight betrayed by such demonstrations, we must nevertheless ask what made these gentlemen who normally "kept their hands in their trouser pockets" itch for a fight.

The cause is, again, that grievous split between thinking and feeling which affects all levels of society and which must never be underestimated. One highly developed method of thinking (science) is valued in every quarter. Quite another attitude is taken up in regard to the realm of feeling (art). The art of the "ruling taste" as we have termed it has now become part of the dream world of the masses and their representatives. Here it lives on and gives rise to nostalgic images with which they oppose impotently, arrogantly and with loathing, all expressions of truly creative art whose roots reach back through the ages.

This is the real reason why such malicious antagonism was provoked by the movement expressed by the Bauhaus and by the work of the artists who were associated with it.

Gropius Leaves the Bauhaus

I attended the Bauhaus Week as a simple spectator and was astonished at all I saw. I knew no one there. Finally, accompanied by a friend, I took courage to go and see Gropius. We found him standing in the center
Fig. 57 of his office beneath a tubular lamp which hovered provokingly in mid-air.

---

[8] Cf. "*Das Werk*", Vol. X, 1923, p. 288.
[9] Cf. "*Das staatliche Bauhaus in Weimar und sein Leiter*", Weimar, 1924, pp. 32 and 34.

My friend described to Gropius my plans for the future and I his. Gropius listened to us quietly and looked at us with some scepticism and reserve – that was all.

In the following years our relations drew nearer, particularly through Moholy-Nagy who became a close friend. In 1926 I went to Dessau to see the Bauhaus under construction, but my next visit was not until February 1928, by chance on the day that Gropius announced his resignation.

It was perhaps one of those coincidences that Hans Arp calls "*lois du hasard*" that my first lecture tour in Germany should lead me to the Bauhaus on that particular day. In the afternoon, Moholy-Nagy drew me aside on the stairs and said, "Gropius handed in his resignation to-day, but the students don't know it yet. Please keep this to yourself."

We went through the Bauhaus workshops. Everywhere there was a hum of activity as though it would all go on forever. We visited the faculty houses and called on Paul Klee and other members of the staff.

In the evening, during my address, the news spread through the hall that posters announcing Gropius' resignation were being displayed in Dessau. Later on the evening developed into one of those casual parties that were so much a part of the spirit of the Bauhaus. These served to develop the relaxed and friendly relations between students and teachers that are so helpful in releasing the dormant creative powers of the young. In one corner the Bauhaus band was performing. In the general atmosphere of crazy high spirits there was no hint that anyone knew what had happened. At midnight the band suddenly came to a halt. The most senior student went up to Gropius and said, "You have made many mistakes, Gropius, but there is no one to fill your shoes. You oughtn't to leave us."

Gropius stood up, both embarrassed and moved, and went to the center of the hall. I do not remember much of what he said but the result was unexpected. The student took one of Gropius' hands and Gropius held out the other to the old watchman and his wife who were sitting close by in their carpet slippers. They began to move around in a circle and then suddenly, before he realized what was happening, several students sprang forward and hoisted Gropius onto their shoulders.

The Significance of the Bauhaus

"It was an idea"; this was Mies van der Rohe's explanation of the immense influence of the Bauhaus.

But what was this idea?

It was an attempt to bridge the gulf between the world of the spirit and the world of everyday, between art and industrial production. The whole endeavor of the Bauhaus was to discover similarities between these two conflicting spheres and to make them generally known. To do this it was absolutely necessary to go back to first principles and again to investigate the elemental nature both of art and of matter.

When the world of the spirit and the world of industrial production are split entirely asunder, we find ourselves in the situation of the nineteenth century, whose Janus head faced in two opposite directions. This leads to a schizophrenic division of human life and this duality is what Walter Gropius sought to heal in the Bauhaus. In his first four-page manifesto of 1919 he says:

12. LYONEL FEININGER:
Title page for the first Bauhaus prospectus, 1919.

"The final product of all artistic endeavor is the building. The visual arts once found their highest task in contributing to its beauty and were inseparable constituents of all great works of architecture. To-day each stands apart in independent isolation and this situation can only be changed through conscious cooperative work. Architects, painters and sculptors must again come together and study the many-sided nature of the building both as a whole and in all its several parts. Only then will their work again express the spirit of great architecture and be freed from the dead hand of academicism."

On the front page of this manifesto was an expressionistic woodcut by Lyonel Feininger[10] which gave utterance to the same thought. It showed a cathedral over which shone three bright stars – symbols perhaps of the three visual arts.

---

[10] Cf. "*Bauhaus 1919–1928*", p. 19.

The Bauhaus had, of course, no intention of building cathedrals, but the basic principle of bringing about a unity between the arts that could overcome the split existence of man remained its dominant objective. As Kandinsky put it:

"This fragmentation will be slowly replaced by integration. 'Either or' must be replaced by 'Both together'."

Creative Art

It is the same with art as with science. One cannot arrive at the truth of the matter by following the most obvious route. Art, like science, must first strip off all outer coverings before it can penetrate into the real nature of things.

Both artistic expression and scientific research have now come to employ methods that completely dematerialize the object they are investigating. Both seek to study primary elements: science concentrates upon particles so infinitely small that they can only be apprehended intellectually, art upon the very simplest formal shapes. Both are thereby creating a new image of the world.

One of the functions of contemporary art is the re-awakening of our consciousness of simple but forgotten primary elements. This has given rise to a remarkable situation. In the first place it can readily be seen that contemporary means of artistic expression have an inner relationship with those of prehistoric art[11]. At the same time the work of those artists who are most successful in opening our eyes to long-forgotten symbols, such as Joan Miró or Paul Klee, shows an unexpected similarity to the most up-to-date research techniques of applied science. In "*Mechanization Takes Command*"[12], it is shown how the chronocyclograph, employed in time and motion studies, traces much the same pattern of complicated tracks as can be found in Paul Klee's concentrated figurations.

To sum up, the idea of the Bauhaus consisted in exploring the means of bringing the repetitive work of the machine into harmony with the eternal laws of the nature of material.

Henry van de Velde, now over 90, the founder of the School of Arts and Crafts in Weimar and its head until the outbreak of the 1914 war against Belgium, has said that, when in 1918 he recommended Gropius as his successor, he was well aware that Gropius would conduct things quite differently from the way he had done. Nevertheless, he had been confident that Gropius was the one man in Germany for the task.

There was an inner meaning in Gropius' merging of van de Velde's School of Arts and Crafts with the Weimar Academy of Fine Arts. To accomplish

---

[11] The author is in the midst of preparing a book on this subject; in the meantime, reference may be made to an address "*Prehistoric and Contemporary Means of Artistic Expression*", S. Giedion, International Congress of Prehistoric and Protohistoric Sciences, Zurich, 1950, p. 81.
[12] Cf. "*Mechanization Takes Command*", pp. 110–111, figs. 58 and 60.

the aims he had in view he required, in any case, different influences. But the deliberate amalgamation of art, the germ cell of vision, with the shaping of everyday objects, was in accordance with Gropius' basic ideas.

Thus, it came about that Gropius was able to assemble around him artists whose whole outlook was oriented towards a return to an elemental approach. By working with them the students were able gradually to restore their own damaged vision and to look with fresh eyes not only upon themselves but also upon the objects around them. This was the purpose of the " *Basic Course* " that served as a forerunner to later teaching methods at the Bauhaus[13].

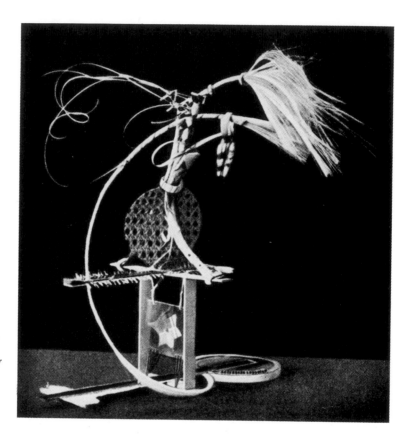

13.   *Classroom study of materials, 1923. Rhythmic composition of various materials as part of a study of their complementary properties; made by a student, M. Bronstein (from " Staatliches Bauhaus in Weimar ", 1919–1923).*

The Basic Course at Weimar was started in 1919 by *Johannes Itten,* who had been running an Art School in Vienna. Itten developed further the methods taught at the Stuttgart Academy by the Austrian, Adolf Hölzel. These included freeing the hand of the young artist from inhibiting stiffness; analyzing pictures by breaking them down into their basic elements; and, above all, heightening artistic sensitivity by stressing the contrasts in structure of different materials. This emphasis upon the structural nature of objects appears again and again in contemporary art, and was basic to the teaching program of the preliminary course at the Bauhaus.

Itten's work in Vienna was first recognized by the art historian, Prof. Hans Tietze: Adolf Loos made him famous overnight, and Alma Mahler, Walter Gropius' first wife, who had an extraordinary instinct for the recognition of unknown talent in all fields of art, brought him to Gropius' notice.

---

[13] Cf. " *Bauhaus 1919–1928* ", pp. 36–37.

When Itten left the Weimar Bauhaus, in 1923, the course was taken over by L. Moholy-Nagy with Joseph Albers, who had been entirely educated in the school. They proceeded to develop it further in their own way. This was again extended by Moholy-Nagy in 1937 in the "*New Bauhaus*", later the "*Institute of Design*", in Chicago[14]. Joseph Albers[15] has also had a great influence upon the education of artists and architects in the U.S.A. since 1933 through his work at Black Mountain College, then at Harvard University and finally at Yale University.

For this return to first principles in the elements of art and the basic nature of materials, particular kinds of creative artists were necessary.

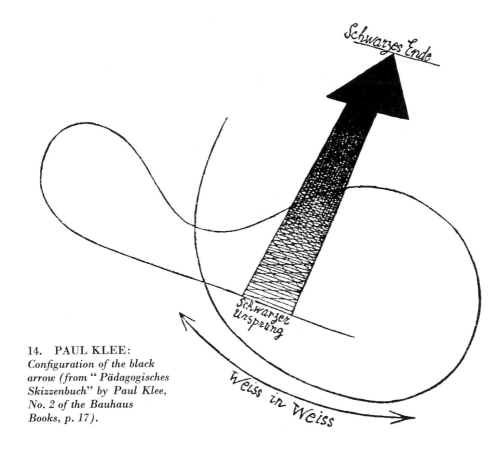

14. PAUL KLEE:
Configuration of the black arrow (from " Pädagogisches Skizzenbuch" by Paul Klee, No. 2 of the Bauhaus Books, p. 17).

Walter Gropius and those nearest to him knew how to seek these out. As a result *Paul Klee* joined the Bauhaus staff in January, 1921 and *Wassily Kandinsky* in June, 1922.

Paul Klee possessed the same penetrative, divining vision of complex structure in the realm of the human spirit as Leonardo da Vinci in the realm of science. It seems remarkable that so deeply intuitive an artist was able to stand the "incessantly explosive atmosphere" of the Bauhaus almost throughout its existence. Certainly, following the demands of his very being, he continued to keep himself apart and to take no part in the Bauhaus' endless battle for existence. He just stayed on. Nevertheless, as Gropius has repeatedly affirmed, he was always "the final moral arbiter of the Bauhaus".

---

[14] Cf. "*Bauhaus 1919–1928*", pp. 90, 124–126.
[15] Ibid., pp. 91, 116–123.

The reason why Paul Klee continued to remain at the Bauhaus was his profound instinct for and understanding of the interdependence of all the things that go to make up life. With the students, as in his own work, he was able to weave a silver web of poetry around the most banal of things. When he was in charge of the weaving class, the warps and wefts of the looms blossomed into pictures such as "Ancient Sound" and, later, "Efflorescence", through whose dynamic parallelograms flickers the light of the inner principles of matter. In his "*Pädagogisches Skizzenbuch*" (Teacher's Sketchbook) instead of the usual rigid textbook presentation of the ele-

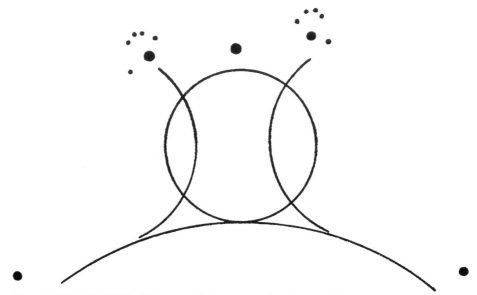

15. W. KANDINSKY: *Diagram of the leap of the dancer, Palucca: arms and legs were outspread; the circle denotes her flaring ballet skirt and the dots her head, feet and hands (from "Punkt und Linie zu Fläche" by W. Kandinsky in the Bauhaus Books).*

Fig. 14 ments of geometry, his students experienced the magical excitement of their first discovery.

Klee was soon followed by Kandinsky with whom he had been in close sympathy since his early days in Munich. Kandinsky with his cosmic vision rooted in his Russian background, and his penetrating insight into artistic problems, made an excellent counterpart to Klee's work and personality. But in one major respect they were alike. Both had plunged deeply into a study of elemental matters and, because of this, both were well fitted to construct the bridge by which the Bauhaus idea could be made accessible to the everyday world.

Dessau, 1925–1928

During the Dessau period the long laboratory work of the Weimar days – the "close contact with primary materials" as Klee described it in his lectures – began to bear fruit. The dual control that had been necessary in Weimar days, when every workshop had to have both a director (an artist) and an instructor (a craftsman) could now be set aside. A new generation had grown up fully trained in the Bauhaus atmosphere: *Joseph Albers*, who gave the Basic Course[16]; *Herbert Bayer*, who taught typography[17], *Marcel Breuer*, carpentry[18]; *Gunta Stoelzl*, weaving[19]; *Hinnerk Scheper*, mural painting; *Joost Schmidt*, sculpture. Other staff members also, such as Moholy-Nagy, now directed their workshops on their own.

On the basis of this systematically sound foundation new prototypes for mass production were now developed. The origins of their design must be sought in the seemingly sequestered work of the art studios. Now this became absorbed into industrial production and distributed around the world. An outstanding example is the tubular steel chair first designed by Marcel Breuer in 1925. Many other examples come to mind including typography, lamps and textiles.

Fig. 52–62

Fig. 56

The kind of work that was coming out of this German educational institution is called in the U.S.A. "product design": in other words, giving form and shape to mass-produced objects, which has become one of the most important problems of highly mechanized industry.

Architecture in the Bauhaus Curriculum

There was, as yet, no direct reference to architecture, though the Bauhaus building itself at Dessau (1925) stood as Gropius' greatest achievement. Even so, architecture stood silently behind everything done at the Bauhaus – for everything was always considered in relation to "the whole".

In the early Weimar days, when Gropius was collecting private funds to build the House on the Horn (1923) he hoped that this would have led to other buildings in accordance with the general layout plan he had prepared. If this had materialized, the students would have had an opportunity for actual practical experience – the "fieldwork" upon which Gropius was later to insist so strongly at Harvard.

Fig. 266

He could only take such opportunities as then offered to develop certain architectural ideas, in collaboration with his old partner Adolf Meyer who had joined the Bauhaus staff in 1919. This resulted in schemes produced by Farkas Molnar, Marcel Breuer and Fred Forbat (who has later built up a considerable practice in Sweden). The atmosphere thus created enabled Marcel Breuer in 1924, while still a student, to give shape to his ideas for the house as a narrow slab[20]. This is clear evidence of the way in which apparently pointless studies of materials provide the substance which, in the hands of a really talented student, can germinate into prototypes that set a new standard.

The only thing Walter Gropius could do, under the circumstances, was to find positions for his students in connection with any building on which he was himself engaged. He was not able to develop his own ideas on architectural education to any extent until he took over the Graduate Course

---

[16] Cf. "*Bauhaus, 1919–1928*", New York, 1938, pp. 116–123.

[17] Ibid., pp. 148–152.

[18] Ibid., pp. 128–134.

[19] Ibid., pp. 142–147.

[20] Ibid., p. 78.

at Harvard University in 1937. The great influence he there exercised over a whole generation of young architects (far wider than the student enrolment at Harvard) cannot yet be fully estimated.

Walter Gropius resigned from the Bauhaus in 1928 on many grounds. The daily never-ending struggle for existence had sapped his strength; in addition, he had the idea that much of the enmity aroused by the school was directed personally against him. The number of buildings he was able to execute in this period was small, apart from the Bauhaus group and the Toerten housing project, and he was very keen to resume active practice. The years immediately following his departure from the Bauhaus saw the realization of several projects. Walter Gropius had a decisive influence upon the German housing movement, which was at that time the most important field of architectural activity. But, in the main, everything had come too late for Germany. Too much time had been taken up with efforts to convince people intellectually, by means of diagrams, carefully worked out statistics and calculations.

Contact between the two poles of those artists furthest removed from exact calculations and the meticulous precision of the rational intellect: this was the aim and the achievement of Gropius and the Bauhaus.

EXHIBITIONS AND LIFE

The Period of World Exhibitions

Exhibitions have played an important part in the life of Walter Gropius. Exhibitions often serve as a proclamation to the general public of new developments in the fields that interest it most. Almost every period seems to have developed an inner relation to some particular kind of building. In Gothic times it was the cathedral; in the Baroque period, the ducal palace; and after the middle of the nineteenth century, when industry had become the focal point of general economy, exhibition buildings took on this rôle. The problems changed and the form and content of exhibitions changed with them. After the middle of the nineteenth century they acquired a new importance. In the earlier years the foreground had been dominated by industrial production, but the theme now became the comparison of competitive products from different countries for the purposes of encouraging higher standards of performance.

Between 1850 and 1890 the arching roofs of the great halls of the World Exhibitions, themselves the products of industry, provided an opportunity to display the creatively constructive activities of the nineteenth century. These "universal" exhibitions, as the first of them was named, flaunted the banner of free trade, which they intended should wave over the entire earth. They flourished as long as there was complete confidence in the onward march of progress and the apparently limitless possibilities of an ever-increasing industrial production.

The Great Exhibition in London (1851) with its Crystal Palace and display of "*Industry of all Nations*", and the World Exhibition in Paris (1889) with its Eiffel Tower and grandiose "Halles des Machines", marked the beginning and the end of this development[1].

From this time on Industrial Exhibitions diminished in outward appearance and inner meaning, for the public no longer marvelled at every new industrial development. They were still held, it is true, but historically speaking they were less important than other much more modest exhibitions. These too were concerned with industrial production but in quite a different sense. The problem now became the incorporation and adjustment of the machine to the way of life of contemporary man. A movement in this direction was behind the reformist activities of William Morris and his followers in the last decades of the nineteenth century. Henry van de Velde also worked untiringly on these lines, starting in 1890 in Belgium and then working from 1897 to 1914 in Germany. This resulted in considerable action in Germany

---

[1] Cf. "*Space, Time and Architecture*", 10th Edition, 1954, p. 473 ff.

expressed by the energetic efforts of the Werkbund, founded in 1907: a late but active descendant of the English "Arts and Crafts Movement". The theme always remained the same: to eradicate lifeless and imitative objects and bad materials from the human environment and to replace them by objects more cleanly and honestly fashioned. The results were perhaps more impressive in Germany than anywhere else. The change of outlook around 1900 was as sudden and intensive as the earlier decision, of around 1870, to concentrate all effort upon the development of major industries. Since this time Germany had perhaps fallen to greater depths than other countries in the mis-use of forms and of materials. Now however determined efforts were being made to awaken in industry a feeling for cleaner and more functional forms. This period was disastrously brief. It was cut short by the first world war. Its peak, reached in the *Exhibition of the German Werkbund, 1914*, lasted but one short summer[2].

The Werkbund Exhibition, 1914

H. van de Velde,
J. Hoffmann,
P. Behrens

At this exhibition the work of two quite different generations, which had both battled against the architecture of the nineteenth century, could suddenly be seen. Under the leadership of the Werkbund, everything creative then existing in Germany was assembled together. By far the most important product of the older generation, then at the height of its creative power, was the theater with its tripartite stage built by Henry van de Velde, who was then about fifty years of age. J. Hoffmann, who was born in 1870, built the Austrian Pavilion with a temple-like façade of columns which were still fluted though without base or capital. They somewhat resembled the grille before one of the Viennese "Werkstätte" jewel boxes[3]. The Exhibition Hall, built by Peter Behrens (1868–1940), suffered from the peculiarities of that architect whenever he struck a monumental note. Compared with the audacity of his A.E.G. factory, it was sadly disappointing.

None of this first revolutionary generation had yet launched an attack upon the ponderousness of the building structure. In this they were very different from the younger generation, who approached things in quite another way. These wanted above all to loosen up the building and to make it transparent. Their aids were glass, steel and ferroconcrete. Behind them stood the anonymous engineering tradition of glazed ironwork exhibition halls. Before them was an awareness of certain half-unconscious feelings that provided the impetus.

Bruno Taut

This was certainly the case in the Pavilion built by *Bruno Taut* (1880–1938) for the German glass industry. This was, as he himself said, "a space enclosed by glass prisms, glass ceiling, glass paving, glass tiles, (glass stairs)[4]". The translucent, prismatic qualities of glass were here exploited, rather than its transparency. The building appeared like a magic crystal; like the embodiment of a poem by the fantastic poet Paul Scherbart, who was a close

---

[2] For further information see Peter Jessen, "*Die deutsche Werkbundausstellung, Köln, 1914*", in the "*Jahrbuch des Deutschen Werkbundes*", Munich, 1915, p. 1ff.
[3] The Viennese "Werkstätte" (craftsmen's centers) were elegant counterparts of the German Arts and Crafts Centers, and were closely associated with Josef Hoffmann.
[4] See Bruno Taut, "*Die neue Baukunst*", Stuttgart, 1929, p. 28.

46

friend of Bruno Taut. In his pamphlet *"Glasarchitektur"* (Glass Architecture), published by Sturm in Berlin, 1914, the poet utters the following optimistic lines, "Glass architecture which turns the humble dwellings of men into cathedrals will exert the same beneficial influence over them[5]".

The polygonal glass pavilion of Bruno Taut was a manifesto! Its glass cupola, composed of many facets like the eye of an insect, was constructed like a wicker net with no supporting pole, and was, as Bruno Taut later remarked, a fore-runner of the space-frame that was only to acquire its full architectonic expression in the middle of this century.

The greatest architectural excitement was aroused by the so-called "factory" of young Walter Gropius. It says a great deal for the spiritual development of Germany at that time that a man of thirty should have been given the opportunity to develop his own architectural ideas upon such a prominent site. The structure, which was a model factory for a medium-sized firm, consisted of an administration building with attached car-ports and a large workshed. It was interesting to see the hand of the architect in those open garages (or car-ports as they were later named by Frank Lloyd Wright) which appeared here in 1914, as well as in the factory area to the rear with its wide central nave, pitched roof and curved top lighting. "The form and construction of this hall shows the value of close collaboration between architect and engineer, and also that the assistance of the architect does not necessarily increase the costs of the building[6]."

Walter Gropius' "Factory"
Fig. 32–40

Most important however was the architecture of the administration block with its transparent staircase, the glass-walled offices with continuous glazing round the corners, and the roof terrace. Here the architect subordinated the engineer.

Fig. 37

Even in his factory at Alfeld, Gropius had enveloped the stairway with glass and had 'dematerialized' the corners of the building. In the glass-walled staircase of Cologne, however, which has been so widely imitated, the idea was greatly developed.

The Glass-Walled Staircase

The transparency of the glass produced an astonishing effect. The staircase, relieved of its accustomed shell, now seemed to hover in space. The spiral stairway appeared as if in momentarily arrested movement. This use of the possibilities of transparency was something quite new in architecture. The effect was strengthened by the juxtaposition of the windowless front wall of yellow limestone.

Fig. 32

The glass-walled staircase led up to a covered roof terrace that was carefully detailed. The wide sloping cornices of the two taller structures sheltered dance floors. They were linked by a roofed-over restaurant. These were building elements that became architecturally further developed by others at a much later date.

Fig. 36

A contemporary opinion was expressed as follows: "A marvelous effect is achieved by two staircase towers which he had enveloped entirely in glass. For window-gazing youngsters these glass towers possess a number of

Assessment of 1914

---

[5] See Bruno Taut, *"Die neue Baukunst"*, Stuttgart, 1929, p. 118.
[6] See *"Bautechnische Mitteilungen des Stahlwerk-Verbandes"* (Building Techniques Bulletin of the Steel Workers Society) Dusseldorf, July, 1914, vol. 1, p. 8.

47

attractions, but other than that they have no use." Of the glass windows of the offices "One can't suddenly apply a principle disliked even by prisoners (i. e. being overlooked) to buildings for honest townsmen[7]".

To-day other theories have become current. One, that is everywhere repeated, is that in many of the details of this building complex one can see the influence of Frank Lloyd Wright. For the most part – and this is the real significance of the work – notes were sounded for which F. L. Wright has no ear: such as the use of transparency which only appears in his work very late and very rarely: to some extent for instance in the glass tower of the Johnson Wax Factory in Racine, 1949.

The artistic assimilation of new materials and new possibilities, which in the nineteenth century were mostly used only for engineering purposes, is here given a new range of possibilities. Some of the immediately previous generation had also worked in this direction (one has only to mention *Auguste Perret*, born in 1873, and *Tony Garnier*, born in 1869). Gropius' model factory at the Cologne Exhibition, with its emphasis on lightness, transparency and simplicity of form showed more of the essence of contemporary architecture than anything that had yet happened in Europe.

Bauhaus Exhibition, 1923

The "factory" of 1914 slipped into the war. After that was over, five long hard years followed during which the organization of the Bauhaus was built up. The demonstration undertaken by the Bauhaus in Weimar in the summer of 1923 was a form of defence against the attacks from its immediate environment. The intention was to seek world-wide opinion upon its performance and inner workings. In the opinion of those present the result was probably the most interesting "Exhibition" with which Walter Gropius was ever associated. This was due to the close association of the work of the school with stage performances in the newly re-organized theater as well as performances of the newest works of music. Further information can be found in the chapter on the Bauhaus.

"Open-Air Life", 1928

One cannot omit the exhibition that Gropius set up in close collaboration with L. Moholy-Nagy in the summer of 1928, shortly after he had left the Bauhaus. This was an open-air exhibition in which Moholy-Nagy, in the most unobtrusive manner, employed both sunlight and artificial light together to cast shadows and to "paint with light", just as he did in his pictures. It is very seldom in our time that a painter and an architect have been able to work so harmoniously and understandingly together as in these green outdoor rooms displayed with the simplest of materials in a Berlin suburb.

The exhibition consisted of demountable, half-open, wooden stands which
Fig. 63 held the view of the passers-by, composing eleven booths, which were alter-

---

[7] See Robert Breuer, "*Die Kölner Werkbundausstellung*" (The Cologne Werkbund Exhibition), "*Deutsche Kunst und Dekoration*", vol. XXXIV, April – September 1914, p. 435.

nately open to the street and to the court. Those that opened to the street had large windows, but those facing the court were completely open. Comparisons were shown of old and new methods of living, new building techniques and building materials and, at the end, completed buildings. The most important aspect was the manner in which these different problems were presented.

It may be permitted to add here a few unpublished remarks of L. Moholy-Nagy, which explain how closely the methods of the Bauhaus circle of 1928 approach modern exhibition techniques:

"Moveable walls lettered with new slogans, rotating color filters, light projectors, signal demonstrations and reflectors: transparency, light and movement all in the service of the public. Everything so arranged that it can be handled and understood by the simplest individual. Then also the exciting use of new materials: huge sheets of celluloid, lattice work, enlargements, small and large sheets of wire meshing, transparent displays, with lettering suspended in space, everywhere clear and brilliant colors."

Paris, 1930

In reality, all the exhibitions put up by Walter Gropius and his companions centered around the same theme. They were *demonstrations of a new way of life*[8]. Whether or not this was always apparent, they all in fact showed a part of a new form of dwelling – of a way of living that had not yet come into being. The greatest stimulus to this new approach was given by the Paris Exhibition, held in the Grand Palais at the invitation of the "*Salon des Artistes Décorateurs*" in the middle of May, 1930. It was the first time since the war that Germany had been officially invited to take part. This was, as I wrote at the time[9], "certainly a matter of no small political importance; but the thing that struck one most was how it had come about that the Foreign Ministry, instead of taking the job on itself, handed it over to the German Werkbund. The procedure of the Werkbund was then typical: instead of nominating a many-headed committee, they appointed one man to take over complete responsibility, and that man was no irresolute, compromising type, but: Walter Gropius."

The German Werkbund, who were entrusted with the Paris Exhibit, handed over the task to Walter Gropius, as has been said. He was the commissioner for the exhibit and, as such, was deliberately one-sided in his selection of the objects to be shown, for he was clear from the start that this would achieve a far more effective result. He chose as his assistants Marcel Breuer, Herbert Bayer and L. Moholy-Nagy and organized the job as a form of closely cooperative teamwork, with each member responsible for a particular aspect. The Exhibit consisted of a display of the products of German industry, each carefully selected as showing a practicable human standard for future mass production. The catalog, laid out and illustrated by Herbert Bayer, was in itself a minor typographical masterpiece.

An Exhibition of a New Way of Life

[8] E. g. The Exhibition of "*Non-Ferrous Metals*", Berlin, 1934, and the *Pennsylvanian Pavilion* at the New York World Fair, 1939.
[9] S. Giedion, "*Eine offizielle deutsche Ausstellung in Paris*" (An Official German Exhibition in Paris), *Cicerone*, May 8th, 1930.

The exhibit proved a great success in Paris, and this was mainly due to the fact that it placed before the spectators the "*squelette d'une vie nouvelle*" as *Figaro* termed it[10]. The space in which everything was displayed was itself the reproduction of a "common room", or community center, for one of the unbuilt slab-like apartment houses which Gropius and his companions were then actively engaged in working out.

Main Theme of the Exhibit: the Community Center of an Apartment House

The Exhibit also put forward two other ideas: the case for standardization, and the case for a form of housing not limited to the individual dwelling unit. The immediate impression I received from those days in Paris may here be quoted[11]:

Fig. 64–68

"The '*section allemande*' is situated at the farthest end of the Grand Palais. On approaching the exhibit, one's eye is at once caught by the glass walls of a swimming-bath and gymnasium. It seems at first sight astonishing to have a swimming-bath right in the foreground; but later one realizes that this first impression is thoroughly right, since it at once gives the French a sensation that this exhibit touches on fundamentals... It shows that Walter Gropius had a very subtle instinct in opening the exhibit with this overture. The entire exhibit is conceived as a single entity which takes the form of the "community center" of a ten-story apartment house. Marcel Breuer has been responsible for the organization of an actual apartment in this residential hotel, Moholy-Nagy for the lighting effects and Herbert Bayer for the arrangement of the various mass-produced objects... As has been said, Gropius was himself responsible for the entrance area with its swimming-bath, gymnasium, bar, dance floor, reading and playing corners, library, radio-gramophone nook, and bulletin board. A metal bridge in the form of a ramp rises over the swimming-bath, with an open lattice-like construction of galvanized steel.

Fig. 135, 141–147

Fig. 5

"Moholy-Nagy, who was in charge of all lighting, from reading lamps to theater illuminations, demonstrated a great number of different lighting effects through the skilful use of a variety of standardized German lighting fixtures, from bedside lamps to large reflectors. In one place one sees the effect of light upon a sensitized surface (photography); farther back, light used as the animating element in a theater (Moholy-Nagy displayed a mobile lighting apparatus – the light modulator); finally one can see an actual theater (the model and plans for Walter Gropius' famous 'Total Theater', 1926; figures from Schlemmer's 'Triadic Ballet', 1923; Moholy-Nagy's stage settings for the 'Tales of Hoffmann' and other productions). In the center of the community area is a self-operated projector which shows pictures of the New Germany. This is shielded from light by three walls of a new material (Trolit). The back wall forms the approach to Herbert Bayer's area, and here one discovers an array of porcelain crucibles and medical instruments. Two things strike one most forcibly about Bayer's section. One is the effective display of woollen fabrics, which are stretched over invisible square frames that hover in space. The other is the display of mass-produced chairs (designed by Breuer, Mies van der Rohe, Schneck, Thonet, etc.) that stand out at right angles from the wall, all the way up to the ceiling. Another way in which

[10] *Le Figaro*, May 16th, 1930.
[11] S. Giedion, "*Der Deutsche Werkbund in Paris*" (The German Werkbund in Paris), *Neue Zürcher Zeitung*, June 17th and 18th, 1930.

Bayer catches the eye of the visitor is by the projection of magnificent enlargements of new buildings upon a hollowed-out surface, so that the beholder appears to be enclosed within the space.

"The success of the exhibit is due in no small measure to Marcel Breuer, as in his section the public are able to obtain a very direct sensation of reality. (All the French were delighted with the excellent finish of the furniture.) Breuer's model apartment of the ten-story apartment house contains a general living area, bathroom, kitchen, men's study and ladies' boudoir, and a workroom (office). Its many technical refinements, such as the revolving standardized cupboards, well-sprung chairs and movable writing-desk, give the general public an opportunity to get acquainted with a new form of living in a way that has hitherto been impossible for them.

"It is very pleasant to realize that the minds of creative men are everywhere moving in a similar direction, and that we are slowly approaching a period of universal cultural understanding...

"The thing that impresses the French most about the German section of the exhibition is that they have found the emphasis laid upon just the opposite from what they had expected – namely lightness. 'The first and most striking feature of the German exhibit is its lightness' *('Ce qui frappe au premier abord dans la section allemande du salon des artistes décorateurs, c'est la légèreté.')* writes Vaillat in '*Le Temps*'[12]. Lightness instead of heaviness. 'This exhibition has one most important aspect', Vaillat continues, 'which none can escape and which we require to study very carefully... In 1910 another exhibition was set up by German artists in the Grand Palais... How much has happened between then and now... Munich, which has now become the most reactionary city of Germany, was then the headquarters of the Werkbund. Now Berlin has taken its place. The bold experiments that came from Munich before the war now arrive from Berlin... It is certainly not an exaggeration to say that the '*section allemande*' is not only a '*salon*' – a salon among many others – but that it again, in very truth, shows us the face of Young Germany...'

The French view of the German Exhibit

" Is it not astonishing that even in *Figaro* (May 16, 1930) Arsène Alexandre, the biographer of Daumier, whose outlook had always been in quite a different direction, could not deny the importance of the exhibit? He touches upon an important point when he enquires: 'Is this really, in the exact meaning of the words, an exhibit of Arts and Crafts? *Non, c'est plutôt une nouvelle conception des lignes, surfaces, contenances, pour une vie abstraite, disciplinée sans restrictions, ni souci d'atténuer la vie même...*'

"The success of this exhibit in the delicate air of Paris betokens one thing above all: a belated recognition of the work fostered by the Bauhaus. The anger and vituperation that has been vented against the Bauhaus for ten years in Germany is here shown, with the utmost clarity, to have been due to a deplorable shortsightedness and lack of instinct. This exhibit is less of a leap into the future than the culmination of ten years of work. International judgement of it, although not in the hands of particulary friendly critics, has restored the balance of opinion and has tipped the scales in favor of Germany."

The success of the German Exhibit

---

[12] *Le Temps*, May 21st, 1930.

The German diplomats, who had been very nervous of the "radical" character of the exhibit, were astounded by the delighted comments of the Parisian press. Encouraged by this success, the German Ambassador invited the organizers of the exhibition to a large reception in the palatial Embassy – an Empire mansion formerly owned by Prince Beauharnais. Walter Gropius laid before him the list of French artists who should be invited, to which – shaking his head the while – the Ambassador agreed. At the head of the great stairway stood the "*chef de réception*" in his red livery, and banged his tall staff upon the floor each time as he announced: "Monsieur Perret; Monsieur Mondrian (in a borrowed frock coat and cravat); Monsieur Le Corbusier; Monsieur et Madame Delaunay; Monsieur et Madame Arp; Monsieur Vantongerloo; Monsieur Léger; etc." All people who would not normally be found in this environment. And it was a superb party!

This Paris exhibit was a beginning and at the same time an end[13].

Fig. 69, 70

[13] Gropius, who was then living in Berlin, took part in every exhibition that was possible before the change of regime (1933). In the *Berlin Building Exhibition*, 1931, Gropius and his group employed the same theme as at Paris: "*The Community Center of an Apartment Building*" (see "*Moderne Bauformen*", vol. VIII, 1931, pp. 388–89). Graphically detailed exhibits show its close connection with his basic conception of the "*tall apartment house amid greenery as a future form of city life*" (see W. Gropius "*Zentralblatt der Bauverwaltung*", May, 1931). The Building Crafts Exhibition, 1931, finally destroyed the view that the German dwelling house must lie closely attached to the ground, and tried to excite a greater interest in the new possibilities of housing settlements.

BUILDINGS FOR EDUCATION

The power to diffuse his influence over his surroundings is an attribute of a great educationalist. Walter Gropius was predestined for this rôle. Being also an architect, it is not surprising that the buildings in which education is carried on are a matter of deep concern to him. Indeed the commission to build the Bauhaus gave him the cue for his most significant building.

This multiform complex of the Bauhaus in Dessau was the first building to make a radical break with the space conception of previous centuries. Here, at one blow, the space-time conception of our period became manifest. Here, two years before Le Corbusier's famous but unexecuted designs for the League of Nations at Geneva, the discerning eye can glimpse the shape of things to come. In accordance with his faith in teamwork, Gropius has designed most of his buildings in close collaboration with others. Is it a mere accident that in the case of the Bauhaus, his signature stands alone?

The Significance of the Bauhaus

The Bauhaus complex is no isolated phenomenon. Certain smaller, unexecuted projects, such as his scheme for an International Academy of Philosophy at Erlangen (1924), already include some of the same features. In this project, two years before embarking on the Bauhaus scheme, Gropius had an opportunity to work out the complex relationships between living and studying under the same roof; it was here that the first steps were taken to achieve new kinds of relationships in space by the interplay of planes at various levels and the varied disposition of volumes of different heights.

Fig. 77–79

In the competition scheme he prepared for an Engineering School at Hagen, Westphalia[1], (1929), a reinforced concrete structure, both the differentiation of the various functions and the aesthetic problem of loosening up a massive block are organically related. A dominating main block facing the street contains the administration offices, conference rooms, library, laboratories and the students' canteen. Stretching back from this building, in the quietest position with the best orientation, lies the elongated classroom wing. Here the rooms almost all face southeast or southwest and part of the roof is also made accessible. The main block facing the street and the classroom wing stretching away from it together form a "T", to which the various special-purpose structures are attached. One is linked to the main block by means of a bridge, a feature that appears again and again in the work of Walter Gropius.

Fig. 80, 81

The machine laboratories with their different heights and the transformer house stand at right angles to the classroom block. This loosening-up of

[1] Cf. "*Zentralblatt der Bauverwaltung*", 1929, No. 47.

the main structure and clear articulation of the parts is a feature that can be traced in Gropius' work up to and beyond the Harvard Graduate Center of 1949.

The Bauhaus, 1925–26[2]

The building program for the new school in Dessau was extremely complicated. First, there was the Bauhaus itself with its various departments; a trades school for the further education of craftsmen and a students' hostel with studio-bedrooms. Then, in addition, there had to be an auditorium with a stage, a canteen, administration offices and a private studio for Gropius himself. Houses and studios for the Bauhaus faculty were to be built in the adjacent pine-woods. Gropius' chief aim was to demarcate each of these elements quite distinctly without isolating one from another, and at the same time to give an architectural unity to the whole. The chief accent falls on the Bauhaus itself with its famous glass curtain-walls.

Fig. 82–91   It contains workshops, lecture rooms and exhibition halls, some of which can be thrown together.

Fig. 82, 84, 88, 90   The students' studio-dormitory, known as the "Prellerhaus" is a taller
Fig. 92   six-story block containing 28 rooms. These rooms, though extremely simple, are spacious and were designed to serve both as bedrooms and studies or studios. In front of each a concrete slab, jutting out into space, forms a small balcony.

Fig. 87, 91   Connection to the main building, the Bauhaus itself, is across a single-story bridge-like structure, raised on piers. This supports canteen, auditorium and stage, and opens through into the foyer of the main building. These spaces could also, to a large extent, be thrown together. Another bridge, containing the administration offices, leads to the trade school, standing at right angles to it. The whole group builds up into a marvelous
Fig. 76   complex consisting of two dissimilar "L" shaped forms interpenetrating
Fig. 87   and intersecting one another at different levels. The use of *passerelles* and piers lifts the weight from the building complex (functional basis: short, time-saving, communicating passages). This lightness is given further emphasis by the glass walls of the Bauhaus itself.

The Bauhaus and the New Space Conception

These glass curtain-walls, that are drawn around the corners of the main Bauhaus building, dominate the scene. Lecture rooms and exhibition halls are on the third floor, above the different workshops. The chief difference
Fig. 87, 89   between these glass façades and those of the nineteenth century (such as Eiffel's Exhibition Hall in the Paris World Exhibition of 1878) is that these façades are no longer composed of enlarged windows fitted into rigid supporting frames. Instead, they wrap round the building at the most critical points of its structure, giving it a crystalline translucence. Structurally they also contribute to that process of loosening-up a building which now domi-

---

[2] Cf. W. Gropius, "*Bauhausbauten Dessau*", Vol. 12 of "*Bauhausbücher*", Munich, 1930.

nates the architectural scene. The 'dematerialization' of the corners indicates, as in the Fagus factory, that the structure itself should be sought within; in this case the structure consists of a reinforced concrete frame with cantilevers: rather over-heavy owing to the regulations of the German building by-laws.

These glass walls flow into one another precisely at the point where the human eye is accustomed to see a supporting column. Here, for the first time on any large scale, is a proclamation of the interpenetration of inner volume and outer space. As has already been described in "*Space, Time*

16. *View from the main staircase to the workshop building (Bauhaus Books).*

and Architecture", this is an expression in terms of architecture of the same abandonment of the single viewpoint of the Renaissance that had already occured in painting: in Picasso's Arlésienne (1911–12) the head is shown simultaneously full face and in profile.

The Bauhaus complex has no definite frontal façade. The interplay of transparency and the piercing of space by bridges leads to an interpenetration of horizontal and vertical planes that makes it impossible to grasp the whole of the complex from any single viewpoint, and results in an unprecedented effect of simultaneity that accords with the space-time conception.

Significance of Bauhaus Building Program

The complexity of the Bauhaus program with its combination of students' living quarters with teaching quarters and with the faculty houses a stone's throw away, was most unusual on the European continent. There, unfortunately, a sharp division usually separates living from studying, even in the Universities.

The Bauhaus buildings were not, however, intended to carry on the medieval traditions that have persisted in Oxford or Cambridge. The intention was based rather upon a passionate endeavor to create an island of concentration in total contrast to the chaotic confusion of the world around: a moment of unity in a world already almost in flames. Only now, in retrospect, are we able to recognize that the aims, then limited to the teaching program of the Bauhaus, are identical with those slowly becoming accepted as the aims of our whole way of life, the reconciliation and interpenetration of the individual and communal spheres.

Impington Village College, Cambridge, England, 1936

It was ten years after the completion of the Bauhaus before Walter Gropius, then in exile, built another building for education in partnership with

Fig. 94–98

Maxwell Fry. This was the Impington Village College, Cambridge, England[3], which was designed to provide for the social activities of adults as well as classes for the children. This is a combination that has always borne fruitful results. The correctly oriented, single-depth classroom, that Gropius had already developed in his project for Hagen, has now become generally accepted architectural practice. This was linked to the single story height which has been adopted in so many of the English and American postwar schools. Here at Impington is an early example of both these trends, with its great glazed openings that give free access to the open air.

Impington College is a secondary school for 240 children between 11 and 15 years of age. Linked to the classroom block is a slightly curved building. This contains rooms for adult courses as well as those for recreation and play. There is a hall seating about 360 which serves as an auditorium for the children by day and for adult assemblies, theatricals and so forth in the evenings. Adjoining this is a dining-room with kitchen attached; a common-room; rooms for table tennis and billiards; a library; small lecture rooms and, in addition, workshop space with a smithy.

The principle of loosening-up and articulating the volumes is here continued.

School Buildings in the U.S.A.

A new chapter opens for Walter Gropius with the invitation to head the Graduate School of Design at Harvard and his consequent arrival in America. This does not, however, bring about any change in his methods of approach. The general line of thought continues to be followed, as it was first formulated, but it now becomes responsive to the living and educational patterns of the U.S.A.

Wheaton College Art Center 1937

His early schemes, such as the one for Wheaton College[4] (1937) which, though premiated, was never built, unquestionably served as pioneering

[3] Cf. "*Architectural Review*", Dec. 1939, pp. 227–234; also A. Roth, "*Das neue Schulhaus*", Zurich, 1950, pp. 107–114.
[4] Cf. "*Pencil Points*" *(Progressive Architecture)*, Sept. 1938, pp. 144–149.

projects. They opened the way to convincing at least some of the trustees of American universities that the imitation of Gothic colleges from Oxford or Cambridge is no indication of spiritual independence, and that there are other ways of dealing worthily with large student dormitories than to build them as Colonial-style mansions.

Fig. 103–105

In 1937 it was still impossible for the Wheaton College scheme to break through this wall of prejudice. In its stead a thoroughly respectable brick building was selected which has a light, wood-paneled auditorium, good acoustics, Aalto furniture and modern paintings on the walls. As I was being shown round by the teacher of art history, while the girls drifted about upon their own affairs in carelessly casual garments, she remarked: "You can be sure that in a few years these girls will be demanding that their parents, or their husbands, give them a modern home and hang modern pictures on the walls."

Gropius' and Breuer's Art Center, which also had to fulfil certain social functions, would, if it had been built, have been one of the finest evidences of their collaboration. Lighter and more freely articulated than any previous education building, this Art Center was a fitting symbol of the unconstrained behavior and way of life of an attractive New England college.

Although the design for the Wheaton College Art Center won only second prize in the competition and was in no danger of being built, a great change was already in the air. In 1939 Mies van der Rohe was appointed sole architect to lay out the large campus of the Illinois Institute of Technology in Chicago and to design all the buildings. In 1947 Alvar Aalto was able to persuade the trustees of the Massachusetts Institute of Technology, Cambridge, to accept his revolutionary design for a student dormitory on the Charles River, and in 1949 Walter Gropius together with his associates was entrusted with the task of building the *Harvard Graduate Center*[5] for "America's oldest and most respected educational institution."

Harvard Graduate Center, 1949–50

Fig. 75, 117–128

This group of dormitories and community center (commons) was required to be built extremely rapidly. Gropius and his young partners in TAC, " *The Architects Collaborative*", completed this extensive assignment within the short space of a year, 1949–50. The funds also, in comparison with those available for similar projects in the past, including Aalto's MIT dormitory, were exceedingly short. Although this made things difficult for the architects it was more in tune with the simpler way of life of the post-war generation.

Seven dormitories and the Harkness Commons were built by this group of eight architects, with Gropius as the "job captain" or responsible leader.

These Harvard dormitories, which house approximately 575 graduate students, are situated just beyond the Faculty of Law. They are in no way fenced off from their surroundings. The loosening-up of building masses by free planning of their component units is carried further here than in the earlier examples, and results in an interplay of solids and voids that belongs to the feeling for spatial experience inherent in our period. The two-and three-story dormitories have a reinforced concrete frame with yellow infill-

Students Dormitories Harvard *Fig. 121*

---

[5] Cf. "Harvard Builds a Graduate Yard" in *Architectural Forum*, 1950, Vol. 93, pp. 61–71; also "The Graduate Center" in *Harvard Alumni Bulletin*, Oct. 1950.

ing, in contrast to the usual red brick masonry of Harvard buildings. The buildings are linked by covered passageways and their elongated horizontal planes and slender widely-spaced supports confer simultaneously a sense of movement and a feeling of coherence. The intention of the architects can be readily discerned: to articulate the space through the interplay of the different horizontal planes. The flat two- and three-story dormitories, the curved single-story communal building and the sunken garden before it, together place a new spatial interplay before the onlooker whether, he is conscious of it or not.

Fig. 120, 127

The Dining Area as a Community Center
Fig. 120
Fig. 122, 123

The walls of the upper floor of the curved communal building – steel frames, limestone infilling – are mainly of glass. It has become the social center of student life. A free-standing concrete ramp, which forms a sort of spine for the whole building, leads directly into the cafeteria. The large dining area is divided into three by means of wooden screens so that there is no impression of mass feeding (1200 at a sitting).

The planning of the rectangular kitchen block with its ancillary service rooms is handled in a most accomplished manner. Silently and unobtrusively it plays its part in the life of the whole.

Contemporary Art and the Harkness Commons

Fig. 124, 128

One more thing must certainly be mentioned: the resolute way in which contemporary art has been incorporated into this center of student life. Walter Gropius and his associates realized from the beginning that these students, whose education had left their optical psychic nerves quite undeveloped, could not at once be receptive to the works of Joan Miró, Hans Arp, Herbert Bayer, Joseph Albers and others. They were nevertheless convinced that the lack of a visual education cannot be accepted as an insurmountable obstacle. The student needs only to be shown the stirrup by which he can mount the horse. Surely he will then wish to ride – he needs but time and opportunity.

It has already been said that finances for the Graduate Center were exceedingly limited. It is perhaps therefore interesting to relate how it became possible to find funds to commission these works of modern art. Easter Sunday, 1950, I was at Gropius' house in Lincoln. That afternoon he had to go to Boston to meet with the donors of the Graduate Seminar and to ask them to pay for this work, on the basis of some preliminary sketches. This was a good deal to ask from men who had more than likely a wholly different attitude towards art. Late in the evening he returned and simply said, "Miró and Arp were not accepted[6]". But next day at lunch a leading figure at Harvard came over to his table at the Faculty Club and said, "An anonymous donor has subscribed the missing sum. You can go ahead!"

Walter Gropius' daring in demanding that the works of creative artists should become the daily companions of student life was based on the same insight that he exhibited in 1920, when he invited Kandinsky, Klee and other artists then held in popular contempt, to come and teach at the Bauhaus – a government institution.

At the sixth Congress of CIAM in 1947, at which Gropius participated, the problem of contemporary aesthetics was discussed and, in particular,

---

[6] The fact that just these two artists, Joan Miró and Hans Arp, were selected as two chief prize winners at the Biennale in Venice, June, 1954, shows the rightness of Gropius' choice.

why it was so difficult to-day to obtain full cooperation between painter, sculptor and architect. This difficulty can perhaps be sensed in the Harkness Commons – a difficulty that arises from one simple reason: they did not work together from the beginning.

The fact that one courageous act leads to another can now be seen in the new University of Caracas in Venezuela. Here the architect Villanueva brought in sculptors, such as Henry Laurens, Alexander Calder, Hans Arp and Antoine Pevsner, and painters such as Léger at an early stage in the development of his plans. This made it possible for some of them to realize their ideas on a scale that had hitherto not been possible.

Another project of "The Architects' Collaborative" was a design for the Hua Tung Christian University, Shanghai, which they undertook in collaboration with another former student of Gropius, J. Ming Pei. The first scheme had already been drafted in 1946. This consisted of a widespread building complex to house three separate Christian denominations. The three parts lie separate from one another around ponds studded with small islands, but are interlocked by covered open walks. The actual academic center, focussed round the library, lies to the south[7].

Hua Tung Christian University, Shanghai, 1948
Fig. 112–116a

The Harvard Center proved to be the first of a series of commissions for schools from the young partners of the Architects Collaborative, who set out to convince educationists that it is both more human and more economical to tailor schools to meet the needs of the children than to intimidate them by enormous and palatial mansions.

Junior High School, Attleboro, (Mass.) 1948

The manner in which these schemes have been wholeheartedly praised by certain educationists shows their satisfaction in finding that these schools, with their relaxed ground plans that spread out lightly over the landscape, have not only given better educational results but have also proved more economical both in construction and in maintenance.

With all due recognition to teamwork, the Junior High School at Attleboro, Mass, stands as a thoroughly mature work of architecture. The freedom of its plan symbolizes unconstrained American youth, and this is intensified by the irregular site which has permitted the use of different levels.

Fig. 129–134

The airview of the model at once reveals the whole organization of the plan. The classroom wings with their firm lines are distinctly separated from the other elements. The gymnasium, to the left, and the higher auditorium display their independence, while at the same time they are clearly interlocked within the total complex.

Fig. 130

The lines of the carefully considered connecting passages between the elements can easily be discerned from the model, without the need of a ground plan. A distinctive mark of a good architectural composition is that it can be reproduced with a few strokes of the pen. The position of the low, projecting bicycle shed of the Attleboro School is reminiscent of the Municipal Employment Office at Dessau, where the bicycle shed was also incorporated within the total architectural composition and not treated as an extraneous necessary evil.

Fig. 133

Fig. 131

---

[7] Cf. Hua Tung Christian University, Shanghai, in "*Interiors*", Vol. III, Jan. 1952, pp. 66–79.

Fig. 129   The main entrance with its free cantilevered canopy and shallow steps
Fig. 133   invites entry, and the gently rising ramp, whose great glass panes open
onto the landscape, helps to facilitate the transition from freedom to
discipline.

A school needs a certain degree of concentration and seclusion in order to
function and this is well expressed by the half-open, half-closed court that
Fig. 134   lies between the classroom wings, enclosed by glazed corridors. As in the
Harvard Graduate Center, this-half open, half-closed contact with the outer
world has been given a distinctive architectonic character. In the court at
Attleboro, life is given to the complex in a new and intensive way. The
void has become as important as the solid.

THE MODERN THEATER: INTERPLAY
BETWEEN ACTORS AND SPECTATORS

During the short period of cultural flowering in Germany before her fall, Walter Gropius conceived one of his most interesting schemes: the "Total Theater".

His aim was to achieve an interplay between actors and spectators through the use of modern techniques. In a speech at a Congress in Rome in 1934 Walter Gropius dealt with the general problems of the theater and then stated "the aim of this 'Total Theater' is to draw the spectator into the drama. All technical means have to be subordinated to this aim and must never become ends in themselves[1]."

Significance of the "Total Theater"

This conception, like many of Walter Gropius' most important ideas, is as yet unrealized. Whether he or someone else will be given the opportunity to call into being this new conception of theatrical space cannot be foreseen. But it is quite certain that the idea of the "total theater" with a direct interplay between human beings, as it was put forward by Walter Gropius and some others around the end of the nineteen twenties[2], is in the line of current trends; and that its need is becoming more and more apparent following the long intervention of the cinema.

From the time of the Renaissance until the present day, the theater has developed along the lines of a fixed viewpoint, a fixed perspective, oriented towards a framed, enclosed stage. Basically it is all designed for one spectator seated on the central axis. It is only problems of access and of social hierarchy that have necessitated the provision of banks of seats off the main axis. The perfect position for the spectator is in the pit, lower than the stage and at some distance from it. To create the frame, the stage must be elevated above the auditorium. This has the effect of pushing the spectator away until he can see into the frame.

A theater in keeping with our general trend of development must endeavor to break down the passive role of the spectator in his distant seat, and use every possible means to turn him into an active participant in the proceedings. This entails a new conception of the construction of the theater itself. Instead of the peep-show, boxlike stage with its fixed and static perspective, a neutral but dynamic space must be created, though easily transformable into all former types of theater: the spatial stage[3].

---

[1] Walter Gropius: "Theater Building", in "*Convegno di Lettere*", October 1934, *Reale Accademia d'Italia*, Rome, 1935, p. 160.

[2] F. Kranich, "*Bühnentechnik der Gegenwart*", Munich-Berlin, 1933.

[3] Frederic Kiesler, who was already concerned with the creation of a dynamic theater in 1923–24, writes that he "first used the term 'spatial stage' in the History of the Theater included in the program for the production of O'Neill's 'Emperor Jones' in Berlin, 1923". See Hans Curjel's "*Gegenwartsprobleme des Theaterbaus*" (The Problems of Contemporary

Fundamental Types of Theaters

There are two fundamental types of theater: the Greek theater in which the stage projects into the auditorium and can be seen from all sides, and the framed stage of the Renaissance and Baroque theater designed to be seen from one single viewpoint. The tendency today is to create a synthesis between these two types by giving a dynamic flexibility to each of them.

The Greek Theater   The circle was the first of all regular forms. The dance was the start of all theater.

In early Greek times the spectators were grouped around a circular dancing place and could observe the rhythmic movements from every side. From the rural districts, where the cult of Dionysos[4] originated during the agricultural period, the dance floor moved into the cities. In the sixth century BC the dancing place *(orchestra)* in the Agora at Athens consisted of an unenclosed circle of rammed earth[5]. It was a place for spontaneous improvization.

The highly developed Greek tragedies of the fifth century BC also had their origin in the cult of Dionysos, whose altar stands in the center of the great circular arena of the theater at Athens.

The *orchestra*, or acting area, later became surrounded by raised seats for the spectators *(theatron)*. The extension of these seats round more than half the circle indicates the importance given to drawing the spectator into the performance, during which the choir acted as an invisible intermediary. The *orchestra* stood at a tangent to the articulated front of the *skena* or stage *(skena* = tent).

The *skena* was then developed in the fifth century BC with the advent of actors for performances of the tragedies of Aeschylus and Sophocles. Soon it served to support simple indications of the site of the drama, painted upon wood or linen. Machinery was then built up behind the *skena* to allow for the appearances of the Gods (thence *"deus ex machina")* and steps going down to the *orchestra* served for apparitions from the underworld.

These concentric banks of stone seats still give the spectator a powerful impression of the unity of the scene. To this was added the religious inspiration of the great tragic dramas and a close relationship with the curve of the heavens and the distant landscape – for the early theaters were open to the sky[6].

The Greek theater, in which the religious cult becomes more and more humanized, leading finally to comedy, and in which a democratic unity of

Theater Design), special number of *"Bauen-Wohnen"*, Vol. 11, 1951, p. 3. Here also can be found the ground plans of Kiesler's "Limitless Theater" of 1923–24; the studies for his double theater with a shared stage, Brooklyn, 1926; and his "Universal Theater" for Woodstock, U.S.A.

[4] Even in prehistoric engravings the animal charmer dances with his flute to draw the creatures after him or push them before him.

[5] William Bell Dinsmoor, *"The Architecture of Ancient Greece"*, 3rd Edition, New York, 1950, pp. 119–120.

[6] The great circuses at Rome for chariot racing were developed from the Greek *stadion* or race track, which was generally U-shaped with one end rounded: see Dinsmoor, op. cit. pp. 250–251.

For physical combat, oval types were created, like the Colosseum at Rome. Both originated, in their simplest forms, from parts of the Greek *gymnasion*, not from the theater.

"living the play" links stage and audience, is one of the greatest discoveries of the democratic spirit – unthinkable in any earlier period.

It is the desire to recreate this lost unity and to give it a point of crystalization that gives importance to Walter Gropius' "total theater" – designed before adequate plays had been written to perform within it. It stands as the impassioned plea of an architect.

The type of theater that grew from the Renaissance conception of perspective (a long U-shaped room with perspective concentrated upon the framed stage, a back stage, and a separating curtain) was fully developed in Italy by the middle of the seventeenth century. The famous *Teatro Olympico* of Palladio (completed by Scamozzi in 1585), though it retains the half-circular raised seats of classical times, has already a highly developed deep stage. The Renaissance and Baroque Theater was an enclosed space designed for a limited audience, a " court theater " in which the general public were allotted only the poorly placed seats. The religious and cosmic aspect had disappeared and, with it, the unity of actor and spectator.

The Renaissance Theater

The, as yet unrealized theater of our period is a response to our unconscious need to create again a *vita communis*, a form of life which transforms the passive spectator into an active participant. Walter Gropius' "total theater" expresses this concept in terms of architecture. He builds with light and creates an abstract space.

The "Total Theater", 1927

"The task of the theater architect to-day, as I see it, is to create a great and flexible instrument which can respond in terms of light and space to every requirement of the theater producer: an instrument so impersonal that it never restrains him from giving his vision and imagination full play, and a building whose spatial treatment lifts and refreshes the human spirit.

Gropius' Conception of Contemporary Theater

"The heart of the theater is the stage. Its shape and position to the spectators is of utmost importance for the development of the dramatic action and the effect this has upon the senses. This must be the starting point of the new conception of theatrical space[7]."

The dimensions of Walter Gropius' "total theater" arise from such a clear perception of the possibilities of spatial transformation and are so exact that they could be protected by a patent[8]. The shape is oval. Within this shape, and touching it tangentially, is a large circular turntable upon which are rows of seats and another smaller turntable, also eccentric and also touching tangentially. By turning these discs the position and the character of the stage can be completely altered. Gropius explains this himself as follows[9]:

Fig. 142

"My 'total theater' makes it possible for the actors to play during the same performance upon a deep stage, an apron stage, within the central arena, or simultaneously upon all three. The oval auditorium is supported upon twelve slender columns. At one end, between the columns and partly en-

Gropius' Explanation of his "Total Theater" [10] Fig. 145–147

---

[7] "*Convegno*", op. cit., p. 155.
[8] Deutsches Reich, Reichspatentamt: Patent No. 470451, allocated 15th January, 1929.
[9] E. Piscator, "*Das Politische Theater*" (The Political Theater) Berlin, 1929, p. 125.
F. Kranich, "*Bühnentechnik der Gegenwart*" (Contemporary Stage Production), Vol. 2, Munich-Berlin, 1933, p. 348.
[10] "*Convegno*", op. cit.

closing the front rows of seats, is the deep stage, which is in three sections that can be used separately or together[11].

"The smallest turntable can descend to the basement, where the seats can be removed so that it can rise again to serve as an apron in front of the deep stage. It is then almost completely surrounded by the audience and the actor, by descending some steps, can walk directly among them...

"A complete transformation of the theater occurs by turning the larger turntable through 180°. Then the former apron stage becomes a central arena entirely surrounded by the rows of spectators. This can be done even during the play... The mechanical apparatus to effect these changes of scene is complemented by changes in the light projection. Special consideration has been given to Piscator's demand that projectors and screens should be placed everywhere, and I am personally of the opinion that light projection can make the simplest and most effective modern stage setting: upon the neutral space of a darkened stage one can literally build with light...

"Screens are stretched between the twelve columns of the auditorium upon which twelve films can be projected from cameras situated behind them. The audience can thus suddenly find itself in the midst of a raging sea or surrounded by a rapidly advancing multitude.

"The aim of this theater is not to assemble a number of ingenious devices. All of these are merely means to attain the supreme goal – *to draw the spectator into the drama*."

Diorama, 1827   Is it not curious that, just a century earlier, Carl Wilhelm Gropius, in the service of quite a different space conception, should have projected scenes upon transparent screens by means of his diorama, 1827? There the spectators, standing in total darkness upon a revolving turntable, passed in turn before a series of different scenes, as has already been described in an earlier chapter. The difference is that, while Carl Wilhelm Gropius was able to make his diorama a center of Berlin's artistic coterie, the circumstances a hundred years later were such that Walter Gropius was unable to make more than a model of his much more far-reaching project, and even this model was destroyed in an air raid upon Cologne.

Competition Project for Theater in Kharkov, 1930

Fig. 148–152   Walter Gropius' competition project for the Ukrainian State Theater of Kharkov, 1930, to seat 4,000 is without doubt, both in interior and exterior treatment, one of his most perfectly balanced compositions. If it had been built it would, in many ways, have given a new impulse to the stagnant art of theater design. Although the program did not permit an application of the principle of the "total theater", the stage has been made so flexible that it can be reduced to a small surface for intimate scenes, or the action can be transferred at will into a large apron stage projecting into the midst of the audience. A great circular backdrop increases the depth of the stage.

---

[11] Henry van de Velde's "simultaneous stage" in three parts at the Werkbund Theater, Cologne, 1914, where three stages were also placed adjacent to one another.

Despite the large scale of the building, every seat has good acoustics and a good view: all are oriented directly upon the stage, with the same angle of sight, which compensates for the long distance. The rows of seats form arcs of a circle exactly following the curved line of the stage, and the same curve is repeated by the outer walls.

Above all, the entire project is an architectural achievement with a rare monumental simplicity. The transparency of the glass-encased staircases at Cologne Exhibition of 1914 envisioned future possibilities. In the Kharkov Theater, 1930, transparency is used to strengthen the whole architectonic idea of the intricate organism. Here the segmental, protruding glass screen of the main entrance and the recessed glass curves of the side entrances, the use of ramps and free-standing stairs inside and outside, stand waiting to be filled with pulsing life. It is an architecture, humble and without vanity, in the service of man, in the service of the masses. *Fig. 32, 148–152*

Upon the publication of the project Gropius set down the principles of the new theater so clearly and concisely that they cannot be omitted here[12]. **Principles of the New Theater**

"The principles of the new theater are... a *community theater* linking the people together – *architectural integration* of all space-forming elements with the intention of bringing about a *human integration* between actors and spectators – *abolition of separation* between the 'fictitious world' on the stage and the 'real world' of the audience – *audience participation* in the action of the drama to stir up and awaken their dormant creative capacities – by erasing the distinction between 'this side' and 'that side' of the footlights, between the stage and the auditorium: by bringing the events of the drama among the audience: by animating the theater through the creation of a three-dimensional space instead of a flat 'stage picture': by giving an appearance of movement to the walls and ceiling with the aid of projections and films to extend the scene being enacted on the central stage, so as to encompass the spectators and bring them in some way within it: also by creating a projection *space* instead of a projection *screen*, whereby the entire auditorium, being surrounded on all sides by the built-in projection lights, itself becomes a stage, an area of illusion...

"*An instrument of the theater so impersonal, amenable and flexible* that it never hinders the producer of musical or dramatic performances, but leaves him free to develop to the full his own artistic conceptions..."

Walter Gropius again employed the form of a segmented circle in his competition design for the Palace of the Soviets at Moscow in 1931. **Competition for the Palace of the Soviets, 1931** *Fig. 156*

Almost all the modern architects entered these two competitions but none of their compositions won any of the prizes.

In 1930 Russia was already in the grip of a frozen academicism, just as the United States had been at the time of the international competition for the "Chicago Tribune" in the twenties.

If a new publication were to assemble the competition drawings for the Palace of the Soviets and the Theater at Kharkov it would give an immediate insight into the diversity of impulses inherent in the modern movement *Fig. 153–157*

---

[12] "*Bauwelt*", vol. 35, 1931, p. 51.

65

around 1930. The schemes ranged from Le Corbusier's starkly constructivist project to the almost organic conception of the sculptor Naum Gabo[13].

Fig. 136–139 The only project that Walter Gropius was able to realize was the transformation of the modest theater at Jena, which was opened for the historic Bauhaus Week of 1923. Its tiny stage then saw performances of Oscar Schlemmer's Triadic Ballet, a Pantomime by Kandinsky and a Mechanical Cabaret by Kurt Schmidt.

Fig. 94 As part of a more elaborate complex, Walter Gropius built the theater for Impington Village College in Cambridgeshire with Maxwell Fry, 1936. During the day this theater serves as the school assembly hall and for instruction in dancing and gymnastics: in the evenings it is at the disposition of the adults. But Gropius' main objective, to build an experimental contemporary theater, where ventures in drama could be accompanied by ventures in its spatial setting, has never been fulfilled.

---

[13] See *Gabo-Pevsner*, The Museum of Modern Art, New York, 1948, p. 21.

BUILDINGS FOR INDUSTRY

Gropius' industrial and office buildings do not show the same continuity of development as his school buildings or his plans for the changing structure of the city. Their occurrence is somewhat sporadic, owing to the circumstances and the period during which he has worked. However the Fagus Works of his youth, and the Boston Center on which he worked forty years later, are important milestones of his career. Thus this book opens and closes with structures for business purposes.

On seeing the Fagus Works one would not immediately realize that this represents the first occasion upon which someone had dared to explore the consequences of employing steel-frame construction as a means of artistic expression. Though the building is audacious, it makes no great gestures and now seems a natural part of the present period.

The Fagus
Factory, 1911

A photograph especially taken for this book, in 1953, needs special mention. It shows how well this early building was constructed and that its outward appearance remains as good as ever. In great contrast to the wilful destruction of F.L. Wright's Larkin Building at Buffalo, 1904, – one of his finest works – the Fagus Factory is to-day classified as one of the historic monuments of Germany.

Fig. 28

It is significant that Gropius' first office building, the Municipal Employment Bureau in Dessau, 1928, should have owed its existence to the economic crisis. It was built as an employment registry during a period of high unemployment. The problem was to find a suitable ground plan for a building to meet the special conditions of that time: that is to say to enable the fewest number of officials to serve a large number of unemployed from many different occupations in their search for work. "To meet this condition", writes Gropius in his description of the building[1]," the ground floor plan takes the form of a half circle, with the large waiting-rooms around the periphery split up segmentally into smaller rooms for each occupational trade, and the special consultation rooms towards the center... The inner rooms are lit by concentric bands of sloping skylights. Their function is limited to supplying light, as ventilation is provided for by a separate system.

Municipal
Employment
Office, Dessau,
1928
Fig. 164–168

In the interior a pleasant relationship exists between the flat glass ceilings, the walls and the separating partitions. These do not brutally abut the ceiling, but stop short and are linked to it by a transparent glass band.

The general scheme gives a very coherent appearance due to the careful placing of the taller office wing and to the architectural insight that led to the prolongation of the semi-circular waiting halls to form another wing, pri-

---

[1] "*Bauhaus Books*", vol. 12, p. 212.

marily intended as a cycle shed for the unemployed, instead of cutting the building short at the diameter of the circle.

Chicago Tribune Competition, 1922 *Fig. 169* Gropius had earlier entered a competition scheme for McCormick's Chicago Tribune building, 1922. This competition, organized in that year by the newspaper, offered very high prizes – amounting to a million dollars.

The site that had already been reserved for the building was just outside the business section of Chicago, in which stood the buildings of the first "Chicago School". Historically speaking, this competition took place at a moment when the modern movement in architecture was striving to develop its vocabulary, but when America had lost heart and soul to the *Ecole des Beaux Arts*. It was the time when the finest architect of the first Chicago School, Louis Sullivan, was almost starving of hunger in the city and when a commission of the American Institute of Architects, sent to study the construction of earthquake-proof buildings in Japan, 1922, made no mention in its report of Frank Lloyd Wright's Imperial Hotel in Tokyo.

The Chicago Tribune later issued a large publication containing all the competition schemes. An analysis of this, exemplifying the absurd situation which then existed, would make an excellent subject for a university thesis. The Americans at that time admired only secondhand imitations of European achievements. They had momentarily forgotten all that they themselves had created upon the prairie lands between 1883 and 1893. For the *avant-garde* of Europe – in Germany, Holland, Denmark and France – the word "America" was synonymous with "sky-scraper" and with possibilities that were unrealizable in their own countries. Several entries from this European "*avant-garde*" appear in the Chicago Tribune publication. To mention only a few: there are entries from the Dutch architect Dujker, who died far too young; from the Danish architect Lönberg Holm, who soon afterwards emigrated to America; and from the German architects Bruno Taut and Walter Gropius. Although very different from one another, these projects were all very close to the spirit of the "Chicago School", whose buildings were quite unknown to the European competitors. They were united by the universal spirit of our period. Gropius' composition, for example, contains several of the constituent elements of the Chicago School: the three divisions of the so-called "Chicago Windows", the functional honesty of the building form, and its clearcut lines.

This early scheme for the Chicago Tribune is also important in that it gives evidence of Walter Gropius' unconscious inner relationship with American architecture.

The schemes awarded the prizes give a good insight into the American attitude towards architecture around 1922. A pamphlet fell into my hands one day when I was in Harvard in which a humorist stated that the 'Celestial Jury' (as it called itself) remarked of the Gropius project "This must be the man who invented the mouse-trap".

Fig. 170–175 *Fig. 176–180* It is not necessary to expound at length upon the threads that unite this early project of 1922 with office buildings for the American Association for Advancement in Science in Washington, 1952, and for McCormick and Company in Chicago, 1953. One need but observe the loosening-up of the ground floor treatment to see the strides made in contemporary architecture during the intervening thirty years.

SINGLE-FAMILY HOUSES

Family Houses for the Bauhaus 1925-26

Gropius' special interest lies in the inter-relationship of things. It is therefore natural that he should be more interested in the design of large complexes than individual houses.

A few early houses exist, the first of historic importance being those he designed for members of the teaching staff of the Bauhaus in 1925–26, after the school had moved to Dessau. These are not so much independent private houses as the homes of fellow members of an organized community.

There were altogether four buildings: one detached house for Gropius and three duplexes (semi-detached) which were designed for the other staff members (Kandinsky, Klee, Moholy, Schlemmer, Scheper and Muche). "They stand about 65 feet apart along a line running from east to west in the unfenced clearing of an open pine-wood"[1], and were built of cinderblocks.

Fig. 182, 184–186

These duplexes occupied by the teaching staff demonstrate a theory of construction that Gropius first developed while still at Weimar and which he has maintained throughout his life: the creation of identical and, in the later period, standardized component units that can be assembled or combined together in a great number of different ways, so that the final products, while fully mechanized, can have an intrinsic flexibility and an external variety of appearance, or, as Gropius himself puts it: "Alterations can be made of the same basic unit by repeated horizontal and vertical additions: the guiding principle being to combine the greatest possible standardization with the greatest possible versatility[2]."

The special needs of an artist's dwelling, such as a north-facing studio, were also taken into account: staircase, kitchen, dining-room and bathroom face north, and the bedrooms and living room south.

In the "L"-shaped detached house, which had no studio, both bedrooms and living quarters were on the ground floor. Like the others it was composed of translucent, superimposed cubes with terraces at different levels.

Fig. 187–192

The principle on which these houses were built is greatly in advance of the Muche house in Weimar, 1923, which was entirely concentrated upon the

---

[1] Cf. Walter Gropius, "*Bauhausbauten Dessau*", No. 12 of the Bauhaus Books, Munich 1930, pp. 85–151.
[2] "*Staatliches Bauhaus Weimar, 1919–1923*", Munich 1923, Fig. 109–111, also No. 3 of the Bauhaus Books, Munich, p. 13.

interior plan. Now, in these houses, the recent artistic clarification of the "de Stijl" movement and the work of Le Corbusier has been taken into account, though the conception of design is quite different.

Van Doesburg and van Eesteren conceived a house as a series of interpenetrating planes or slabs – a peculiarly Dutch point of view.

Distinction
between "De Stijl"
and Le Corbusier

Le Corbusier's conception of a house was, from the outset, founded upon a free plan in which the interpenetration of the levels expressed the interpenetration of inner volume and outer space (Maison Laroche, Auteuil, 1923–24 and, one year later than the faculty houses at Dessau, the house at Garches, 1926–27). This conception was primarily derived from the reinforced concrete skeleton which Le Corbusier accepted as his consistent point of departure (design for Maison Domino, 1915). Apart from anything else, the large cinder blocks which Gropius employed for the Bauhaus houses would have made such an interpenetration of space quite impossible.

The particular historic significance of the faculty houses at Dessau is due to the rare unity that they display between the building and its equipment, which came about through the cooperative teamwork of the various sections of the Bauhaus. The furniture was both designed and constructed in the joinery workshops of the Bauhaus under the direction of Marcel Breuer; the lighting fittings came from the metal workshops under Moholy-Nagy and the carefully thought-out polychromatic treatment of the walls was the work of the mural decoration department under H. Scheper. An impressive account of the design of every detail – from the double doors to the shoe cupboards – is given by Walter Gropius in No. 12 of the Bauhaus books.

The caption to a picture of an experimental built-in ventilator reads: "To-day many things are considered luxuries that will to-morrow be common practice." The fact that these ventilators, which were actually quite cheap, were then built in over all the cooking stoves – as they have been in every American kitchen since around 1950 – shows the rightness of this early project.

There were no other examples at that time, either in Germany or elsewhere, with such a close unity of structure and equipment. It is apparent to-day that this group of houses displays an enduring validity that is just as much a product of its own age as any domestic building of the Gothic or Baroque periods.

Fig. 267–270

The way in which Gropius extended this approach to the erection of workers' lowcost dwellings can be seen in his row houses at Toerten, Dessau, 1926[3].

Gropius and American regionalism

An entirely new situation met Walter Gropius when he set about building a house for himself in New England (1937–38), shortly after his appointment to Harvard.

---

[3] Cf. "*Bauhausbauten, Dessau*", op. cit., pp. 184–187.

This house is closely related, both in structure and conception, to all truly contemporary architecture: respect for the natural conditions of a particular region and the ability to fashion these to meet contemporary living requirements. This desire to create a harmonious relation between the present and the eternal – between the cosmos and the earthly environment – I have called the New Regionalism[4]. This is a universal trend that can be found in the work of every architect who works with an awareness of the contemporary world, whether he be in South America, Finland, California or Africa. One of the boldest current examples is Le Corbusier's new Capitol at Chandigarh, India, where an oriental vision has become incarnate in reinforced concrete.

The house Gropius built for himself at Lincoln, Mass,[5] stands on one of the most charming sites of New England, on the crest of a hill in the midst of an orchard of 90 apple trees, only half an hour's ride by car from Harvard. Mrs. Storrow, owner of all the land round about, left Walter Gropius quite free to select the site for the house that she was to finance. It is fitted unobtrusively into the landscape while, at the same time, overlooking its surroundings.

The structure of the house consists of the traditional light wood frame of New England, sheathed with white painted clapboard siding: only in this case the siding runs vertically instead of horizontally. Rough fieldstone walls, like those employed in the seaside house built around this time at Cohasset, are here not yet incorporated into the structure of the house itself.

Construction

It is perhaps interesting for a moment to examine in this house the ways in which New England traditions and contemporary means of expression have fertilized one another. The first thing in the American scene that seems to have attracted the attention of the architect was the use made of the large traditional front porch, screened by mosquito nets, as an auxiliary living room. In general, the traditional porch is built within the bounds of the house itself, but in the Gropius house – very typically – it projects into the outer space. In the summer this area actually becomes the living room and in winter it is occupied by a large ping-pong table which is put to daily use. The outer space also penetrates the upper story by means of a large verandah. A roof slab, detached from the house, protects the southern front from the summer sun and permits free air circulation. Each one of the four sides is differently modelled: the whole inner organization can be read from the exterior. On the approach side a welcoming canopy, partly protected by a glass wall, projects at an angle. A free-standing spiral stairway of cast iron bears witness that there is little need to fear burglars in New England!

New England Traditions and Contemporary Architecture

Fig. 193, 200, 201

Fig. 199

Fig. 193

A large wooden trellis for climbing plants juts boldly out into the garden at right angles to the brick wall beside the large screened porch.

Fig. 198

All this is indicative of the methods of approach of a contemporary architect. Proven and long familiar elements are handled in a new way. In the

Fig. 199

[4] S. Giedion, "*Architectural Record*", January 1954.
[5] All buildings between 1937 and 1941 were signed jointly by Gropius and Breuer. Although it would be quite possible to distinguish the work of one from the other, this would neither be pertinent nor desirable.

Lincoln house the properties of the traditional thin wood frame have been exploited to achieve a new lightness and to perforate the building cube. Regional features, such as the big front porch, have been given a new spatial significance. The projecting canopy, spiral staircase and wooden trellis break up the compact solid of the house-form, and also provide it with tentacles that reach into the outer space. Compared with the faculty houses at Dessau 1925–26, this house at Lincoln has subtly and unobtrusively achieved a far greater loosening-up of the total volume.

The reaction of a Boston patrician to this new regionalism has been described by Gropius himself[6]:

"By building near Walden Pond[7] in the New England countryside we became the neighbors of John Adams, one of the direct descendants of the presidential family, and we were rather worried over what, we thought, might have been a very sour reaction from a family so steeped in history. But old Mr. Adams took one good look and to our surprise stated that he thought this modern house was actually more in keeping with the New England tradition of simplicity than quite a few other solutions that had been tried. He was little disturbed by the unfamiliar sight of a flat roof[8] and other unconventional characteristics, so long as he could see that the moving spirit behind it was facing the problem in much the same way in which the early builders of the region had faced it, when, with the best technical means at their disposal, they built unostentatious, clearly defined buildings that were able to withstand the rigors of the climate and that expressed the social attitude of their inhabitants..."

Within the House   As with so many of Gropius' buildings – from the Fagus factory of 1911 onward – their inherent rightness becomes ever more apparent with the passage of time.

Fig. 197   Within Gropius' house at Lincoln there is nothing that stresses its modernity. Living has simply, in some new and subtle way, become pleasanter. The flow of space through the studio, living-room and dining space on the ground floor is agreeably relaxing.

The house has neither too much nor too little glass. The surrounding landscape is seen in segments. One long window wall takes in both living room and dining space, but even here one has the comfort of a low retaining wall. This window looks out into a paradise for the many-colored birds of New England. Cock pheasants strut there fearlessly with their hens, and tiny humming birds while still in flight sip sweetened water from glass tubes. In the guest room the visitor is awakened at daybreak by the cries of birds demanding their daily food from the mistress of the house. Beyond the glass screen is a constant, ever-changing spectacle that the occupants of the house never weary of watching. This is as much a part of the life of the house as the electric dishwasher or the automatic garbage disposal in the kitchen.

---

[6] Speech by Walter Gropius at a reception in his honor at the Illinois Institute of Technology, May 18th, 1953.
[7] This is a charming little wood encircled lake immortalized in the writings of Thoreau.
[8] Around the turn of the 19th century all self-respecting houses in New England appear to have had flat roofs.

On my first visit to the house in the autumn of 1938, soon after it was completed, it was a central topic of discussion. It was constantly overrun with visitors, as it was at that time unique in New England and no other modern house existed for miles around. Since then it has become an accepted part of the landscape, has made friends with the animals and the trees and given an impetus to the development of the contemporary movement.

Other houses

The house for another Harvard professor, the late James Ford, was built in 1938 at the far end of the same orchard, in the hollow of the valley. This was followed soon after by a bachelor residence for Marcel Breuer. Here mezzanine floors were used, a feature which later became popularized under the name of "split-level houses", one of the most useful catchwords for the speculative builder. The house of Mr. and Mrs. Chamberlain at Sudbury, Mass., 1939, only a few miles away from Lincoln, bears the impress of the hand of Marcel Breuer.

Fig. 202–204

Fig. 205, 206

More family houses were built after the founding of "The Architects Collaborative" (TAC) in 1945, the most interesting perhaps being in the small settlement at Six Moon Hill, Lexington, Mass., built since 1947. Here, on a sparsely wooded hill, Gropius' partners started to erect some loosely articulated wooden houses for themselves and their families. They were soon joined by other people of similar tastes, so that at the present time about 30 houses have been built there by TAC.

A most friendly atmosphere has developed in this settlement. I saw this in operation one May evening in 1953 when people gathered together in the house of B.C. Thompson and I was again able to experience the art with which Walter Gropius can bridge the gulf between the different generations.

THE PREFABRICATED HOUSE

Gropius has taken greater interest in the prefabrication of houses than any of the other pioneers of contemporary architecture. In Germany before the first world war almost all houses were built of solid brick construction by manual labor. It would have been impossible there in 1900 for a young architect, such as Tony Garnier, to have prepared plans for the construction of a complete town, "*La Cité Industrielle*", in the new building material, ferroconcrete. In Germany concrete was employed only for large and daring structures. It never came into question for domestic buildings, much less for small private houses as in France.

The work of Le Corbusier certainly had its source in the imagination. On the other hand it could never have been developed in a region that had not such a high level of technical skill in the use of ferroconcrete – a skill that Auguste Perret used to such good effect around the turn of the century.

Gropius'
Proposition, 1909

There was only one solution for the situation in Germany: to shift directly from brick masonry to industrialized production. Gropius grasped the essential principles of the factory-produced house at a very early date, 1909. He knew even then, even if he did not express it in these words, that the house could never be considered in the same way as the car: the house must always remain a personal affair. For this reason the mass production of standardized complete houses offers no solution to the housing problem. The industrialization of the house must be limited to the mass production of standardized components which would not prohibit changes in the form and planning of the house. It was while Walter Gropius was working with Peter Behrens in 1909 that he sent Emil Rathenau, President of the A.E.G. (General Electric Company) a "*Proposition for the creation of a company for the construction of houses on the basis of an artistic unity*".

The concept was described in the following terms: "The idea of industrializing house construction can be realized by the repetition in each building of the same standardized component parts. This would mean that mass-production methods could be employed which would be cheaper for the producer and could result in lower rents for the occupiers.

"The possibilities of varied assembly of these interchangeable parts would enable the Company to satisfy the public desire for a home with an individual appearance...

"It is possible to have an infinite number of variations of every plan-type by differing combinations of the standard elements...

"It is thus possible, both commercially and technically, to satisfy the public's desire for an individually designed house, by the multiple possibilities of combining interchangeable parts, without sacrificing the principles of mass-production."

Throughout his life Gropius has held to this fundamental idea. In a letter to the *"New-York Times"* of March 2nd, 1947, which is reproduced in part at the end of this chapter, it is very clear how this early vision has remained with him through the years. All architects of stature, without exception, concur with the principle. But industry cannot give up its fruitless quest: the mass production of complete houses.

In the Toerten housing project near Dessau, 1926–1929, Gropius produced on the site certain prefabricated parts, such as standardized beams of reinforced concrete and cinder blocks for the supporting cross walls. But the main emphasis in the Toerten project was on the greatest possible coordination of the process of building construction.

Toerten Housing
Fig. 222, 223

The most interesting of the experiments carried out under the Weimar Republic was the Weissenhof Housing Project for the Werkbund Exhibition at Stuttgart, 1927. In his two detached houses Gropius again concentrated upon the techniques of building construction – this time upon dry wall construction: light steel framework, with wall panels of compressed cork covered with sheets of asbestos cement.

Weissenhof Housing, 1927
Fig. 224–229

The most important features of his prefabricated copper houses, 1931, were the large wall panels in which the line connecting the sections runs vertically down the center. The joints between the panels themselves foreshadow the "connectors" developed later for the *General Panel Corporation*. By the varied possibilities of assembly of these separate prefabricated elements, houses could be adapted to suit increasing or shrinking family needs.

Prefabricated Copper Houses, Hirsch, 1931
Fig. 230–238

The Packaged House System, 1943–1948

By far the most interesting undertaking in this field was the Packaged House System of the General Panel Corporation, 1943 to 1948. The basic idea was similar to that of the copper houses at Hirsch, 1931: but this time the wood-framed wall panels were clad with narrow boards of the same material and the panels lost their former unwieldy dimensions and became easy to handle. Every element was based upon the same module: 3 feet 4 inches. The length of the panels was always a multiple of this dimension. The results showed this module to be sufficiently flexible to allow for every type of combination, from a completely open ground plan to a firmly enclosed house block.

The distinctively new feature of the *General Panel Construction* is that the standardized building elements can be assembled in more than two dimensions (unlike the vertical wall panels of the copper houses of 1931). The third dimension has now been brought in. The same panels can be assembled vertically or horizontally, to form walls, floor, ceiling or roof. This has been made possible by a most carefully worked out four-way steel joint or connector. The connecting parts of this joint are built into the panels during their construction so that each can later be assembled at will on the four-way system.

The development of this General Panel system was most carefully studied by Konrad Wachsmann over a number of years in New York, including the total building process and the mechanical and electrical equipment. After experiments had been made in Long Island, New York, mass-production was started in California with considerable financial backing. The system has proved its worth, but it will be some time before its importance and possibilities are fully recognized.

The Present Attitude of the House Purchaser

Gropius' and Wachsmann's Packaged House System, with its carefully worked out designs of standardized building components, is in the direct line of future development, especially in its concentration upon the production of easily transportable and easily assembled multi-purpose unit parts and not upon the production of complete standardized house types. Nevertheless it has had no financial success. Why is this? In large buildings in the United States often eighty per cent of the construction consists of standardized prefabricated parts. But their use for small private houses meets with considerable psychological difficulties[1].

These difficulties, in the last resort, lie with the present attitude of the house purchaser. No matter how identical in plan and appearance his house may be to all its neighbors in its suburban setting, the man building his own home still likes to believe that he is getting an individual, personal, handmade product.

If, however, he decides to go in for a mass-produced, prefabricated house, he wants to select this from a catalog and to purchase it ready-made like his automobile. This attitude is now common among the general public throughout the western world.

There is, however, no doubt that the time is coming when the ready-made box will no longer be acceptable. The demand will again arise for a flexible arrangement of the house to suit the needs of the owner. But this moment has not yet arrived, either for the house purchaser in Long Island or in Switzerland, where prefabricated wooden chalets disfigure the Alpine landscape. In society as in personal life we only learn as a result of bitter experience. The goal is seldom reached by the shortest road.

The Architect and Industrial Production

Walter Gropius clearly set down his own position in relation to prefabrication in a letter to the "*New York Times*"[2] written in reply to a nervous enquiry by the editor as to whether the housing problem could or should be solved by methods of mass-production. The editor queried "whether we should be so eager to abandon the one great sector of modern existence in which the spirit of mass-production has been most successfully resisted." He finished "The appeal of one's own non-prefabricated, non-standardized home will persist, and perhaps for the ultimate social good it should be encouraged."

Gropius replied: "The true aim of prefabrication is certainly not the dull multiplication of a house type ad infinitum: men will always rebel against attempts at over-mechanization which is contrary to life. But industriali-

---

[1] Another interesting reason, pointed out by Walter Gropius, is that the methods of financing the construction of private houses are still based entirely upon manual labor.
[2] *New York Times*, March 2nd, 1947.

zation will not stop at the threshold of building. We have no other choice but to accept the challenge of the machine in all fields of production until men finally adapt it fully to serve their biological needs...

"Very gradually the process of building is splitting up into shop production of building parts on the one hand, and site assembly of such parts on the other. More and more the *tendency develops to prefabricate component parts of buildings rather than whole houses.* Here is where the emphasis belongs...

"The future architect and builder will have at their disposal something like a box of bricks to play with, an *infinite variety of interchangeable,* machine-made *parts* for building which will be bought in the competitive market and assembled into *individual buildings of different appearance and size.*

"Prefabrication, as a logical progressive process, aimed at raising the standard of building, will finally lead to higher quality for lower prices... Prefabrication will thus become a vital instrument to solve the housing problem economically.

"During the period from 1913–1937 the average cost per family-dwelling increased to 193 per cent (Bureau of Labor Statistics) whereas the average cost of the automobile simultaneously decreased to 60 per cent (Automobile Manufacturers Association)...

"The coming generation will certainly blame us if we should fail to overcome those understandable though sentimental reactions against prefabrication. If we are determined to let the human element become the dominant factor for the pattern and scale of our communities, prefabrication will be beneficial and must be encouraged for the ultimate social good. For it is a logical, progressive means to pull us out of the painful housing emergency."

This warning against an attitude of sentimentality springs from the knowledge that industry, left to itself, inevitably creates independent standardized items that cannot be co ordinated together. Neither the engineer nor the manufacturer – or rather not just these two on their own – should undertake the standardization of building components. The architect must participate from the beginning in the establishment of the forms and dimensions that should be adopted. It is as much his duty to resume his traditional function of coordinating all phases of building activity in this field as it is to see that painters and sculptors are enabled to cooperate from the earliest stages of design for any great public building.

Walter Gropius' first proposition of 1909 can again be heard in his desire to arouse the architect to grapple with the enormous and undirected power of the American industrial machine before it is too late. Much as one of his ancestors might have mounted the pulpit in the 17th century to raise a warning voice, so Gropius, almost pleadingly, addresses his audience in May 1952 in the "*Architectural Forum*". The response was considerable and there are signs that he did not speak in vain.

"To-day the architect is not the 'master of the building industry'. Deserted by the best craftsmen (who have gone into industry, toolmaking, testing and researching), he has remained sitting all alone on his anachronistic brick pile, pathetically unaware of the colossal impact of industrialization. The architect is in a very real danger of losing his grip in competition with the engineer, the scientist and the builder unless he adjusts his attitude and aims to meet the new situation...

"The architect of the future – if he wants to rise to the top again – will be forced by the trend of events to draw closer once more to the building production. If he will build up a closely cooperating team together with the engineer, the scientist and the builder, then design, construction and economy may again become an entity – a fusion of art, science and business."

THE DEVELOPMENT OF THE SLAB
APARTMENT BLOCK

The slablike multi-story apartment block was first conceived and developed by Walter Gropius and Marcel Breuer. It consists of narrow rectangular slabs, eight to twelve stories high, the long side resting on the ground. They do not line the street but are built at an angle to it, thus destroying the solid '*rue corridor*'. They are orientated so that every inhabitant can enjoy the same amount of sunlight. Between them lie wide green spaces. Each thin slab is only one apartment deep. The emergence of this new dwelling type in the late twenties can only be understood in a wider context.

Housing decadence and housing reform

This new building type is a part of an attack against the structure of the great metropolis, as this had developed during the second half of the 19th century. In the forefront stood the elimination of the back-to-back houses and lightless tenement wells which had resulted from rampant land speculation. Other points of attack were the impossible traffic connections between home and workplace and the absence of any clearly formulated building program. The absence of this latter was due to the lack of any clear promulgation of basic human needs. At the outset of the modern movement around 1920, successful efforts were made to humanize a large inner court, such as J. J. P. Oud's working-class apartments at Tusschendiyken in Rotterdam, 1919. Great though the difference was between his wide, carefully designed inner courts and those of earlier tenements, they still had no effect upon the structure of the great city, which remained locked within itself by the rigid pattern of the '*rue corridor*'.

Row-houses and the penetration of sunlight

The next step in the process of loosening-up the city was the adoption of a form known in German as "*Streifenbau*" – row-houses which run at right angles to the street. As far as we know, it was Augustine Rey who first pointed out, at the International Tuberculosis Congress in Washington in 1908, that orientation towards the sun must become one of the basic requirements of any town-planning program, and that the greatest care must be taken that the direct rays of the sun should penetrate every apartment.

Fig. 255–258

Around this time parallel row-houses became prevalent, orientated to catch the maximum amount of sunlight. They stood on lawns or in gardens. Only the narrow end of each terrace fronted upon the traffic stream which passed by unnoticed and undisturbed. Walter Gropius then emphasized the advantages of this solution: "As against the old block plan row-houses have the great advantage that every dwelling receives its proper share of sunlight, that the free current of air along the rows is not obstructed by cross blocks and that corner apartments without cross ventilation disappear altogether[1]."

[1] Cf. Walter Gropius, "*Die Wohnformen, Flach-, Mittel- oder Hochbau*" in "*Neues Berlin*", periodical edited by M. Wagner and A. Behne, April 1929.

Walter Gropius further demanded that in new building laws, restrictions on building heights should be replaced by regulations limiting the density of population. As an example he suggested rows of-ten to twelve-story blocks with eight times wider distances between the units than would be possible with two-story row-houses at the same density. This introduced a new freedom and spaciousness into the city.

Development of the slab apartment block

The slablike block of row-houses gave rise to the slablike high-rise apartment building. This development was assisted by new structural techniques, such as the steel skeleton. The new type first appeared in a scheme by Marcel Breuer, himself educated at the Bauhaus, which he prepared for a competition on low-cost dwellings organized by the Berlin magazine "*Die Bauwelt*"in 1924. In the model of Breuer's apartment house the steel skeleton has had a strong influence upon its artistic form[2].

The principle of these tall narrow blocks was to loosen the structure of the city by creating new free open spaces while retaining the same overall density of population. Walter Gropius summed up this argument in a paper on "Houses, Walk-ups and High-rise Apartments[3]", presented at the third congress of CIAM (Brussels 1930), which was concerned with rational urban planning:

Rationalization and a richer life

"How should the rational height for working-class housing under urban conditions be determined? To formulate the question more clearly it might be as well first to define the notion 'rational' more closely. It would seem one of the duties of this congress to oppose the widely held idea that 'rational' and 'economic' are equivalent. Literally, 'rational' means 'reasonable', and consequently, besides the economic it must include psychological and social factors. The social prerequisites of a building program are without doubt more vital than the economic, since economy, for all its importance, is not an end in itself but the means to an end. Any rationalization is only justified if it makes for a richer life... The city needs to reassert itself. It needs the stimulus resulting from a development of housing peculiarly its own, a type which will combine a maximum of air, sunlight and open parkland with a minimum of distances and communications and minimum running costs. Such conditions can be fulfilled by the multi-story apartment block, and consequently its development should be one of the urgent tasks of city planning.

Outline of future development

"The advantages and disadvantages of a multi-story apartment block are: "One problem, the direct relationship between the apartment and the ground, remains to be solved... A well-run, hygienically improved kindergarten, best sited on lawns between the blocks; and a nursery for the smaller children built on the roof terrace are the desirable aim...; the realization of such things as communal club-room, sports equipment or kindergartens, will not be a great burden, as, in the case of a multi-story block of flats, the cost may be economically divided among a larger number of families. These expenses will, after all, be simply the cost of installations to help the inhabitants convert the time they have saved to that most important of all occupations, *creative leisure*..."

---

[2] Illustrated in W. Gropius, "*Internationale Architektur*", 2nd ed., München, 1927, p. 90.
[3] Cf. "*Rationelle Bebauungsweisen, Ergebnisse des 3. Internationalen Kongresses für Neues Bauen*", Stuttgart 1931, p. 26 ff.

The proper function of the house and garden is however recognized. It must be assigned its rightful place in the structure of the city:

"Houses *and* high-rise apartments both correspond to a real need and must exist *side by side* in order to fulfil their proper function.

"The *family house* with a garden is conducive to greater peace, greater privacy and provides more ample possibilities of relaxation.

"*Walk-up apartments* have the disadvantages of smaller distances between buildings, less sunlight, smaller green areas and less outdoor space to move around in.

"The *high-rise block* on the other hand can be much more airy and sunny: there can be greater distances between buildings and large areas of parkland in which the children can have complete freedom to play and make as much noise as they like...

Fig. 255–258

"*The family house, then, is no panacea* since its logical consequence would be a dispersal and denial of the city. The *loosening* but not the *breaking-up* of the city should be the aim. The two opposites 'town' and 'country' can be brought closer to each other through our use of the technical resources which we have at our disposal, and through the most extensive landscaping of all the available ground, even the rooftops, so that the encounter with nature will become a daily and not merely a Sunday experience..."

Greenery in the city

Between 1928 and 1931 Gropius was examining the various aspects of the high-rise slab. Questions of sunlight, of better use of the ground, of financial soundness, were illustrated by comparative schemes entered for large competitions such as that of Spandau-Haselhorst, 1929, organized by the Government Research Institute. At the Berlin Building Exhibition, 1931, a more popularly designed representation was staged to draw the attention of the general public to the problem. There were models of multi-story blocks with green spaces between them, with, nearby, examples of the attractive community rooms in each block. Projects, such as the staggered multi-story blocks at the Wannsee shore, 1931, in which the organization of communal facilities was best developed, anticipated the future but could not then be realized.

Fig. 279–285
Fig. 69, 70

Fig. 260

Fig. 248–253

All was in vain. No slab apartment block was erected in Germany. There were many reasons for this: practical problems of financing; the lack of precedent for the use of new structural methods – such as the steel skeleton – for apartment houses; the reluctance of landlords to introduce elevators into working-class housing, and similar considerations. On the other hand many projects arose based on the idea of the "*Streifenbau*". In many cases rows of single family houses were grouped with bands of two-, three- and four-story walk-ups. Mies van der Rohe's apartment block which dominated the *Weissenhofsiedlung* in Stuttgart, 1927, employed a steel skeleton and was, to some extent, a partly completed high-rise slab[4].

When Gropius went to England in 1935 he worked with Maxwell Fry on an interesting project. An old park belonging to the Duke of Gloucester, at St. Leonard's Hill in the vicinity of Windsor Castle, was to be developed as a

---

[4] At the *Weissenhofsiedlung* Walter Gropius used for his two detached houses a steel skeleton frame with dry assembled curtain walls.

building site. As usual, the preliminary plan had divided the estate up into small sites for single family houses, thus destroying the existing "*grand seigneur*" aspect of the park. As in Germany, a magnificent representation of the alternative project was placed on exhibition in London and journals such as "*The Architectural Review*" gave ample space to support the idea. All was in vain for the moment. As in Germany, the scheme remained on paper. The reason was obvious: after its great achievements of the 19th century, England had lapsed into slumber and was most reluctant to join the modern architectural movement. Gropius' intentions were quite unacceptable to the English outlook of the 1930's. A segmented landscape packed with single family houses was preferred to the free landscape and communal facilities offered by the tall apartment blocks.

Fig. 261–265

The high-rise building is realized outside Germany

It seems that Holland was the first country to build the high-rise slab, through the efforts of Van Tijen, Maaskant, Brinkmann and Van der Vlugt. In 1933–34 they erected the *Bergpolder*, a nine-story block with gallery access to the two- and three-room apartments in a suburb of Rotterdam. In 1937 they followed this with *Plaslaan*, a ten-story block set beside an artificial lake in a wide level landscape near to an open park. This block had shops at the street level, and a garden on the roof with two screened shelters. The apartments contained one to four rooms[5].

In his master-plan for Amsterdam South, 1934, C. van Eesteren envisaged a whole series of such blocks set in wide green spaces[6].

England, America

Fig. 254

The Highpoint flats at Highgate in North London, designed by the Tecton group in 1936–1938, can also be included in this category. The slab high-rise apartment block has since become a standard type that has spread over the world. It is far more easily integrated into a city plan than the 'tower apartments', developed in Sweden and frequently employed by architects with romantic inclinations.

Fig. 170–175

The sixteen-story McCormick office building in Chicago, 1953, designed by Gropius and his partners (TAC), is also plastically related to the high-rise apartment slab.

The principle has been carried to an extreme in Skidmore, Owings and Merrill's project for two apartment blocks in Central Chicago South, 1951; also in Oscar Niemeyer's design for a week-end hotel for 10,000 people near Rio de Janeiro, which is conceived as an enormously long curved slab.

The plastic evaluation of the high-rise slab

It is true that there were certain practical considerations which prevented the slab apartment block from being built in Germany around 1930. But the decisive obstacles lay elsewhere: in the attitude of mind of the public. The slablike block was a new form of dwelling and as such had to encounter a strong psychological opposition. The root cause of this objection was the demand from the general public and the building promoters for the kind of

---

[5] Fully documented in A. Roth, *The New Architecture*, Zurich, 1940, pp. 91–104.
[6] Cf. "*Space, Time and Architecture*", 10th edition, p. 706.

heavy massivity which they associated with the apartment block around an inner court.

One of the constituent elements of the contemporary conception of space is just this: the slab. Robert Maillart, the Swiss bridge engineer, had to fight all his life against a prejudiced public, to whom his bridges did not seem sufficiently massive. He employed reinforced slabs which permitted an extreme economy in the use of materials. This, in the eyes of some, imbued his structures with a new expressive strength, but to others gave rise to feelings of mistrust and insecurity.

The high-rise slab, when considered simply as a shape, is a narrow rectangular slab posed upon its long or short edge. Plastically, it belongs to the same category as the seventy-story skyscrapers of the Rockefeller Center, 1931–39, which rest on their short edges. Their shape, also, arose from practical considerations. The interplay of their forms portrays – perhaps unknown to their creators – the space-time conception of our period.

Long slablike apartment houses, upright slabs such as skyscrapers, bridges of thin concrete slabs, cubist paintings between 1910 and 1914, all contain within themselves an expression of the new spatial vision[7].

[7] Cf. "*Space, Time and Architecture*", 10th edition, p. 744–758.

THE CHANGING STRUCTURE OF THE CITY

Contact between the individual and the community

Town planning and democracy have a common basis: the establishment of an equilibrium between individual freedom and collective responsibility. This is an ever-fluctuating problem that can never be solved once and for all. It all depends on how far intentions can be implemented. In other words the level of a civilization depends upon how far a chaotic incoherent mass of humanity can be transformed into an integrated and creative community. This requires that the human approach is always given pride of place.

A French sociologist, René Maunier, in a forgotten booklet '*Origine de la Fonction Economique de la Ville*', Paris 1907, recognized then that the essential nature of a city lies in its complexity. He saw that the city was not simply an economic or geographic phenomenon but, above all, a social complex. The city must be recognized '*comme un fait social*' and not '*comme un simple phénomène géographique ou économique*'. If first place is given to questions of financial remuneration and if no more of the human factor enters into the picture than can be enforced by building codes, then we inevitably arrive at the situation as we see it to-day. A cancerous growth spreads through and destroys the inner and outer structure of the city, and the life of the individual becomes atomized.

Contemporary artists do not wait to give expression to the symbols that grow within them until these can be given meaning by changes in our conception of the State, by the rise of a new religion or by a new political order. No more do the creative urbanists wait to form their plans until the conditions are ripe to realize them. Their starting point is the man of to-day, the conditions under which he lives and the terms he has to come to with them. Then from their inner vision they attempt to evolve a form which re-interprets those eternal laws that human nature is bound to follow. The urbanist has the moral responsibility of awakening in man a realization of needs and aspirations that are at present slumbering within him. That this is possible is evident from developments, even in the U.S.A., over the last ten years.

The world situation seems to look in one direction towards a time of utter destruction, and yet in another direction it is clear that there is an ever-developing process of humanization. These two contradictory trends persist simultaneously. Whichever gets the upper hand will determine the destiny of our civilization.

The urbanist, who inevitably stands for humanization, is required to provide an answer to the question: What form should the contemporary city take in order to restore the distorted equilibrium between individual freedom and collective responsibility? His starting point must be the diversified residential unit: in other words the housing group that caters for households of differing social structure and differing circumstances. From this point – as we have seen – new dwelling types are coming into being together with a new social implementation of the human habitat.

It is ever clearer that, despite differences in detail, there is universal agreement as to the kind of operation that the present city structure must undergo to recover those values that have been lost to our period: the human scale, the rights of the individual, the most primitive security of movement within the city. How can one overcome the isolation of the individual, induced, to a large extent, by the chaotic structure of the present day city? How can one stimulate a closer relationship between the individual and the community?

It is a long-drawn-out and difficult process. Massive agglomerations of apartment blocks and sky-scrapers offer no more of a solution than an endless sprawl of single-family dwellings and row-houses. The starting point must be the diversified residential unit. This can provide differentiated dwellings for our ever more complicated social structure: dwellings that take account of the existence of single men and women and that allow for the normal changes of family life – the young married couple, the period of growing children, the later shrinking of the family circle and the period of old age. These needs cannot be met by an endless series of similar cells, whether horizontally or vertically arranged. Right from the start the social needs of the different age groups must be taken into consideration: not merely the requirements of small children, but also those of young people and adults.

The diversified
residential unit

The vocabulary of contemporary architecture was formulated between 1920 and 1930 and the vocabulary of the new city structure in the following decade. This fell outside the normal purview of the layman, and of many architects. Nevertheless a fairly clear picture of the future city can now be envisaged. What is here in process of formation is certainly of greater importance than all before in the contemporary movement: to confront a chaotic way of life with positive action.

It is astonishing, when looking over the developments in methods of town planning during the last two decades, to realize in how short a time uncertain groupings have been transformed into an almost universal acceptance of the form the new city must take. The gradual clarifying process involved can perhaps be seen more clearly in the life-work of Walter Gropius than of any other contemporary.

The first experimental approach can be recognized in his early scheme for a housing project at Weimar, 1922, planned in connection with the Bauhaus. Its scattered single-family dwellings and rudimentary row-housing certainly originated from the desire, at that time of heavy inflation, for individual vegetable plots to provide an element of security. Only one house from this scheme was actually built, the experimental house "on the Horn" that was erected on the occasion of the "Bauhaus Week", in 1923.

Review of Gropius'
urban planning

Fig. 266

Between 1928 and 1931, after his move to Berlin, Gropius became almost wholly absorbed in considering the structural changes necessary for the living environment in a great metropolis. He now, more than at any other period of his life, concentrated upon the development of a better form of dwelling-place and a more rational employment of urban land. From these studies he evolved, as we have seen, the slab apartment block set in a green landscape. That his mind moved beyond the mere economic utilization of urban land is shown by the exhibitions that he made at this time. All set forth the various advantages that can be obtained in connection with the slab apartment block. Everywhere he tried to open the eyes of his contemporaries to the new possibilities of urban living that he then perhaps saw more clearly than the others: the extension of the dwelling, or as we named it twenty years later at a CIAM Congress, the human habitat.

Fig. 248–253 When he was given an opportunity in which his imagination could have free play, such as the never-executed scheme for high-rise apartments along the shore of a lake, he included roofed terraces and, midway up the height of the block, community rooms. Unfortunately he was never himself able to build any such scheme. It is of course well known that it was Le Corbusier who was given the opportunity of creating a resplendent realization of this problem, latent throughout the whole period, in his *Unité d'Habitation*, Marseilles, 1947–52.

In America the general trend of the times enabled Gropius' work to broaden out. The foreground was now occupied by the form the entire city should take to give an expression to the wholeness of human settlement. Pointers in this direction are such studies as "*A Program for City Reconstruction*" which Gropius and Martin Wagner worked upon together with the Harvard students. That this was published at length by the *Architectural Forum*, June 1943, together with all the conditions laid down for the new cities, shows that it is possible to-day to have a link between the work of the student's class-room and the general public. These conditions for 'City Reconstruction' related to new towns whose population was limited to 30,000. The main principles were: the human scale, closer relation of the inhabitants to community life, contact with nature.

In the later years came practical problems: how is it possible to provide for a more human existence within the present metropolis, which cannot be simply swept away? It goes without saying that this sort of planning has nothing in common with a piecemeal replacement of slums by super-slums in the form of massed apartment blocks with no communal facilities. The new planning must take account of the whole city as a social complex, '*un fait social*' as we have said at the start of this chapter, whose interconnected needs must be realized and planned for from the outset. Pointers to this approach are the Michael Reese Hospital, Chicago, since 1945, and the Boston Center, 1953.

Toerten, Dessau
1926–28

Fig. 267–270

Fig. 270 The plan for the Toerten housing scheme at Dessau (for the Government Research Institute) with its lines of row-housing parallel to the street, seems somewhat conservative in comparison with the spatial conception of the Bauhaus. The emphasis of the Toerten housing lay rather in its rationalization of building methods. Even so, certain details portray that here no ordinary hand was at work. In the rectangular space formed by the junction of two streets of row-houses, a rigidly enclosed quadrangle has been split open and new vitality achieved by extremely simple means.

Further the site organization of buildings of different heights – row-houses, a cooperative and a higher apartment block – foreshadows a new animation of space by the coordination of different volumes.

The Dammerstock housing scheme near Karlsruhe was designed one year after the experimental housing project at Weissenhof. It is one of the attempts to achieve a unified scheme produced by a number of different architects, each responsible for a single element, under the general direction of Walter Gropius.

Dammerstock, Karlsruhe 1926–28

Fig. 271–278

17. BERLIN-SIEMENSTADT, 1929. *Row-housing placed amid existing greenery.*

The four prize-winning plans that Gropius made for the Spandau-Haselhorst housing scheme had by far the greatest influence. This was a national competition staged by the Government Research Institute. Gropius drew up four different schemes for the same site. The fourth showed by comparison the great urbanistic advantages of the slab apartment block, and was of course closest to Gropius' real intentions. It was probably this scheme that gave the decisive impetus to the widespread acceptance, a few years later, of this type of urban planning.

Spandau-Haselhorst, Berlin, 1929

Fig. 279–285

The apartment blocks of Siemensstadt are, beyond doubt, the most congenial of all the housing projects actually erected, in the strength of their long clean lines, the retention of existing forest trees, and their incorporation into the open ground plan. As in Dammerstock, several different architects were responsible for the designs of the apartment rows.

Siemensstadt, Berlin, 1929

Fig. 286–292

In the lay-out of a large housing scheme for 5,000 families near Berlin, the use of parallel row-housing at right angles to the street is pushed to the limit. The main traffic arteries are led round the entire project and in-between the three neighborhood units. Despite the stiffness of the whole lay-out, a great deal of care has been taken to see that it is pleasantly set in the midst of a green zone. This plan also reflects the desperate need in Germany at that time for the maximum number of low-cost dwellings.

The first housing scheme with which Walter Gropius was concerned in America was at New Kensington, near Pittsburgh, Pennsylvania, which he built with Marcel Breuer during the war. The houses lay on a hill and were intended for the workers of an aluminium factory in the valley below. One part of the site fell steeply down to the valley, and even the plateau on which the houses were erected was pleasantly uneven. The simple wooden row-houses with their brick cross walls created an uproar in the local press which may have reminded Gropius of his earlier experiences in building Toerten, 1926.

As we have already said, in January, 1942, Walter Gropius and Martin Wagner, together with the Harvard students, undertook a study which was given the significant title "*Housing as a Town Building Problem*". The results were assembled under twelve heads. This "*Program for City Reconstruction*" contains elements of the essential structure of the future city: *limitation of size of population* by the creation of separate neighborhoods: limitation of the size of each of these neighborhoods to the normal range of pedestrian movement. A traffic system encircles the neighborhoods, accompanied by a green zone that can, to some extent, be employed for food production. It was intended that the whole of one of the six neighborhoods envisaged in the scheme, together with its communal facilities, should be built at one time. A civic center was planned to serve all the six neighborhoods.

This new town was planned to be erected in the vicinity of Boston to reduce the 'high blood pressure' of the big city. Such diversified residential settlements seem especially suitable around great industrial centers, so that the ever-shorter working day of the man at repetition work on the assembly line can be offered rectifying balance.

The problem of the great metropolis arises anew. Its future lies in the possibilities of the period and the wishes and desires of the people. But the metropolis exists here with us and we cannot at a single stroke reduce its formless sprawl to the human scale. Even so there are clear evidences of an ever-growing humanization process that will not allow itself again to be suppressed. To-day it has become common knowledge that the unrelated patchwork of isolated slum-clearance projects only leads to even greater chaos.

The new planning can only arise from actual points of crystalization. Possibly the first area to be tackled in this way is the re-development of a very large dilapidated urban area in South Chicago. At the time of the flowering of the Chicago School, during the 1880's, this area had been a fashionable suburb. To-day it is simply an enormous rubbish heap.

This great slum zone is now attacked from several sides by independent planning schemes. Several big private organizations are at work. A large

extension plan has been prepared by the great building complex of the
Illinois Institute of Technology. Another big scheme is centered on the
Michael Reese Hospital, the largest private hospital in Chicago. In addition there are large housing projects sponsored by insurance companies,
and one by the city itself.

The Michael Reese Hospital was founded in 1882. Its entire area covering
about seven square miles is now being replanned – probably the first
undertaking of this sort in the U.S.A. Open spaces, sports grounds, diversified housing, community facilities, are all slowly coming into being.
Walter Gropius, as consultant architect, played a prominent part in the
preparation of this plan[1].

**Coordinated
planning:
The Michael Reese
Hospital, 1945**
Fig. 312, 313

It is just possible that these various large development projects in South
Chicago may form themselves together despite the absence of any master
planning.

In 1953 a new scheme appeared: the Boston Back Bay Center. This is the
largest project in which Walter Gropius has yet been associated. The Stevens
Development Corporation of Cleveland undertook responsibility for the
financing but its realization is handicapped by uncertainty about the tax
rates that will be levied on the new premises.

**Back Bay Center,
Boston, 1953**

Fig. 314–317

It is new in the history of large enterprises that an undertaking of some
75 million dollars should be designed by a group of architects who are
practically all university professors. Twenty years earlier it would have
been unthinkable for a leading real estate developer to have consulted a
university professor in connection with an important building project. This
reflects a far-reaching change of attitude of the business man towards the
teacher of architecture, and it cannot be denied that this change is largely
due to the creative achievements of such architects as Mies van der Rohe
and Walter Gropius. An even clearer example of change of attitude appears
in the acknowledgement by the *Architectural Forum* in September 1943
that the earliest designs for the new Boston Center were made by students
of the Harvard School of Architecture.

The plan for the new Boston Center makes use of the freight yards of the
old Boston-Albany railroad which had become unbearably costly to oper-
ate owing to the ever-increasing tax rates on the property. So it became
possible for an enterprising firm of real estate developers to undertake the
project.

The strength of the spatial planning of the first coordinated group of
skyscrapers – the Rockefeller Center, twenty years earlier – cannot be
forgotten. The Boston project is however, by comparison, a more elaborate
complex and is more urbanistically varied.

A large area has been consciously created for the sole use of the pedestrian,
a protected zone within which he can wander free from danger. At the
entrance to the Forum at Pompeii stands a stone bollard, blocking the
entry of wheeled vehicles. In the Boston Center, three-story car-parking

Fig. 316

---

[1] Until 1953 Reginald R. Isaacs was Director of the Planning Committee. After his appointment to Harvard University he was followed by Jack Meltzer. John T. Black, architect,
Martin D. Meyerson, planner, Frank Weise, assistant architect-planner, and Eleanor Torell,
sociologist, were members of the Planning Commission.

garages are proposed beneath the ground in which 5,000 autos can be stored like garments in a cupboard. At last the pedestrian regains the right he had lost since Antiquity, to move freely within the center of collective life. This is clearly connected with a third principle of urban planning: the reduction in importance of the street frontage and the movement of the shops to their rightful positions; within the traffic-free pedestrian area. Shopping calls for a certain degree of concentration and absence of extraneous disturbance, and here the city dweller of the west has been restored something that (so far) has always continued to be enjoyed in the bazaars of eastern cities: such as the Souks of Cairo or Bagdad.

The significance of this scheme lies in its relation to the changing structure of the city: of the great metropolis which is here with us and cannot be simply dreamed away.

It is this practical aspect that gave rise to the Boston project with its comprehensive building program, which occupies a tongue of land covering some 30 acres[2]. The scheme includes several office buildings, including a 40-story slab which stands transversely across the project and dominates the scene. There is also a hotel, the low buildings of a motel, an exhibition hall and, separated from these by a wide pedestrian way across the traffic stream, a large convention hall for 7,500 people.

From all sides the Center is hemmed in by the dense structure of the great city: gripped as in an iron vice. It stands as an isolated phenomenon closed in upon itself. Its volumes lack breathing space. Even so, from a sociological point of view, this Center is a leap into the future, away from the commonplace business approach, towards the satisfaction of the human needs of twentieth-century man.

---

[2] Further information on this project, including the difficulties confronting its realization, are contained in an illustrated article in the "*Architectural Forum*", December 1953, pp. 103–115.

18.   FAGUS WORKS, Shoe last factory, Alfeld an der Leine, 1911: *View of entrance and main building.*

19.   WORKMEN'S HOUSES, Janikow (Pomerania), 1906.

20.   WORKMAN'S HOUSE, Janikow (Pomerania), 1906: *Completed house.*

21. MAHOGANY CABINET, 1913,
for Dr. Karl Hertzfeld, Hanover.

23. WARDROBE, 1913, for Dr. Karl Hertzfeld:
White enamelled poplar.

22. MAHOGANY DINING-ROOM CHAIR, 1913,
for Mendel House, Berlin.

24. SLEEPING-CAR for the German Railways, 1914. Exhibited in "Werkbund" Exhibition, Cologne. *The zig-zag arrangement of the partition is designed to save space. Upholstery design by Gropius.*

25. DAMASK WALL FABRIC, 1913, for World's Fair, Ghent, Belgium.

26.   DIESEL LOCOMOTIVE, 1913,
for the railway factory in Koenigsberg.
*Front view. The slanted and almost
streamlined hood is well designed for the
exhaust.*

27.   *Side view.*

28

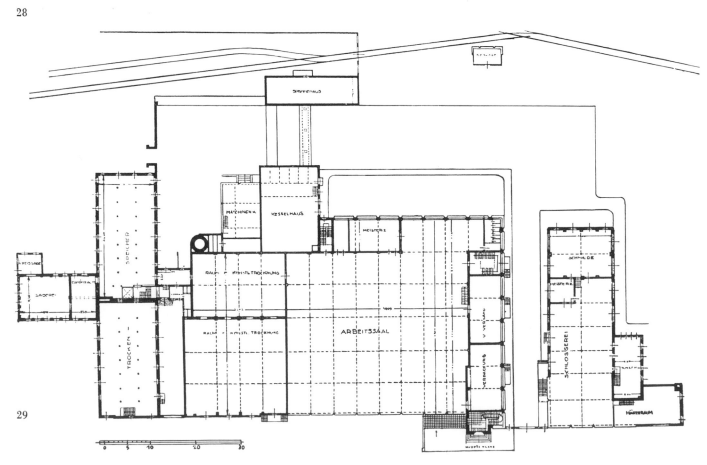

29

30. FAGUS WORKS, *workshop*.

↖ 28. FAGUS WORKS, Shoe last factory, Alfeld an
der Leine, 1911 (with Adolf Meyer): *Cantilevered
skeleton construction. Note omission of corner columns.
This photograph, taken in May 1953, shows the
excellent preservation of this early work of modern
architecture.*

← 29. *Plan.*

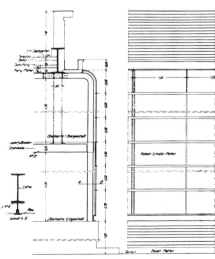

31. FAGUS WORKS, 1911.
View from southwest.

32. OFFICE BUILDING OF THE
"WERKBUND" EXHIBITION, COLOGNE,
1914 (with Adolf Meyer): *Glass-walled staircase
with cantilevered steps.*

33. *Detail of glass partition.*
Vertical section and elevation.
Principle: free-standing glass curtain wall.

34. "WERKBUND" EXHIBITION, COLOGNE, 1914: *General view of office building, workshops and pavilion for Deutz machine factory.*

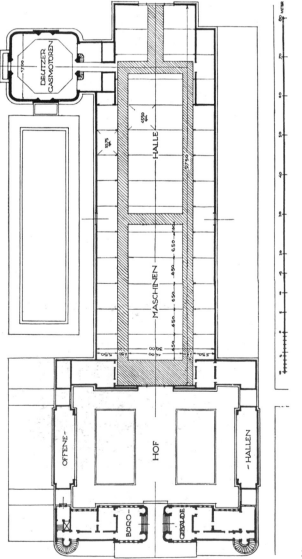

35. *General plan.*

36. "WERKBUND" EXHIBITION, COLOGNE, 1914:
Roof garden and restaurant of the office building.

37. *View, from the court, of the office building with its roof restaurant.*

38. "WERKBUND" EXHIBITION, COLOGNE, 1914: *Rear view of the open garages and office building.*

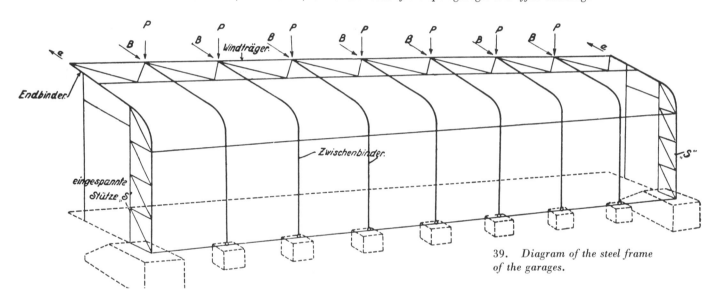

39. *Diagram of the steel frame of the garages.*

40. *View of the entrance to the workshops from the courtyard.*

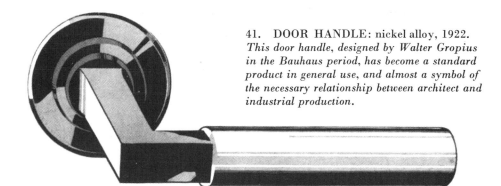

41. DOOR HANDLE: nickel alloy, 1922. *This door handle, designed by Walter Gropius in the Bauhaus period, has become a standard product in general use, and almost a symbol of the necessary relationship between architect and industrial production.*

42. ADLER CABRIOLET, 1930: *Front view.*

43.   STANDARD FURNITURE FOR FEDER STORES, Berlin, 1927.

44 and 45.   Unit furniture for
workers, from the Feder stores, Berlin,
1929: *Standard elements can be
arranged side by side and combined in
order to obtain a series of pieces of
furniture for different uses.*

46. ADLER CABRIOLET, 1930: *Side view.*

47. *Interior of car with two reclining seats. In 1930, long before any large car factory in USA had begun to use reclining seats, the possibility of converting the seats into beds had already been demonstrated by the architect.*

48.   CIRCULAR TRAY FOR THE HARVARD GRADUATE CENTER, 1951. The Architects' Collaborative. Plastic material. *Practical reason for the circular form: space economy. But experience has also shown that round tables are somehow conducive to conversation.*

49.   CAST IRON STOVE, 1931. *This stove became the most saleable product of the Frank Ironworks.*

50.   CHAIR, 1951. The Architects' Collaborative. *Manufacturer: Thonet.*

51. *Symbol for the Bauhaus synthesis: mastery of form, skill of hand, mastery of space. This composition by Herbert Bayer stood at the entry of the first Bauhaus exhibition at the Museum of Modern Art, New York, 1939.*

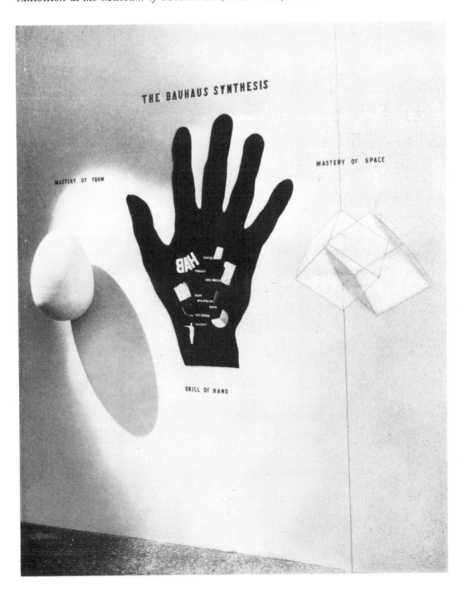

52.   *Desk lamp, 1923. Glass and metal. Design by R.J. Jucker and W. Wagenfeld.*

53.   *Wooden chair, 1922. Seat and back straps of elastic fabric. Design by Marcel Breuer.*

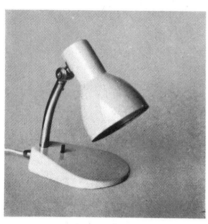

54. *Bedside lamp, 1927. Design by M. Brandt.*

55. *Ceiling lamps, 1927.*

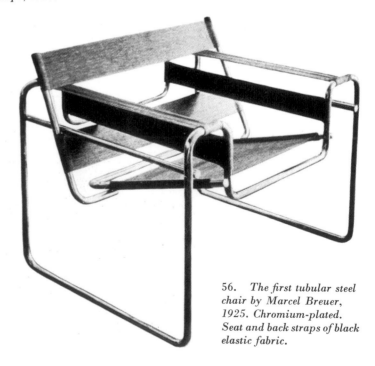

56.   *The first tubular steel chair by Marcel Breuer, 1925. Chromium-plated. Seat and back straps of black elastic fabric.*

57. *Bauhaus director's*
office, Weimar, 1923.
Design by Walter Gropius.

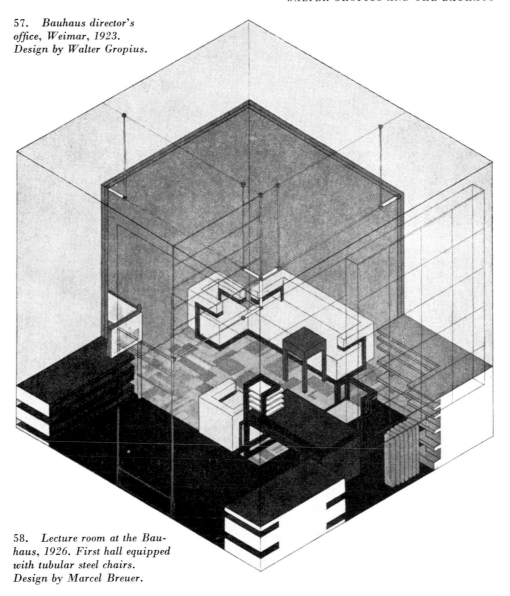

58. *Lecture room at the Bau-*
haus, 1926. First hall equipped
with tubular steel chairs.
Design by Marcel Breuer.

59.   *Four differently shaped teapots, made from identical component parts, 1923. Design by Th. Bogler. This follows Walter Gropius' idea of using economical repetition of machine-made parts to produce a variety of different end products.*

60.   *China, manufactured from Bauhaus models, 1923. Design by Th. Bogler and O. Lindig.*

62.   *Textile piece, hand-woven, as pattern for mechanical weaving, 1923. Design by Gunta Stölzl.*

61.   *Hand-woven fabric, 1922, red-green, black and white wool. Design by Benita Otte.*

63.   EXHIBITION "OPEN-AIR LIFE", BERLIN, 1928:
Type of demountable, semi-open wooden exhibition stand, allowing the passer-by to catch a glimpse of the exhibition beyond.

64. EXHIBITION OF THE GERMAN "WERKBUND", PARIS, 1930
Bar interior. Two-color drawing by Herbert Bayer.

65. EXHIBITION OF THE GERMAN "WERKBUND", PARIS, 1930:
Hall and bar. Large windows with various sets of screens and shades to control the quantity and the color of light.

66. *Entrance to the exhibition.*

67. EXHIBITION OF THE GERMAN "WERKBUND", PARIS, 1930: *Booths in the lounge (for reading, writing and radio) with balcony above.*

68. *Staircase and platform built up from galvanized steel-lattice.*

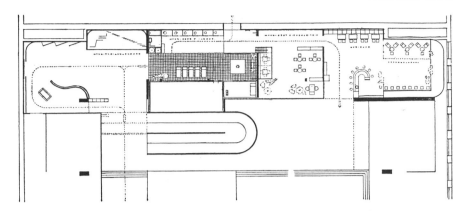

69. "BUILDING" EXHIBITION, BERLIN, 1931: *Plan.*
The Paris, 1930, as well as the Berlin exhibition, 1931, advocated community facilities in slab apartment blocks.

70. "BUILDING" EXHIBITION, BERLIN, 1931: *Gymnasium and swimming pool.*

115

71.   NON-FERROUS METAL EXHIBITION, BERLIN (with Joost Schmidt):
Frame of copper tubes with models of the crystal structures of various metals.

72.   NON-FERROUS METAL EXHIBITION, 1934:
Spiral of different metals and alloys, revolving in a large metallic drum.

117

73.   PAVILION OF THE STATE OF PENNSYLVANIA AT THE NEW YORK WORLD'S FAIR, 1939
(with Marcel Breuer): *Suspended steel bridge inside the pavilion.*

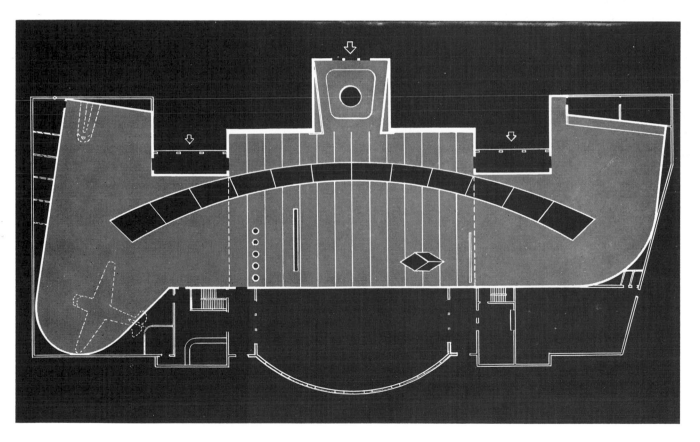

74.   *Plan.*

←

75. HARVARD GRADUATE CENTER,
Cambridge, Mass., USA, 1949: *View from the east
into two of the quadrangles. The open spaces are
as important as the buildings surrounding them.*

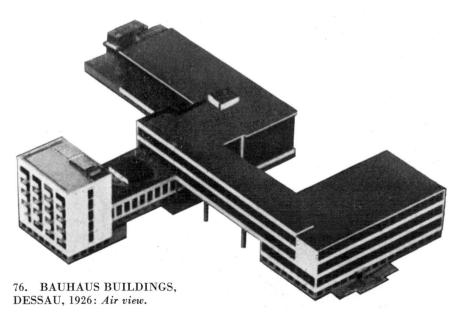

76. BAUHAUS BUILDINGS,
DESSAU, 1926: *Air view.*

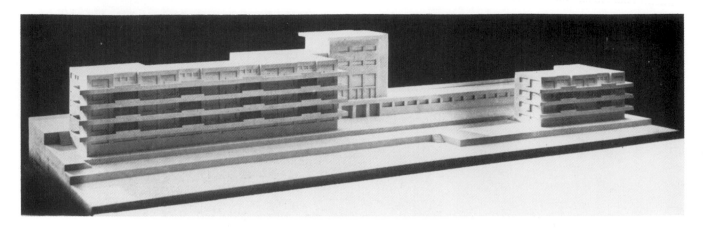

77. ACADEMY OF PHILOSOPHY, ERLANGEN, 1924: Project.

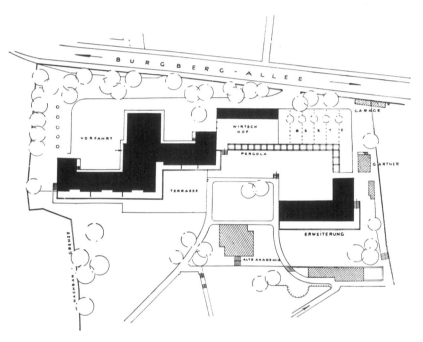

78. *Site plan.*

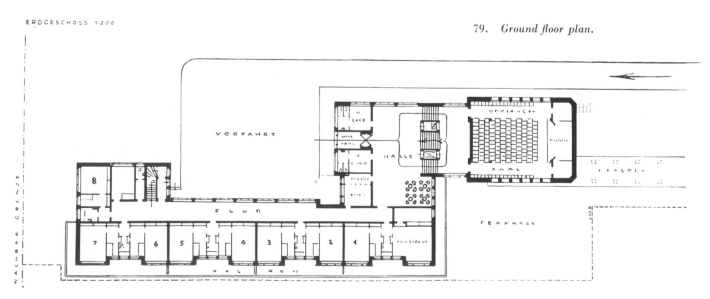

79. *Ground floor plan.*

122

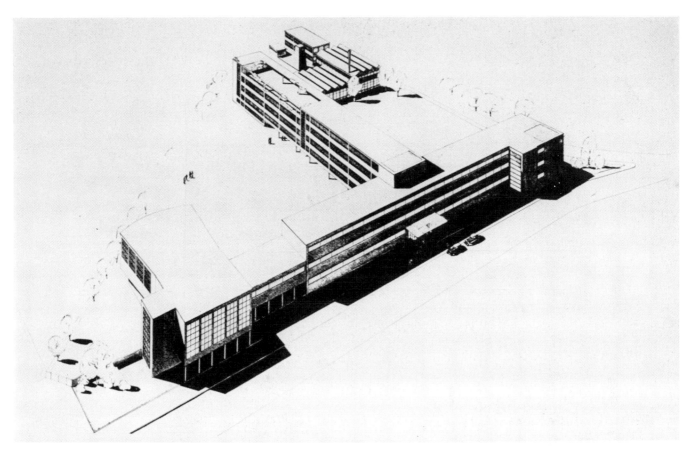

80. ENGINEERING SCHOOL, HAGEN,
WESTPHALIA, 1929. Competition, 2nd prize.

81. *Plan.*

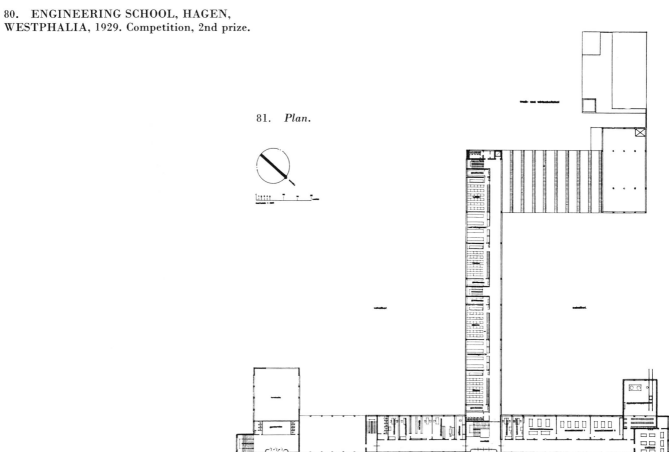

82.   BAUHAUS BUILDINGS, DESSAU, 1926:
*Left: workshop wing; right: studios for students;
center: canteen. Reinforced concrete skeleton and
stuccoed brick walls.*

83.   *Site plan.*

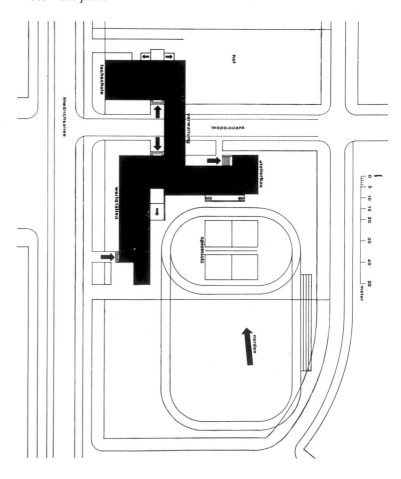

84. *Workshop building for students.*

85. *Ground floor plan.*   86. *Second floor plan.*

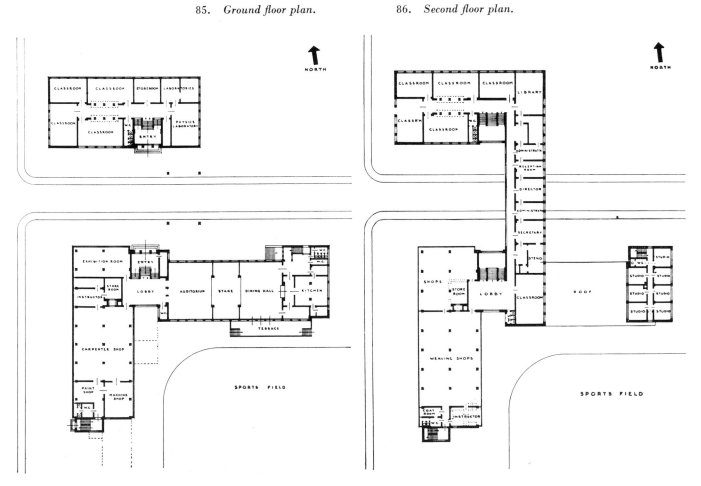

87.   BAUHAUS BUILDINGS, DESSAU, 1926:
Workshop wing with main entrance and connecting link over the street.

89.   *Workshop wing, northwest corner;*
left, entrance to the advanced technical school.   →

88.   *View from the south. Left: workshop wing.*
Right: students house. Center: canteen.

90.   BAUHAUS BUILDINGS, DESSAU, 1926:
View from the east with workshop building in the foreground.

91.   *Workshop wing for students, on the left.*
Center: canteen and auditorium.

92.   *Typical student's workshop and bedroom.* →

93.   *Entrance to the auditorium.* →

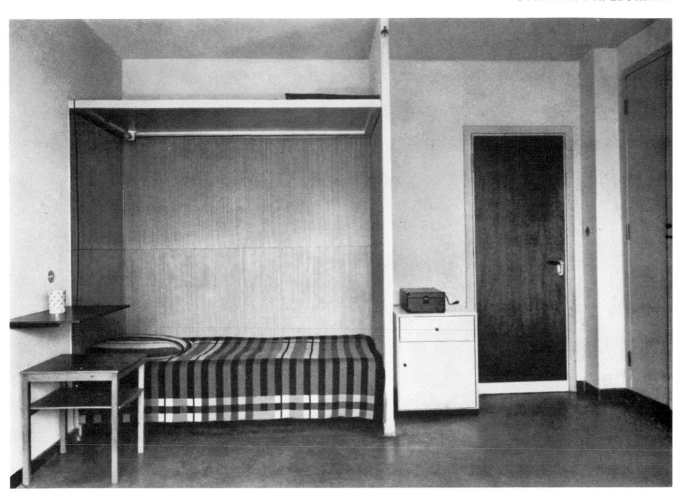

94. VILLAGE COLLEGE, IMPINGTON, Cambridgeshire, 1936
(with Maxwell Fry): Model.

96. *View of the assembly hall.* →
97. *View of classroom wing, from the southeast.*
98. *View into the quadrangle, from the south.*

95. *Plan.*

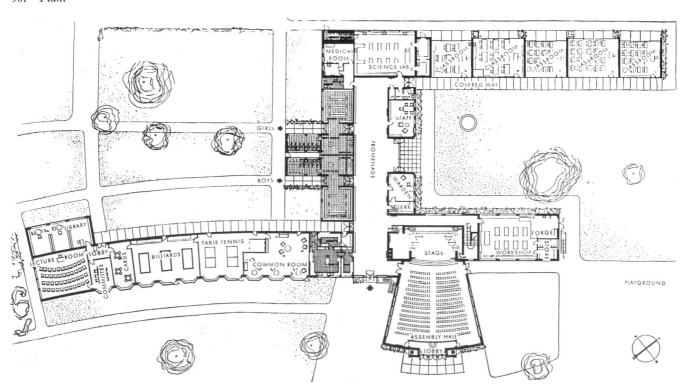

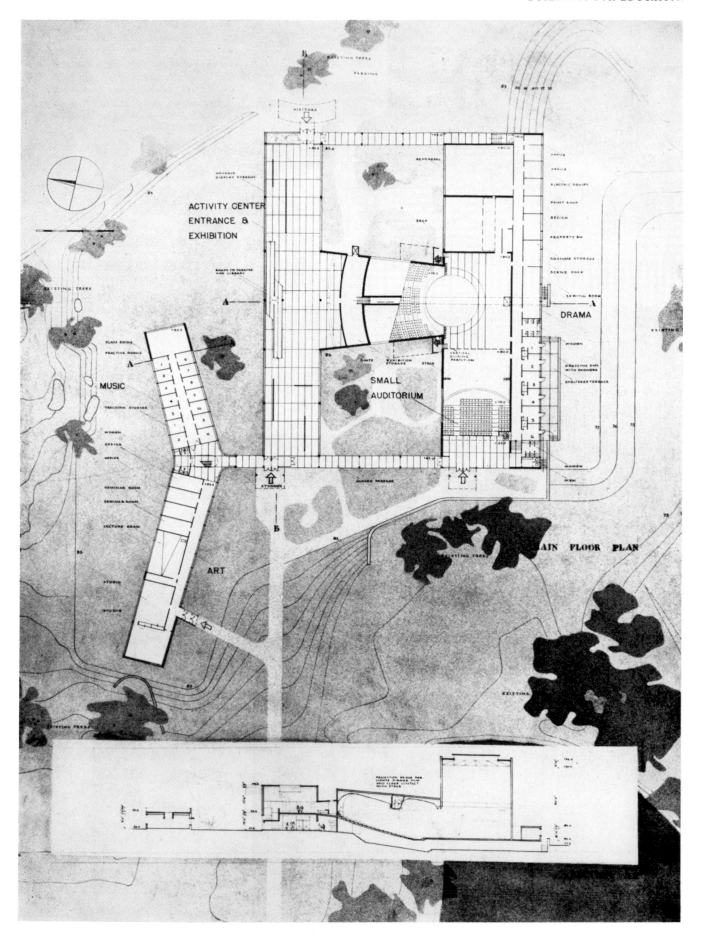

RECREATIONAL CENTER, KEY WEST, Florida, USA, 1940 (with Konrad Wachsmann): *Provisions are made to give adequate recreational facilities simultaneously to all age groups, to children, adolescents, parents and grandparents. Only then can the center fulfil the recreational requirements of the whole family.*

106.   *Entrance. North elevation.*

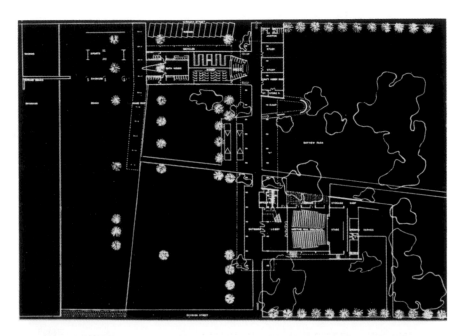

107.   *Plan of ground floor.*

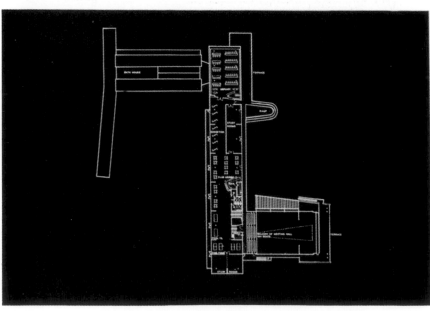

108.   *Plan of second floor with club rooms.*

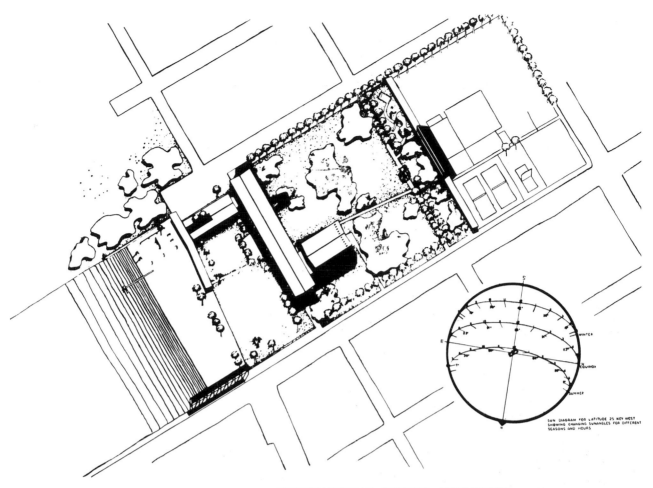

109. RECREATIONAL CENTER, KEY WEST,
1940 (with Konrad Wachsmann). Project. *Site plan.*

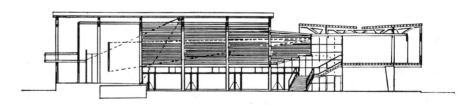

110 and 111. *Section through auditorium. Reinforced
concrete and wood. Double roof for heat insulation.*

111

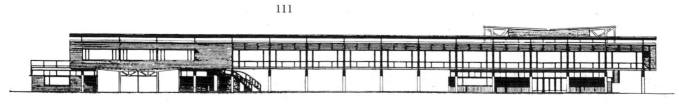

112.   HUA TUNG UNIVERSITY, SHANGHAI, China, 1946: For the United
Board of Christian Colleges in China. Complete campus with dormitories for boys
and girls, and faculty housing. The Architects' Collaborative and I. Ming Pei.
*Elements of design: courtyards, lakes and pools, covered connecting walks, small
buildings in human scale. Local building methods and materials.*

113.   *View of library building
with entrance courtyard.*

114.   HUA TUNG UNIVERSITY,
SHANGHAI, 1946: *Classrooms.*

115.   *Plan of a group of dormitories.*

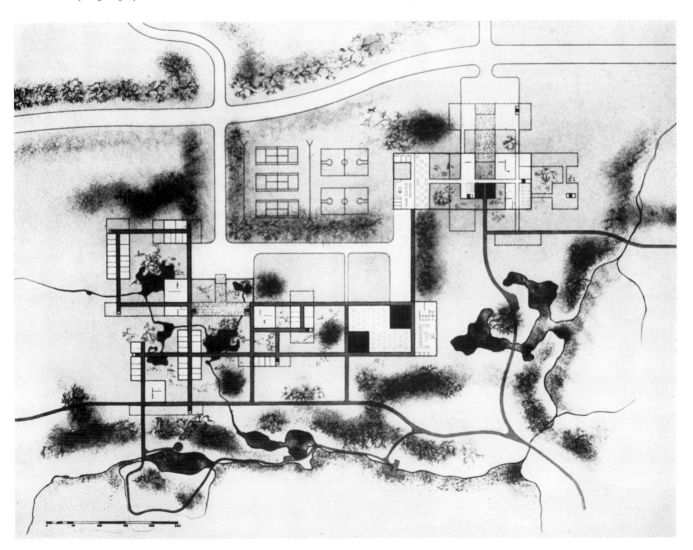

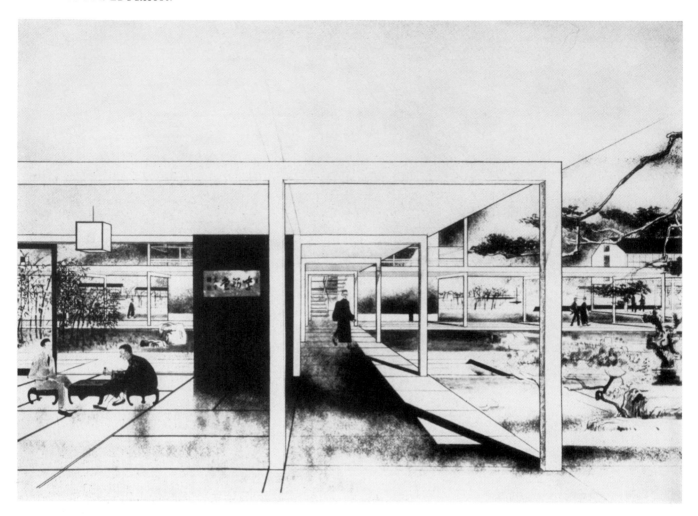

116. HUA TUNG UNIVERSITY, 1946.

116a. *Campus.*

117. HARVARD GRADUATE CENTER, Cambridge, Mass., USA, 1949, composed of seven dormitory buildings for 575 students, and Harkness Commons with lounge rooms and dining facilities for 1200 students. The Architects' Collaborative. *Reinforced concrete structure used for dormitories. Steel skeleton for Harkness Commons. Exteriors: buff brick and limestone.*

141

118. HARVARD GRADUATE CENTER,
Cambridge, 1949: *Air view.*

119. *General plan.*

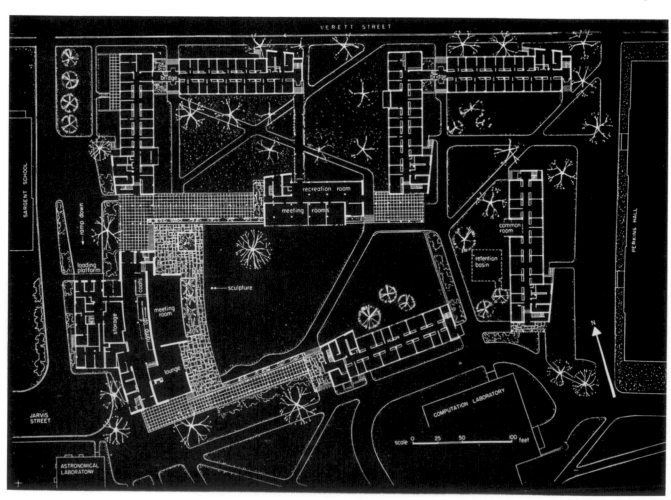

120.   HARVARD GRADUATE CENTER, Cambridge, 1949:
Main view from South with Harkness Commons and dormitories in the background.

121.   *Students' dormitories.*

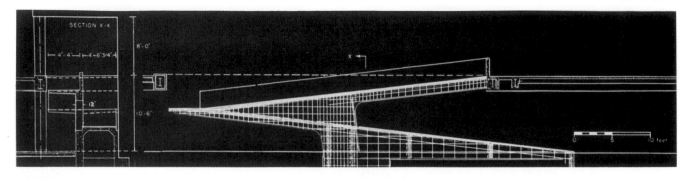

122.   *Section showing structure of the three-way cantilevered reinforced concrete ramp.*

123.   *Entrance hall of Harkness Commons with the three-way cantilevered reinforced concrete ramp leading to the dining-rooms. Curved wall of glazed tile designed by Herbert Bayer.*

124.   HARVARD GRADUATE CENTER, Cambridge, 1949: *Wall painting by Joan Miró in the main dining-room. Oil on canvas, 19 feet long.*

125.   HARVARD GRADUATE CENTER, Cambridge, 1949:
Room for two students.

126.   *Plans of single rooms.*

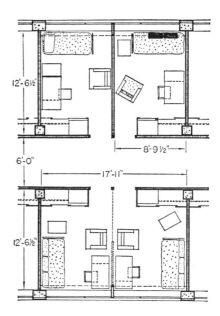

126a.   *Plan of double room.*

145

127. HARVARD GRADUATE CENTER,
Cambridge, 1949: *View towards Harkness Commons with "World Tree", stainless steel sculpture by Richard Lippold.*

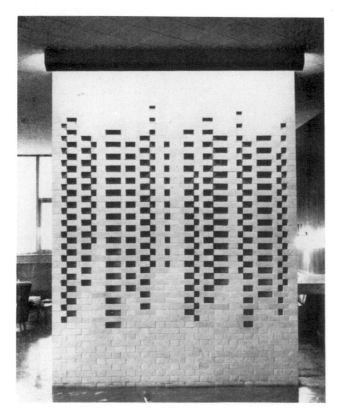

128. Harkness Commons:
Brick relief by Joseph Albers.

129.   JUNIOR HIGH SCHOOL, ATTLEBORO, 1948. The Architects'
Collaborative. Main entrance. *The free suspended, cantilevered canopy and
the few steps undoubtedly create in the visitor's mind an impression of
welcome and intimacy. Just behind, the ramp leading to the classroom wing.*

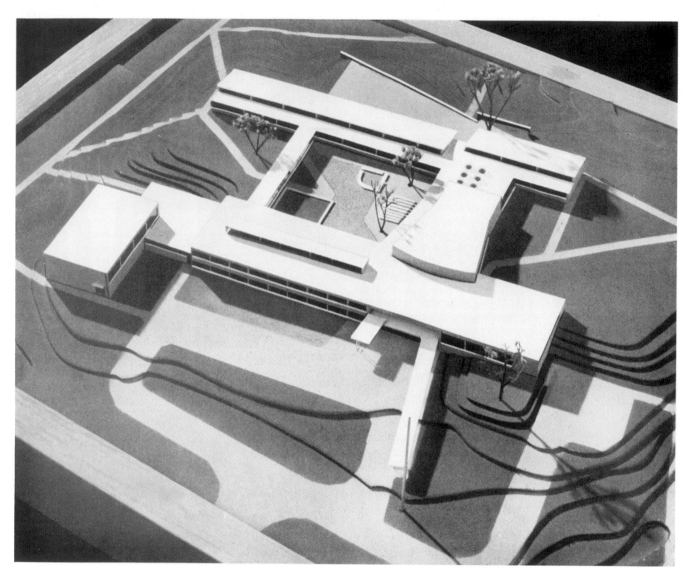

130. JUNIOR HIGH SCHOOL, ATTLEBORO, 1948.
*Air view of model. The lay-out on an uneven site, taking advantage of
the different levels, is as distinctive as the clear arrangement of front
and back classroom wings with skylights. In the foreground, on the left,
the gymnasium, on the right auditorium and library, equidistant
from both wings.*

131. *Main entrance and two-story classroom wing.*
On the right, bicycle shed.

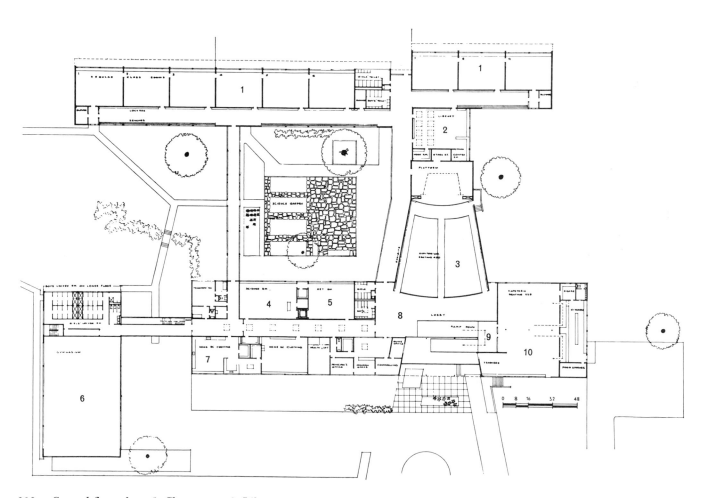

132.   *Ground floor plan. 1. Classrooms. 2. Library.*
3. Auditorium with 450 seats. 3. Laboratory. 5. Art room.
6. Gymnasium. 7. Domestic science. 8. Lobby. 9. Ramp.
10. Cafeteria for 250 persons.

133. *Ramp leading to classroom wing.*
Free view of landscape through the glass wall.

134. *Glass walled, curved passage along*
library and auditorium.

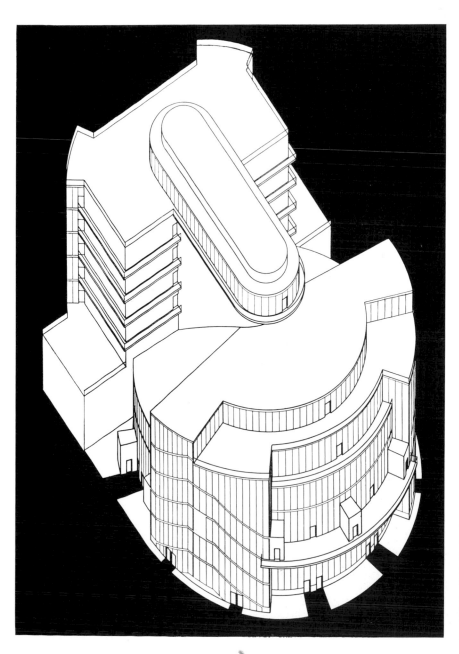

135. THE "TOTAL THEATER", 1927.
*"The aim of the 'total theater' is to draw
the spectator into the drama. All technical
means have to be subordinated to this
aim and should never become an end in
themselves."*
*From a speech by Walter Gropius on theater
building in "Convegno di Lettere",
October 1934, in Reale Accademia d'Italia,
Rome, 1935, page 160.*

136. CITY THEATER, JENA, 1923
(with Adolf Meyer): *General view.*

137. *Foyer.*

138. CITY THEATER, JENA, 1923: *Entrance.*

140. *Interior view.*

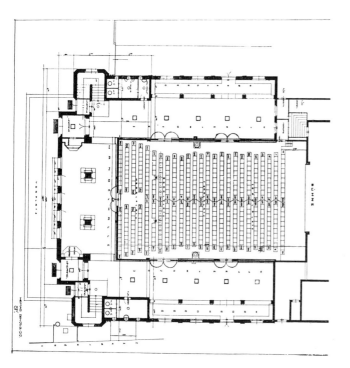

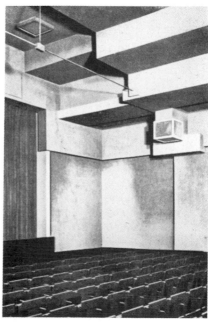

139. *Plan.*

141.   THE "TOTAL THEATER", 1927.
*The principles for the theater of the future and its form are the following: Complete
coordination of all architectural elements leads to a unity between actor and spectator.
No separation between stage and auditorium. Application of all possible spatial
means capable of shaking the spectator out of his lethargy, of surprising and assaulting
him and obliging him to take a real, living interest in the play.*
"Convegno di Lettere", October 1934, in Reale Accademia d'Italia, Rome, 1935, page 159.

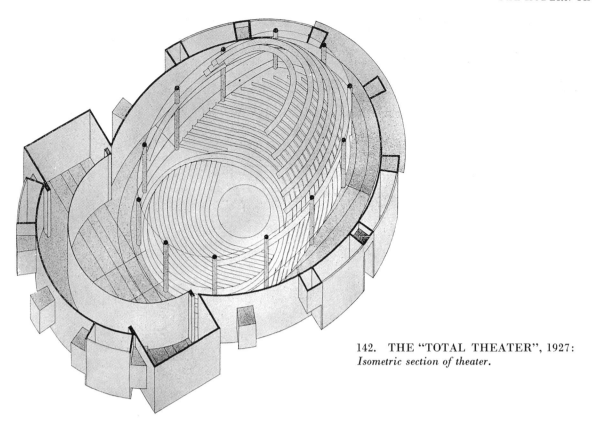

142.   THE "TOTAL THEATER", 1927:
Isometric section of theater.

143.   *Side elevation of the model with entrances.*

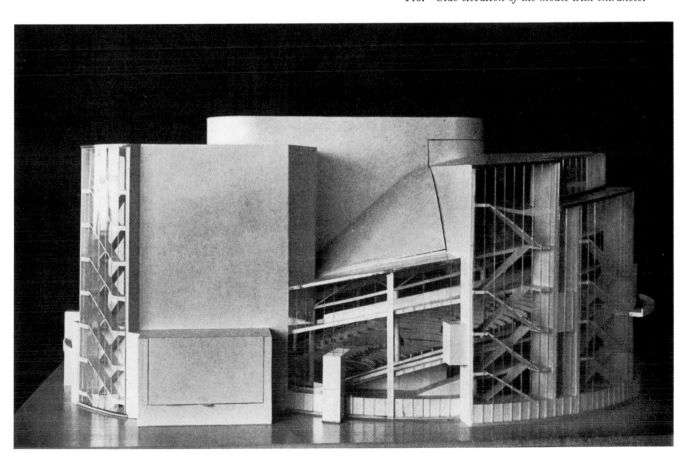

"In my 'total theater', which was originally planned for Erwin Piscator, I have tried to create
an instrument so flexible that a director can employ any one of the three stage-forms
by means of simple, ingenious mechanisms: deep stage, proscenium stage or circular arena."
"Convegno di Lettere", October 1934, in Reale Accademia d' Italia, Rome, page 159.

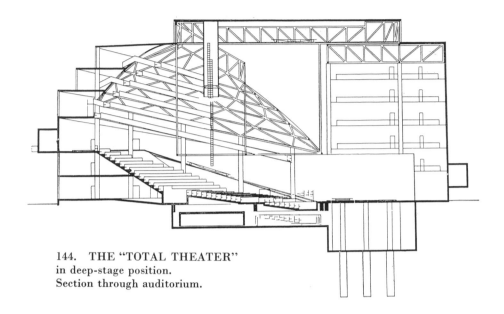

144. THE "TOTAL THEATER"
in deep-stage position.
Section through auditorium.

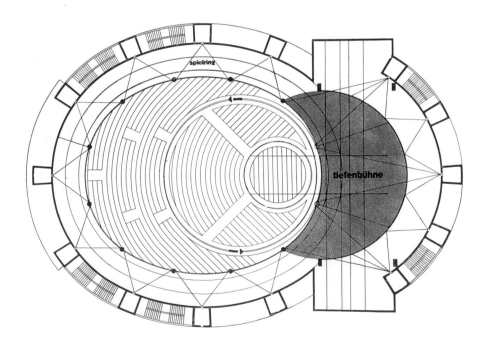

145. THE "TOTAL THEATER"
in deep-stage position. Plan.

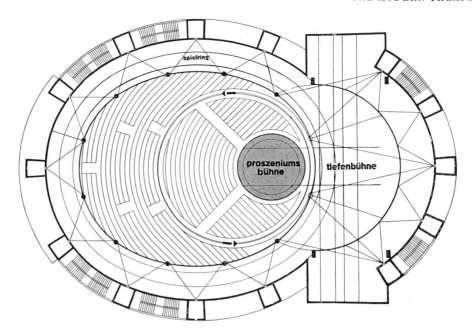

146. THE "TOTAL THEATER"
with stage in front of proscenium.
combined with deep stage.

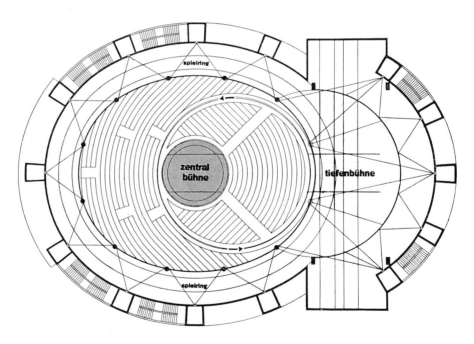

147. THE "TOTAL THEATER"
with arena stage.

"A complete transformation of the building occurs by turning the stage-platform and part of the orchestra through 180°. Then the former proscenium stage becomes a central arena, entirely surrounded by rows of spectators! This can even be done during the play."
"This attack on the spectator, moving him during the play and unexpectedly shifting the stage area, alters the existing scale of values, presenting to the spectator a new consciousness of space and making him participate in the action." "Convegno di Lettere", October 1934, in Reale Accademia d'Italia, Rome, page 160.

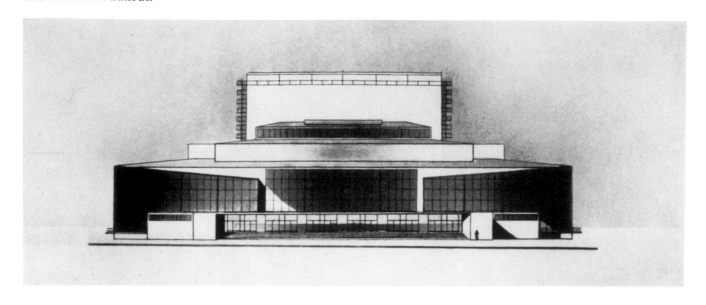

148. UKRAINIAN STATE THEATER,
KHARKOV, 1930. Project. International
competition, 8th prize. *Entrance elevation.*

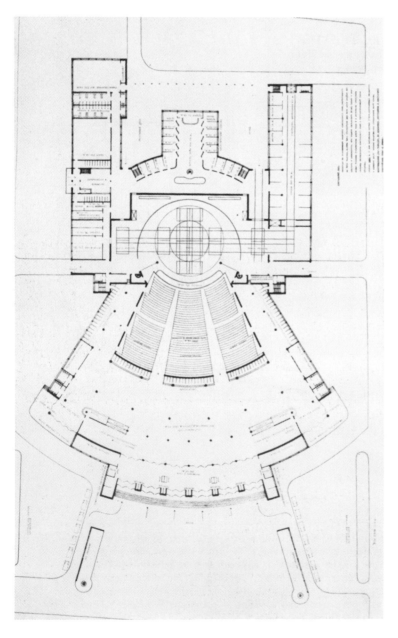

149. *Plan.*

150.   UKRAINIAN STATE THEATER, KHARKOV, 1930. *Perspective.*

151.   *Side elevation.*

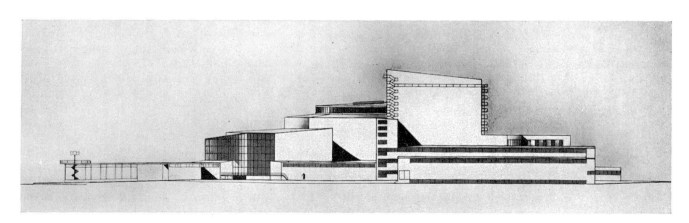

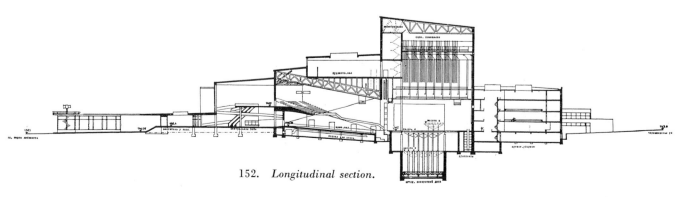

152.   *Longitudinal section.*

153. SOVIET PALACE, MOSCOW, Project commissioned by the
Russian Embassy, Berlin, 1931.
Perspective entrance to theater. Steel skeleton with marble facing.

154. *Front elevation.*

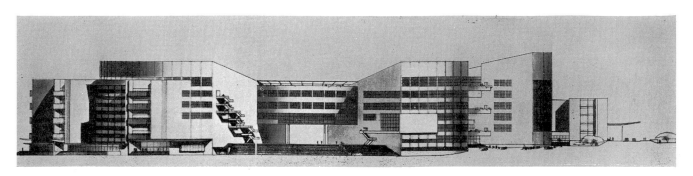

155. SOVIET PALACE, MOSCOW, 1931:
Side elevation of assembly hall and theater.

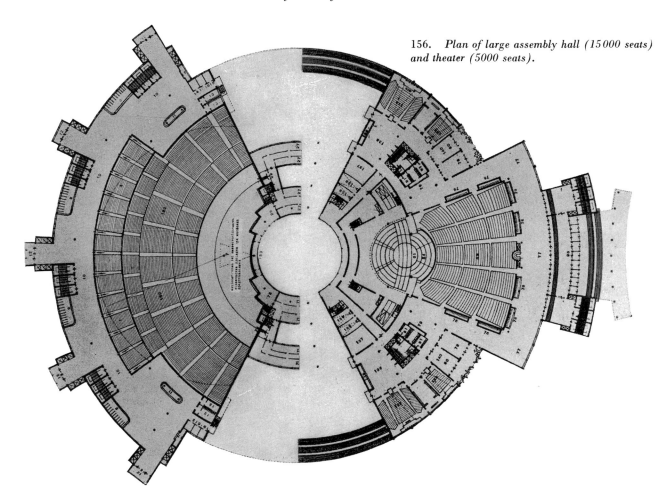

156. *Plan of large assembly hall (15 000 seats) and theater (5000 seats).*

157. *Longitudinal section of assembly hall and theater.*

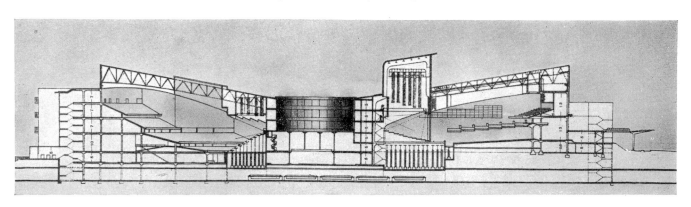

158.   CIVIC CENTER, HALLE an der Saale, 1927: *View from river.*

159.   *Air view with town hall, museum and sports stadium.*

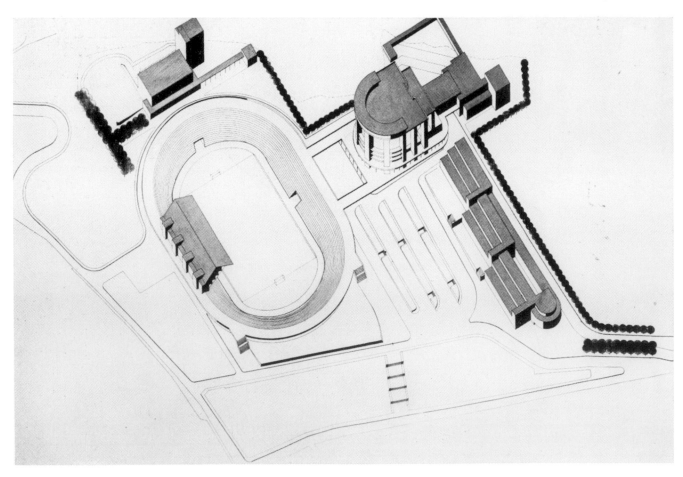

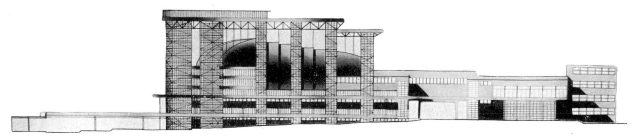

160. CIVIC CENTER, HALLE an der Saale, 1927:
West elevation.

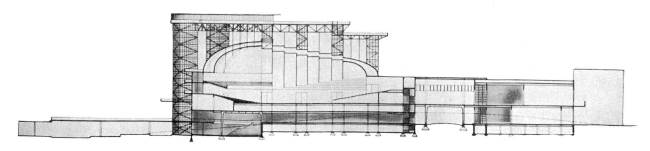

161. *Section of town hall.*
Roof and ceiling suspended from steel towers.

162. *Plan of entrance level.*

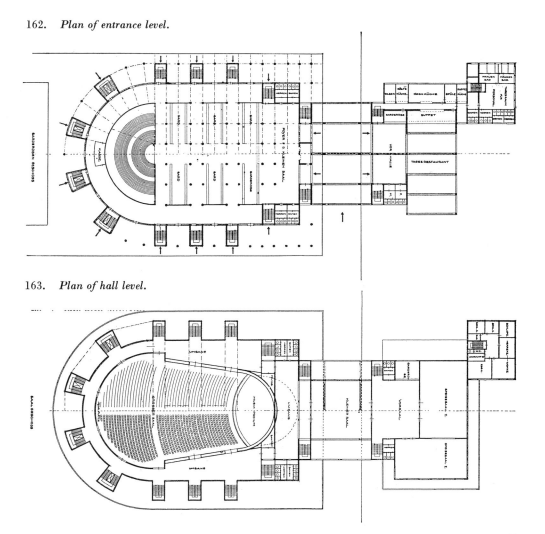

163. *Plan of hall level.*

164. MUNICIPAL EMPLOYMENT OFFICE, DESSAU, 1927/28:
View from northwest with entrances for the various trades round the periphery.
Steel skeleton, top lighting.

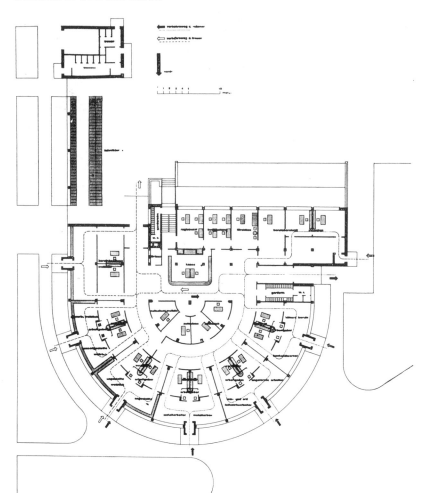

165. **MUNICIPAL EMPLOYMENT OFFICE, DESSAU, 1927/28:** *Plan of ground floor with peripheral entrances arranged to give the utmost space to each of them.*

166. *Site plan.*

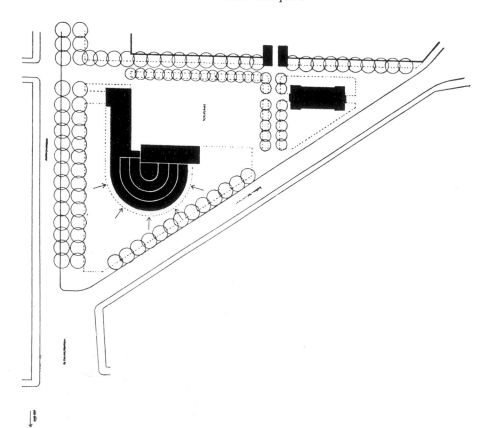

167. MUNICIPAL EMPLOYMENT OFFICE, DESSAU, 1927/28:
Rear view of administration building.

168. *Interior passage.*
Walls of white glazed tiles. Daylighted glass ceiling.

169. OFFICE
BUILDING FOR
THE "CHICAGO
TRIBUNE", 1922
(with Adolf Meyer).
International
competition:
Perspective.

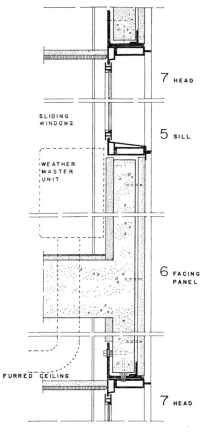

7 HEAD

SLIDING
WINDOWS

5 SILL

WEATHER
MASTER
UNIT

6 FACING
PANEL

FURRED CEILING

7 HEAD

171. OFFICE BUILDING FOR McCORMICK & CO., INC.,
CHICAGO, 1953. The Architects' Collaborative. Arthur Myhrum,
Associate.
*Steel skeleton, glass and marble curtain wall. Since the mechanical
parts of large buildings are increasing in bulk and importance,
they have been deliberately made a part of this composition.
The marble slabs arranged rhythmically under the windows mark
the units for air conditioning and heating.*

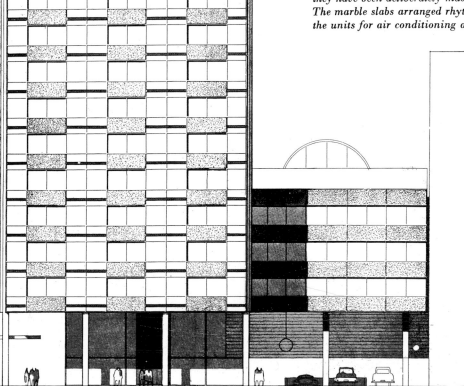

SOUTH ELEVATION

169

172. OFFICE BUILDING FOR McCORMICK & CO., INC., CHICAGO, 1953:
South elevation and entrance to basement garages.

173. *Ground floor with main entrance, shops and restaurant.*
Arcades on both streets.

174. *Ground floor plan.*

175. *Typical floor plan, first to third floors.*

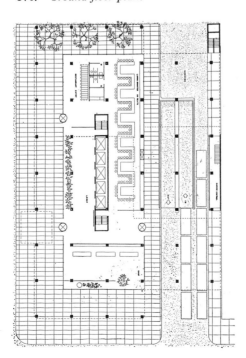

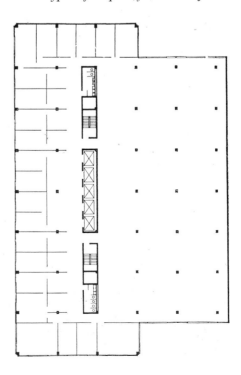

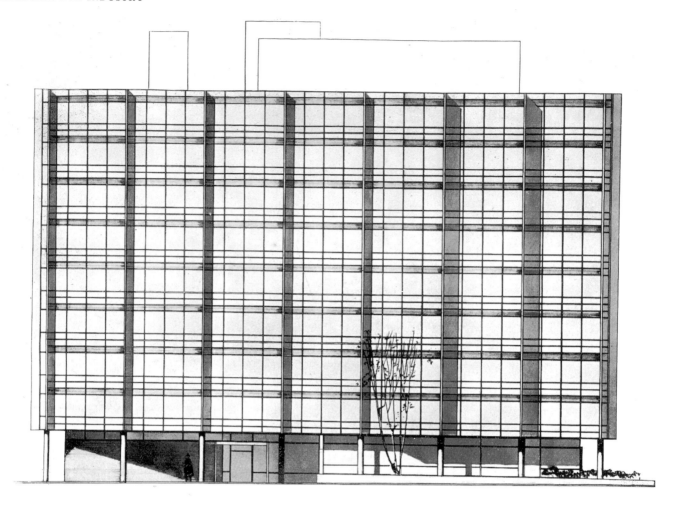

176. OFFICE BUILDING FOR THE AMERICAN ASSOCIATION FOR ADVANCEMENT IN SCIENCE, WASHINGTON D. C. (Scott Circle), 1952: The Architects' Collaborative.
South elevation with sun-shading louvres (brise-soleil).

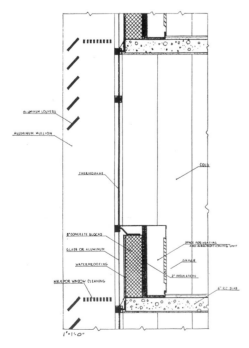

177. *Section through window with sun-shading louvre.*

178. *The polygonal shape results from adaptation to the site.*

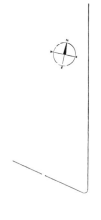
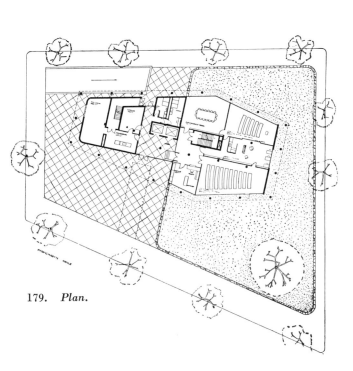

179. *Plan.*

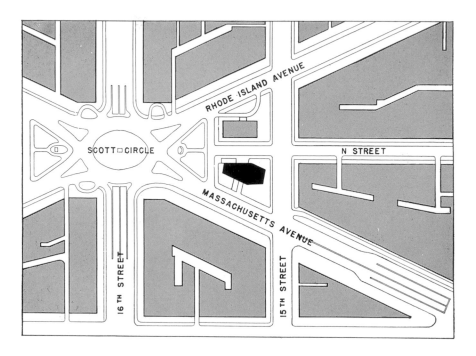

180. OFFICE BUILDING FOR THE AMERICAN ASSOCIATION
FOR ADVANCEMENT IN SCIENCE, WASHINGTON D. C. (Scott Circle), 1952:
Site plan.

181.   SUMMER HOUSE BY THE SEA, 1924 (with Adolf Meyer): Project for Mr. von Klitzing.

182. SEMI-DETACHED FACULTY
QUARTERS, BAUHAUS, DESSAU, 1925:
*Moholy-Nagy's house, view from east.
Cinderblock walls.*

183. Paul Klee in his studio.

184. SEMI-DETACHED FACULTY QUARTERS, BAUHAUS, DESSAU, 1925:
View from south.

185. *Ground floor plan of a semi-detached house.*

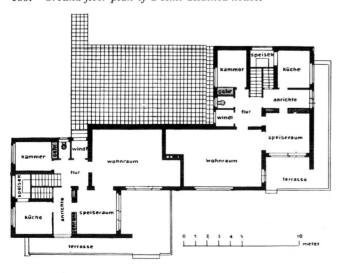

186. *Second floor plan of a semi-detached house. By reversing one of the two equal halves visual symmetry has been avoided.*

187. GROPIUS RESIDENCE, DESSAU, 1925.

188. *Ground floor plan.*

189. *Second floor plan.*

190. GROPIUS RESIDENCE, 1925:
View from northwest.

191. *Verandah outside dining-room.*

192. *Living-dining-room.*

193. GROPIUS RESIDENCE, LINCOLN, MASS., USA, 1937 (with Marcel Breuer):
View of model.

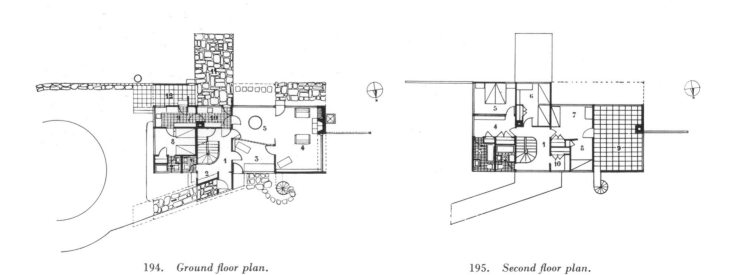

194. *Ground floor plan.*   195. *Second floor plan.*

196. *Second floor terrace.*

197. GROPIUS RESIDENCE, LINCOLN, MASS., USA, 1937: *Living-dining-room.*

198. *Ise and Walter Gropius at breakfast. The screened porch projecting from the house catches the breeze from east or west.*

199. GROPIUS RESIDENCE,
LINCOLN, 1937: *View from south.
The overhanging roof protects the
living-room windows against
the unwanted hot summer sun, but
the welcome winter sun can
penetrate. Frame construction with
painted vertical redwood siding.
Steel casement windows.*

200.   *North view of main entrance
at night.*

201.   GROPIUS RESIDENCE, LINCOLN, MASS., USA, 1937:
View from west showing second floor terrace and wood trellis for climbing plants.
In the background right, the projecting porch.

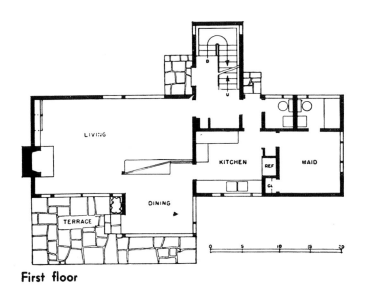

First floor

202. FORD RESIDENCE, LINCOLN, MASS., 1938 (with Marcel Breuer): *Ground floor plan.*

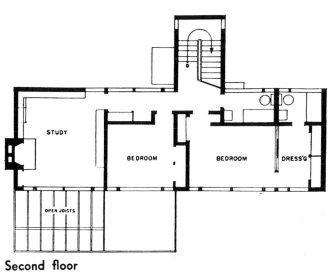

Second floor

203. *Second floor plan.*

204. *Wood frame construction, painted redwood siding. Sun-shading louvres of redwood boards on south side.*

205.   CHAMBERLAIN RESIDENCE, SUDBURY, MASS., 1939
(with Marcel Breuer): *Strutted frame construction, oiled redwood
siding, steel casement windows, local stone substructure.*

206.   *Plan.*

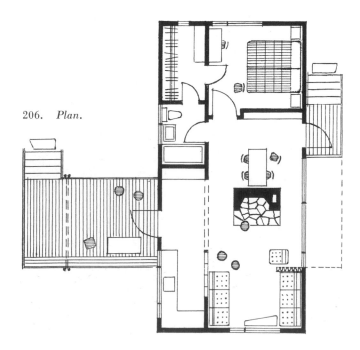

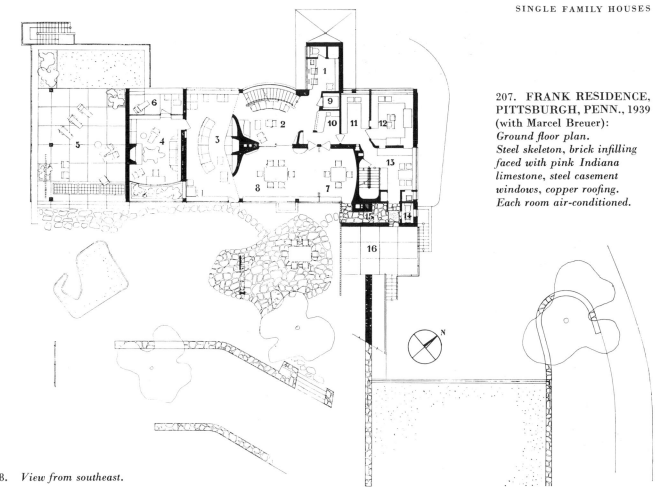

207. FRANK RESIDENCE,
PITTSBURGH, PENN., 1939
(with Marcel Breuer):
Ground floor plan.
Steel skeleton, brick infilling
faced with pink Indiana
limestone, steel casement
windows, copper roofing.
Each room air-conditioned.

208. *View from southeast.*

209. RESIDENCE DR. ABELE, FRAMINGHAM, MASS., 1941
View from southeast. Wood frame construction, painted fir siding, steel casement windows; basement, garage walls and chimney of local stone.

210. *Ground floor plan.*   211. *Second floor plan.*

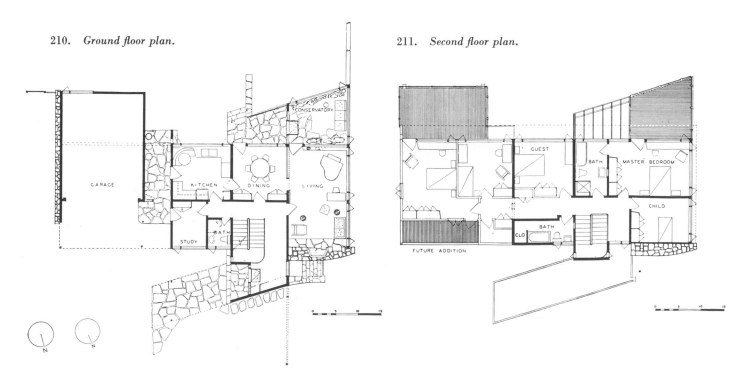

212.   *Southwest view from the lake.*

213.   *South elevation showing proposed extension over garages.*

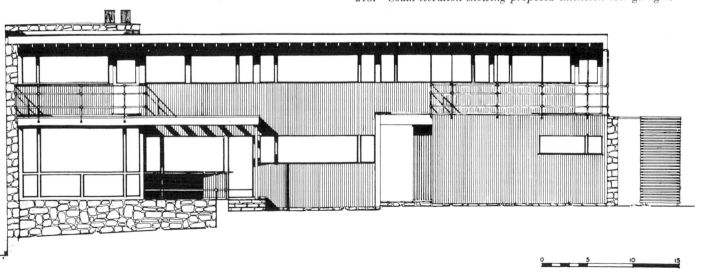

214. HOWLETT RESIDENCE, BELMONT, MASS., 1949:
The Architects' Collaborative. *View from south. Wood frame construction,
"Lally"-columns, oiled redwood siding, steel casement windows.*

215. HOWLETT
RESIDENCE, BELMONT,
MASS., 1949:
View of entrance.

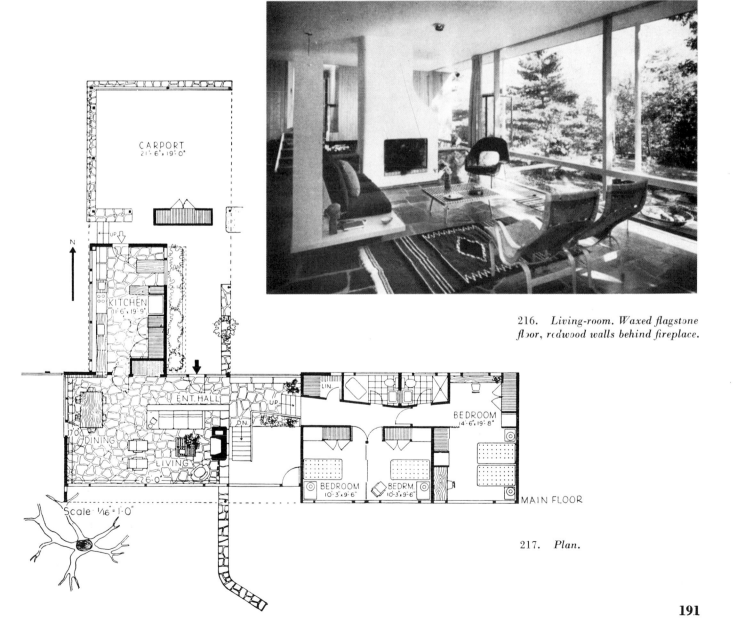

216. *Living-room. Waxed flagstone
floor, redwood walls behind fireplace.*

217. *Plan.*

218. *Walter Gropius and Konrad Wachsmann during erection of a General Panel model house on Long Island, N.Y.*

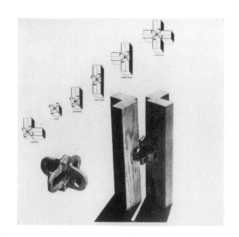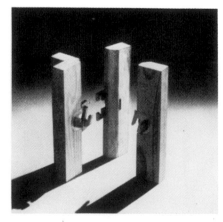

219. PANEL FRAMES OF GENERAL PANEL CORP., 1943–1945
(Konrad Wachsmann and Walter Gropius):
Four-way connection of panel frames by metal-wedge connector.

220. *Same frame parts, disconnected, wedge connector unhooked.*

"The idea of industrializing house construction can be realized by repetition of the same component parts in every building project. By this means the mass production can be made both profitable for the manufacturer and cheap for the customer."
"The possibilities of assembly of these interchangeable parts satisfies the public desire for a home with an individual appearance."   *Walter Gropius, 1909*

221. "THE PACKAGED HOUSE SYSTEM", 1943–1945
(Konrad Wachsmann and Walter Gropius):
Erection and connection of wall, floor and roof elements of the General Panel system.

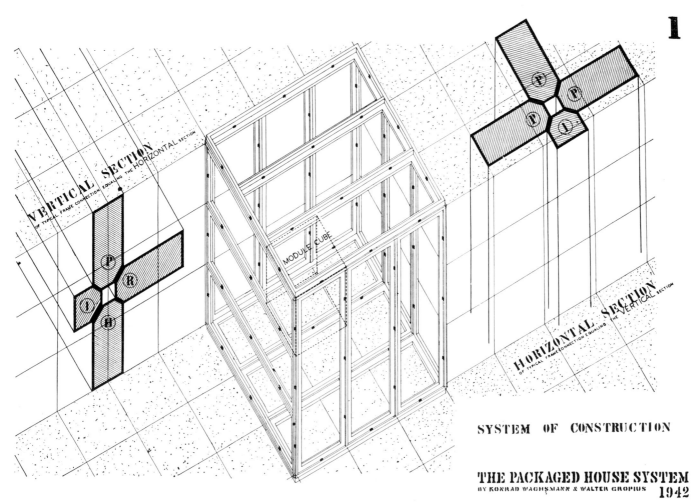

SYSTEM OF CONSTRUCTION

THE PACKAGED HOUSE SYSTEM
BY KONRAD WACHSMANN & WALTER GROPIUS 1942

193

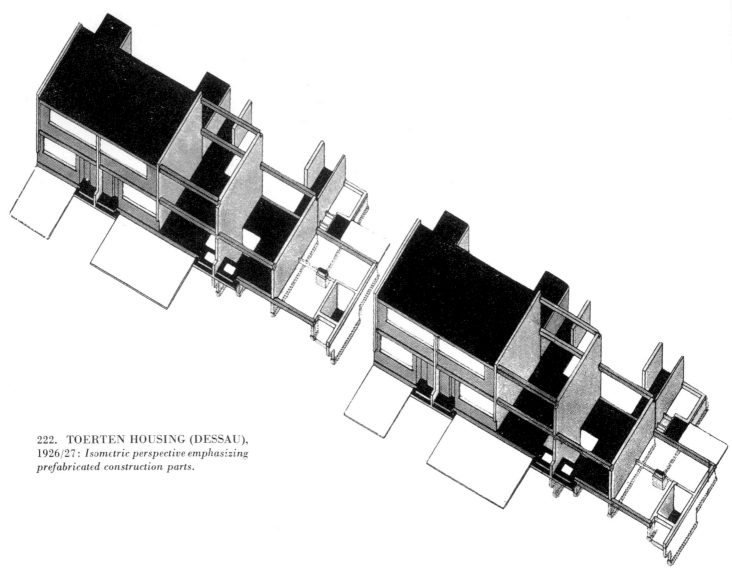

222. TOERTEN HOUSING (DESSAU),
1926/27: *Isometric perspective emphasizing
prefabricated construction parts.*

223.   *Assembly procedure on the site. Structural walls of cinderblock.
Floors and roofs reinforced concrete beams and joists made on the site;
front and rear walls of porous concrete and insulating cellular concrete panels.*

224. WEISSENHOF HOUSING,
"WERKBUND" EXHIBITION,
STUTTGART, 1927:
Prefabricated single-family dwelling.
Dry construction. Light steel skeleton.

225. *Entrance view.*

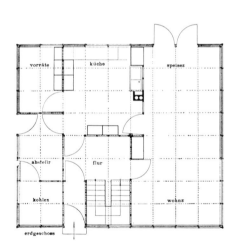

226. *Plan.*

227. *Placing asbestos-cement (Eternit)*
sheets to nailing strips as exterior finish
between steel members.

228. *Non-load-bearing walls*
of compressed cork panels.

229. *Exterior wall section.*

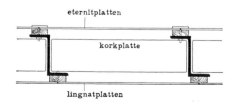

230.   PREFABRICATED COPPER
HOUSES, Hirsch Kupfer- und Messing-
werke AG., Finow (Germany), 1931:
Assembly of prefabricated walls.
Exterior walls wood frame with aluminum
foil insulation; exterior finish of corrugated
copper sheets; interior facing asbestos-cement
(Eternit) sheets.

231.   *Completed basic one-family house.*

232.   *Vertical wall section.*

233.   *Corner closed*
with copper strip.

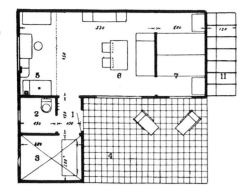

234. *Plan of basic house.*

236. *Plan with four rooms added.*

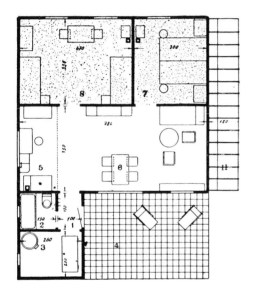

235. *Plan with two rooms added.*

THE EXPANDING AND CONTRACTING HOUSE, MADE POSSIBLE BY USING STANDARDIZED BUILDING ELEMENTS
(Hirsch Kupfer- und Messingwerke AG., 1931)

237 and 238. *Horizontal section of wall connections and window detail.*

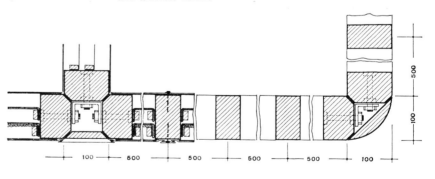

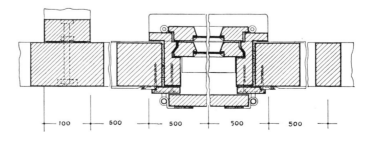

239. *Finished wall panels leave the factory.*

"THE PACKAGED HOUSE SYSTEM",
1943–45 (patented). Manufactured by the
General Panel Corp., New York
(Konrad Wachsmann and Walter Gropius).

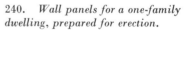

240. *Wall panels for a one-family
dwelling, prepared for erection.*

241. *Floor panels in place, ready for
erection of walls.*

242.   *Walls are erected.*

243.   *The house ready for fixing ceiling and roof panels.*

244.   *View of roof construction.*

245. *Plan of house
assembled with
General Panel elements.*

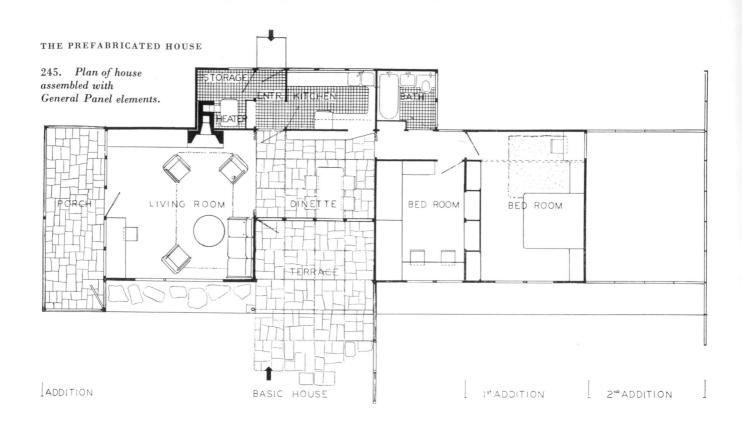

STORAGE ENTR. KITCHEN BATH HEATER

PORCH LIVING ROOM DINETTE BED ROOM BED ROOM

TERRACE

ADDITION BASIC HOUSE 1ST ADDITION 2ND ADDITION

246. *Isometric perspective of a General Panel house interior.
This house can grow and shrink, like the copper houses of 1931.*

THE DEVELOPMENT OF THE SLAB APARTMENT BLOCK

247. ELEVEN-STORY SLAB APARTMENT BLOCK, 1931: Model.

248. SLAB APARTMENT BLOCKS at Wannsee shore (Berlin), 1931:
*Steel skeleton, stuccoed brick walls. Fifteen blocks were planned for 660 families.
All apartments have an unobstructed view which can be blocked by no other building.*

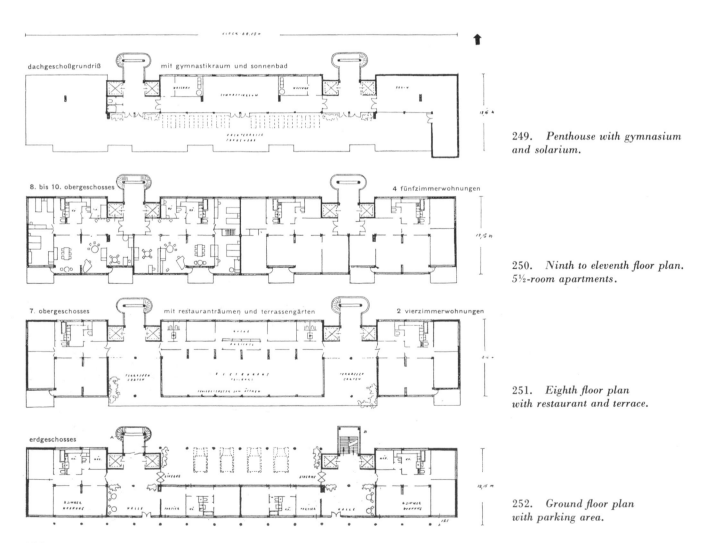

249. *Penthouse with gymnasium and solarium.*

250. *Ninth to eleventh floor plan. 5½-room apartments.*

251. *Eighth floor plan with restaurant and terrace.*

252. *Ground floor plan with parking area.*

253. *Site plan showing staggered position of apartment blocks with communal facilities located between them.*

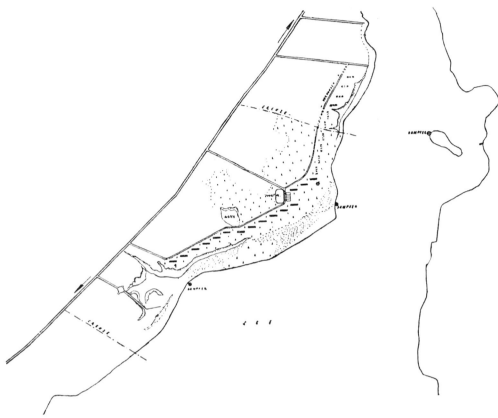

254. TWO DECADES LATER, 1953: "Hudson Terrace" apartment block, New York. Architect: Eli Rabineau. *Slab building with unrestricted view across Hudson River.*

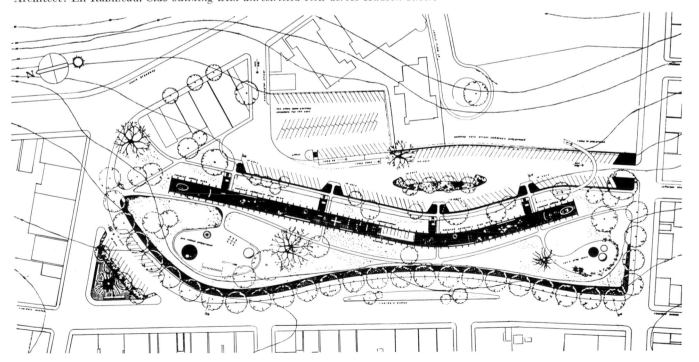

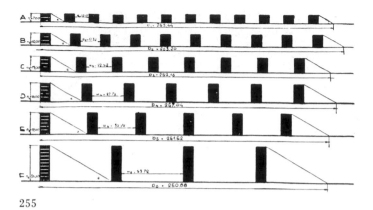

255

256

257

253

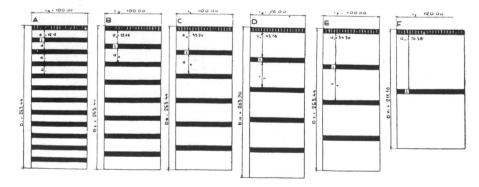

Diagrams illustrating the development of a rectangular building site with parallel rows of dwellings of different heights, from the one-story row houses to the ten-story apartment blocks.

On the same site, slablike, ten-story buildings result in much broader green spaces between buildings than the narrow spaces between walk-ups or row houses.

First example (Fig. 255 and 256):
If the size of the ground and the illumination angle (sun exposure) remain the same, the number of rooms increases with the number of stories.

Second example (Fig. 256):
If the illumination angle and the number of rooms remain the same, the size of the ground diminishes as the number of stories increases.

Third example (Fig. 257 and 258):
If the size of the ground and number of rooms remain the same, the illumination angle diminishes, the sun exposure improves.

259. ELEVEN STORY SLAB APARTMENT BLOCK, 1931: *Steel skeleton and stuccoed tile walls.*

260. Rows of eleven-story slab apartment blocks with intermediate green spaces.

205

261. *View of the park landscape of St. Leonard's Hill near Windsor Castle, England.*

262. APARTMENT BLOCKS, ST. LEONARD'S HILL, ENGLAND, 1935 (with Maxwell Fry): *Plot plan of two slab buildings in the same landscape.*

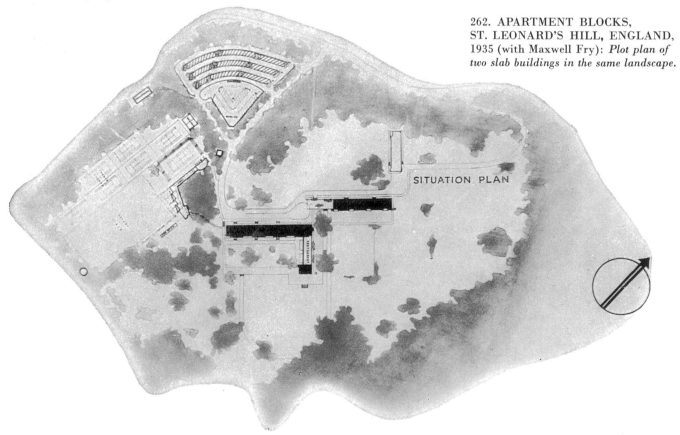

SITUATION PLAN

263.   APARTMENT BLOCKS, ST. LEONARD'S HILL, 1935:
Sketch showing their unrestricted view over the undisturbed park.

264. APARTMENT BLOCKS,
ST. LEONARD'S HILL, 1935:
View over the park from an apartment.

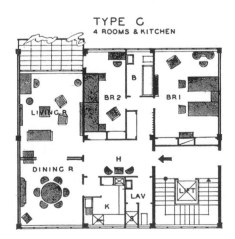

265. *Plan of two-bedroom apartment.*

266. BAUHAUS HOUSING, WEIMAR, 1922. Project.
Vegetable gardens were planned to supply food for the community.

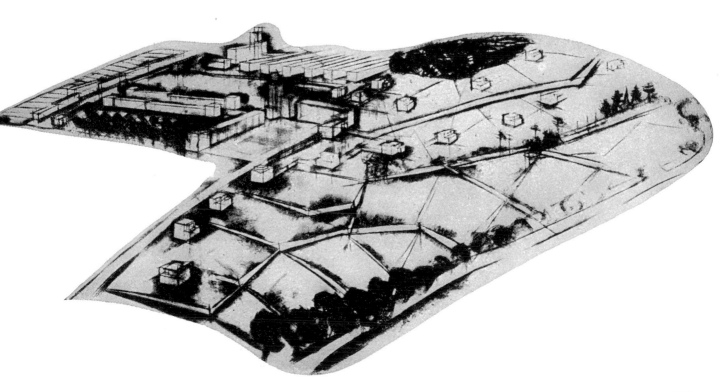

267.   TOERTEN HOUSING, (Dessau), 1926/27:
*Combination of row houses, cooperative stores and
five-story apartment blocks.*

270.   *Drawing of an articulated square
at a corner junction of row houses.*

268.   *Row houses.*

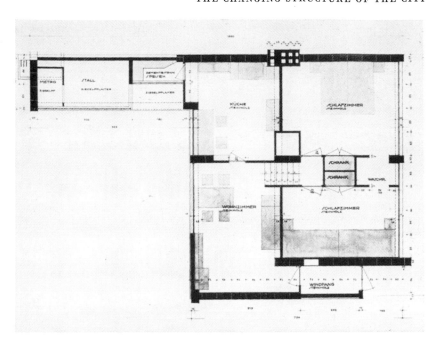

269. *Plan of single-family dwellings.*

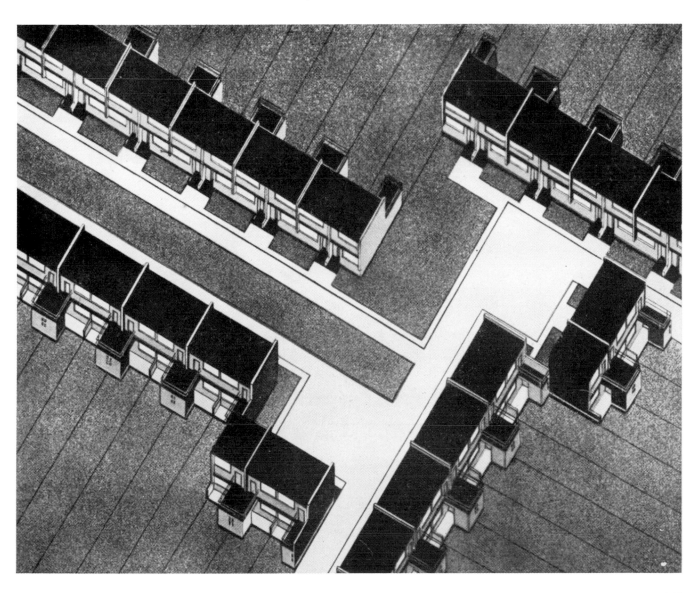

271. DAMMERSTOCK HOUSING
near Karlsruhe, 1927/28. (First prize
in national competition.)
*Gropius acted as a coordinator
for eight architects taking part
in the competition.*

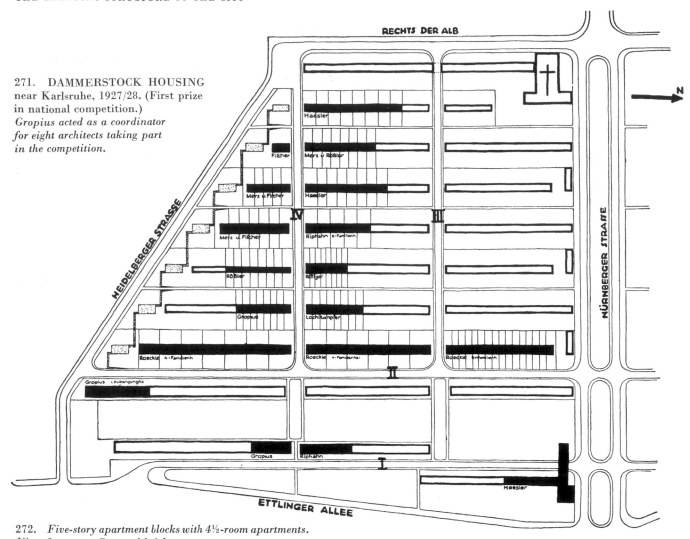

272. *Five-story apartment blocks with 4½-room apartments.
View from east. Stuccoed brick.*

273. *Four-story apartment block,*
outside corridor,
with 2½-room apartments.

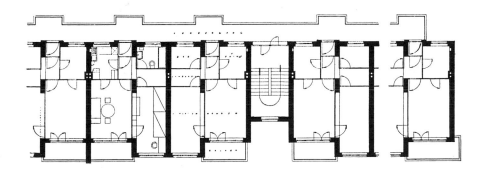

274. *Plan of four-story apartment block.*

275. *Five-story apartment block.*

276. DAMMERSTOCK HOUSING
(near Karlsruhe), 1927/28:
*3½-rooms single-family row houses.
Garden view.*

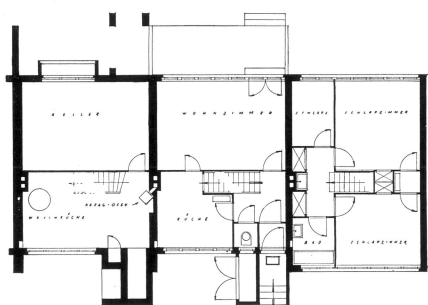

277. *Plan of basement, ground floor and
second floor.*

278. *Single-family row houses.
Entrance side.*

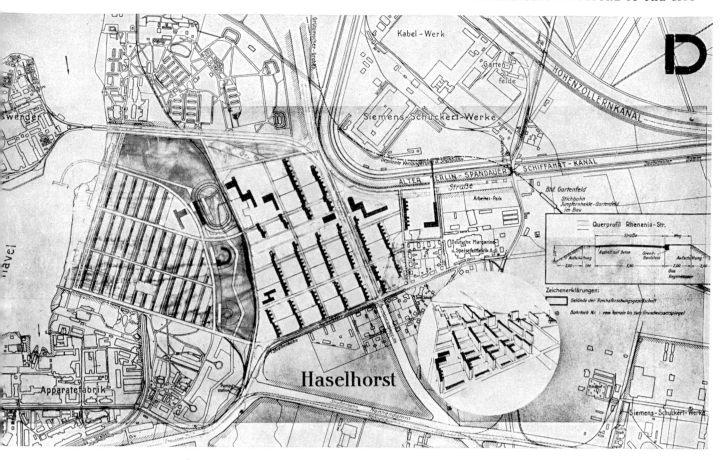

279. MODEL HOUSING, SPANDAU-HASELHORST (near Berlin),
of the Government Research Institute, 1929: Competition, first prize.
Site plan D; one of the four proposed solutions, using twelve-story slab blocks.

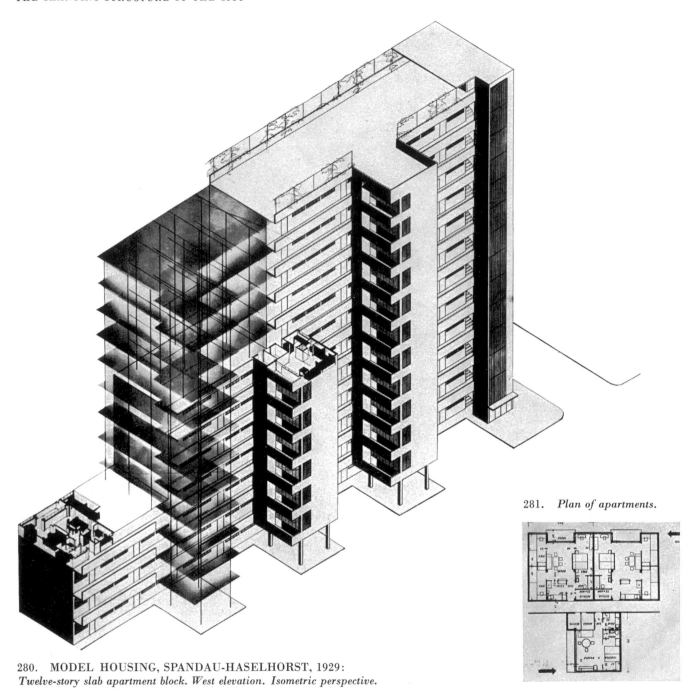

280. MODEL HOUSING, SPANDAU-HASELHORST, 1929:
Twelve-story slab apartment block. West elevation. Isometric perspective.

281. *Plan of apartments.*

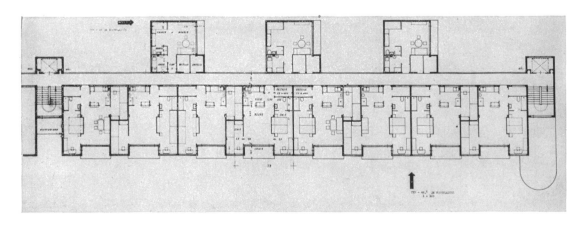

282. *Floor plan.*

283. MODEL HOUSING,
SPANDAU-HASELHORST, 1929:
*Three-story row houses with bachelor
quarters on upper floor
(two-story variation without
bachelor quarters).*

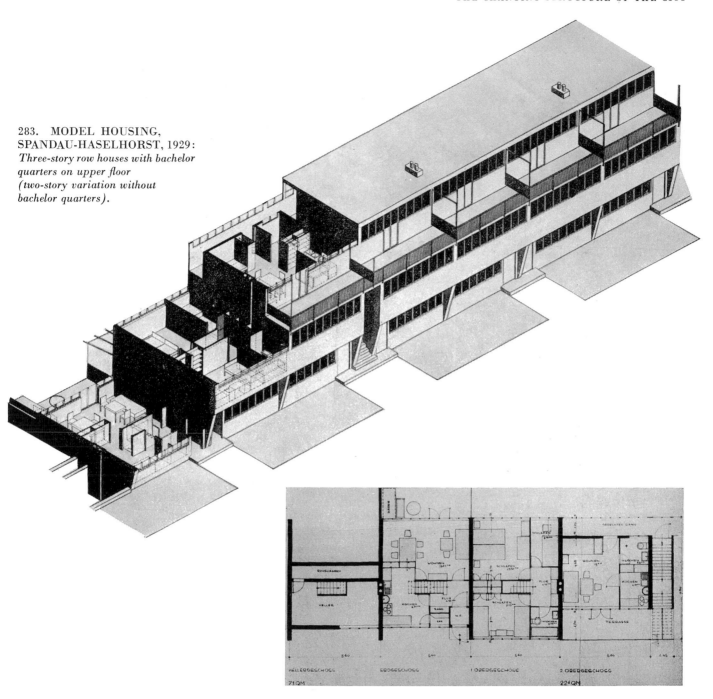

285. *Plan of the different stories.*

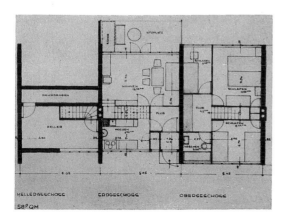

284. *Plan of two-story variation without bachelor quarters.*

286. HOUSING BERLIN-SIEMENSSTADT, 1929:
Four-story apartment blocks. Stuccoed brick.

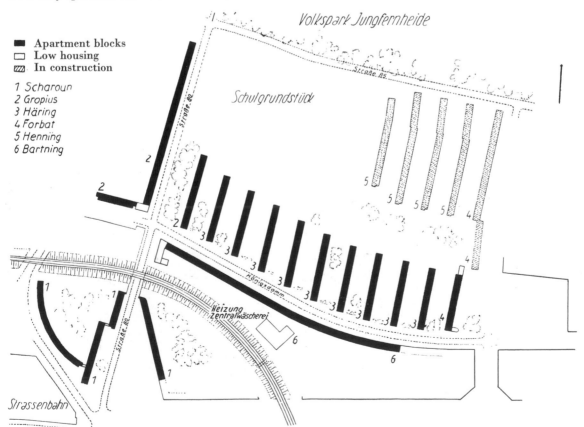

287. *Site plan indicating low housing, apartment blocks and the different architects involved.*

288.   BERLIN-SIEMENSSTADT HOUSING, 1929:
Four-story apartment block, outside corridor. South view.

289.   *Four-story apartment block, outside corridor. North view.*

290.   *Plan of 2½-room apartments.*

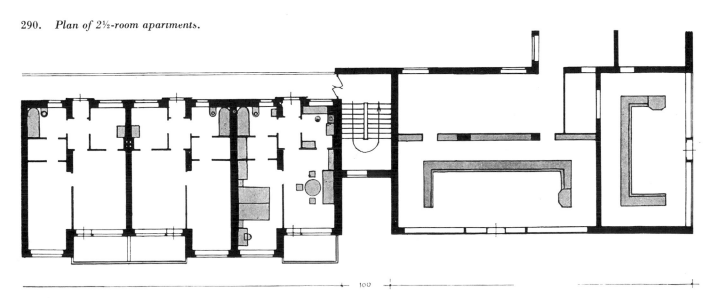

291. BERLIN-SIEMENSSTADT
HOUSING, 1929:
Four-story apartment block. Stuccoed brick.

292. *Plan of 3½-room apartments.*

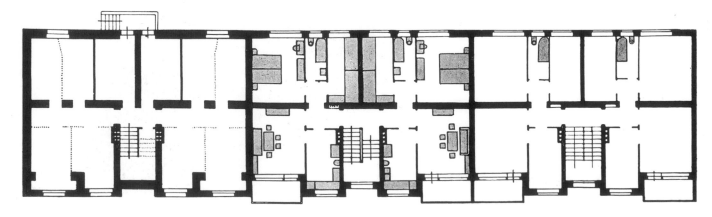

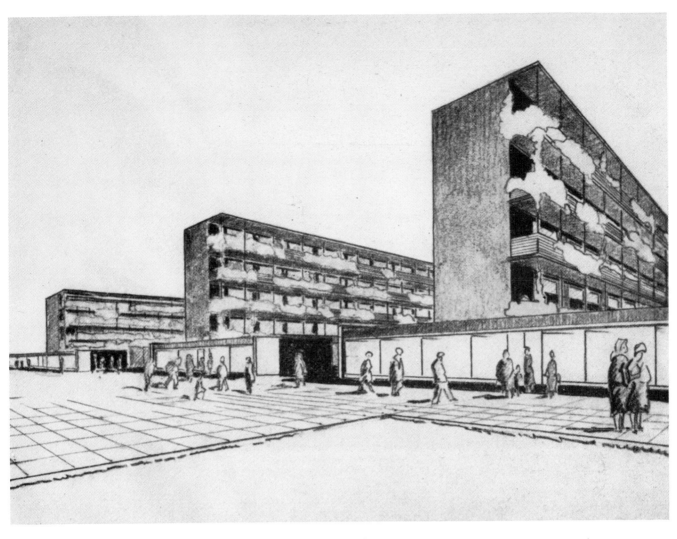

293.   LARGE HOUSING PROJECT NEAR BERLIN, 1929: Project. *Perspective sketch.*

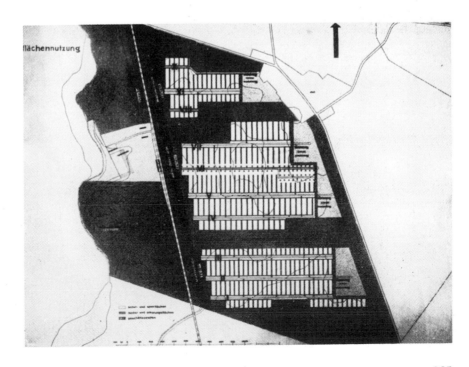

294.   *Site plan. Five thousand families in three neighbourhood units.*

295. LARGE HOUSING PROJECT NEAR BERLIN, 1929: *Perspective.*

296. *Traffic plan.*

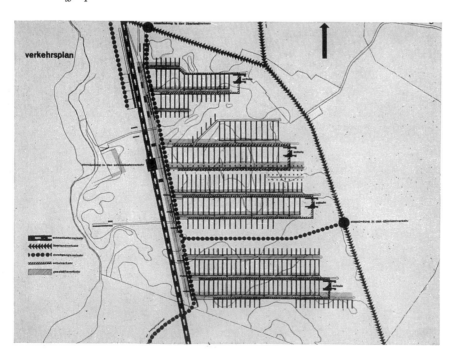

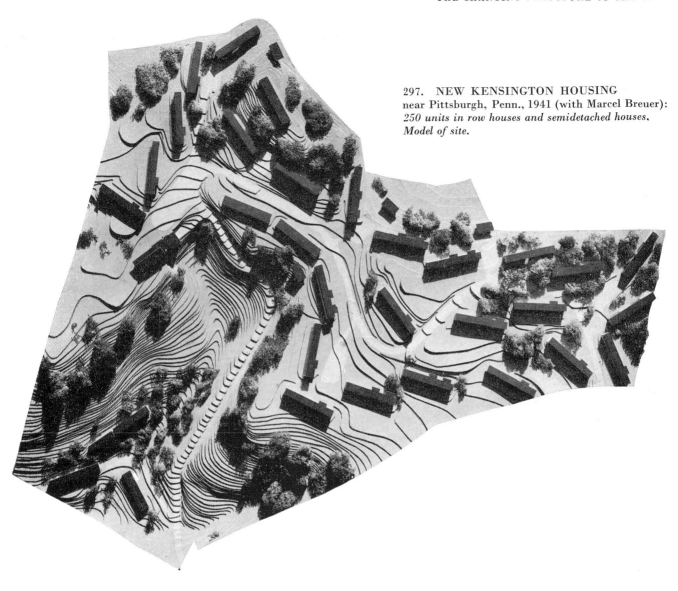

297. NEW KENSINGTON HOUSING
near Pittsburgh, Penn., 1941 (with Marcel Breuer):
250 units in row houses and semidetached houses.
Model of site.

298. *Row houses on hilly land.*

299. NEW KENSINGTON HOUSING, 1941:
*Row houses with six to eight units. Wood frame construction
with vertical oiled siding. End walls buff brick.
3½- and 4½-room apartments.*

300. *View of semi-detached house.*

301. *Row houses, rear view showing tool sheds.*

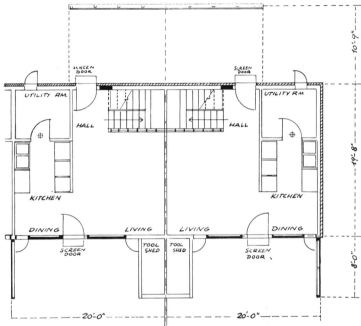

302. *Ground floor plan of living and kitchen areas.*

303. *Plan of upper floor with spacious bedrooms, built-in storage walls and bath.*

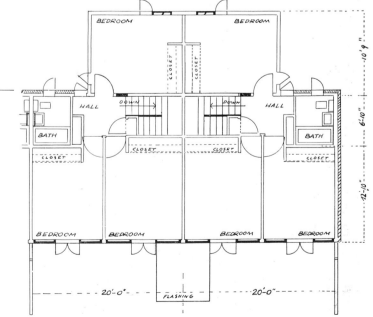

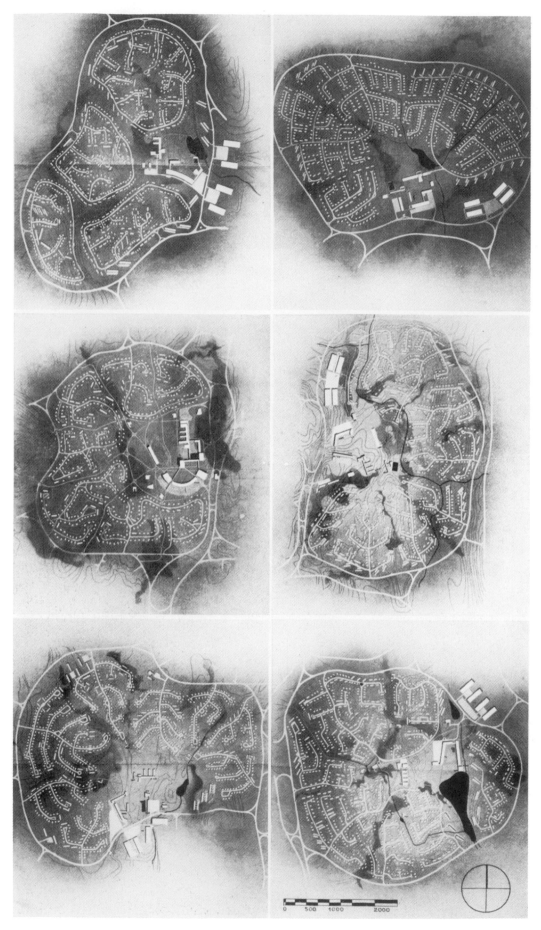

304–309. THE NEW STRUCTURE OF THE TOWN. Six townships for the vicinity of Concord (near Boston), Mass., 1942, prepared by students in the Departments of Architecture and Regional Planning, Harvard University, with Walter Gropius, Martin Wagner and John Harkness. *Each township is calculated for 5000 inhabitants. Traffic is insulated from neighborhood units by green belts.*

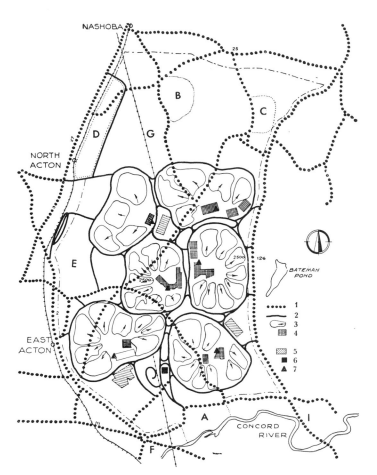

310. THE NEW STRUCTURE OF TOWN.
The six townships with traffic plan.

General plan of the town: 1. Existing roads: 2. Projected roads; 3. Single-family houses; 4. Public buildings; 5. Apartment Blocks; 6. Central administration; 7. Community services; A. Sewage disposal; B. Garbage dump; C. Cemetery; D. Warehousing; E. Railroad yard; F. and I. Access Roads for goods and services.

311. CIVIC CENTER, SUDBURY, Mass., 1951,
for a new town for 30,000 inhabitants. A project by students of the Masters' Class under the direction of Walter Gropius, Harvard University.
The vehicular traffic and parking have been arranged peripherally. The central plaza is reserved for the pedestrian. The Center contains a shopping center, cinema, office buildings and speciality shops, all of which are served from the peripheral road system or by subterranean access roads.

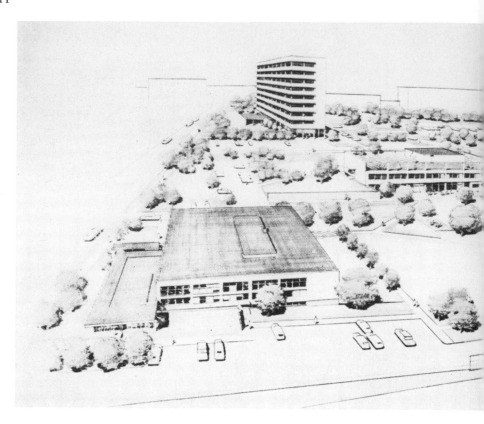

312. THE NEW CAMPUS OF THE MICHAEL REESE HOSPITAL, SOUTH CHICAGO. *The 1953 plans showed the following buildings: Extreme left, Serum Center, designed by A. Epstein and Sons, Inc., Chicago; Consulting Architects, Walter Gropius and The Architects' Collaborative. The low building in the center of the campus is a convalescent hospital, designed by Loebl, Schlossmann and Bennett, Chicago; Consulting Architects, Walter Gropius and The Architects' Collaborative. The high building on the right is a private pavilion with operation rooms, designed by Loehl, Schlossmann and Bennett, Chicago; Consulting Architects, Walter Gropius and The Architects' Collaborative.*

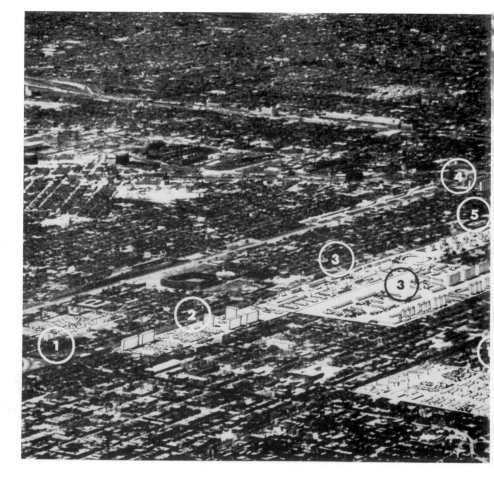

313. NEW PLANNING OF SOUTH CHICAGO. *Many groups have independently undertaken slum clearance and replanning in the South Chicago area. The most important are three private enterprises: the Michael Reese Hospital, whose planning extends over a large district, with apartment blocks and community facilities (figure 8); the expansion of the Illinois Institute of Technology (figure 3), the project of the New York Life Insurance Co. and other insurance companies with large apartment blocks and community building (figure 9). New planning of Chicago town authorities: 1 Wentworth Gardens; 2, 6 and 12 Public Housing; 4 Archer Courts; 5 Dearborn House; 7 Prairie Courts; 10 and 11 Ida B. Wells Homes.*

314.   THE BOSTON CENTER, 1953.
Projected by "Boston Center Architects"
(The Architects' Collaborative, Pietro Belluschi,
Walter F. Bogner, Carl Koch and Associates,
Hugh Stubbins, Jr.); Kenneth C. Welch,
Economic Consultant; Wilbur Smith,
Traffic Consultant.

315.   *Northeast view of projected Boston Center.*
The low building in the foreground is the shopping
center with department store on right. Behind the
shopping center are three office buildings of thirteen,
twelve and seven stories. Further to the right,
a forty-story office building behind a plaza.
On the extreme right, a hotel and motel.

316.   *1.–4. Office buildings; 5. Shopping center;* →
6. Department store; 7. Foodmarket;
8. Permanent exhibitions; 9. Hotel; 10. Motel;
11. Convention Hall; 12. Plaza.

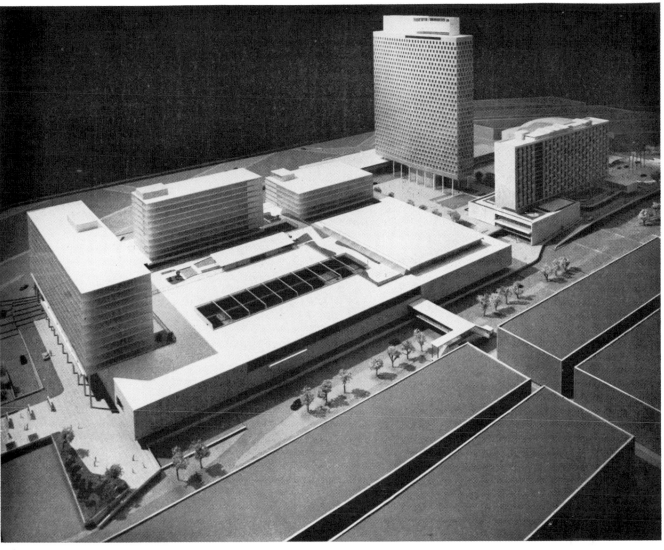

315

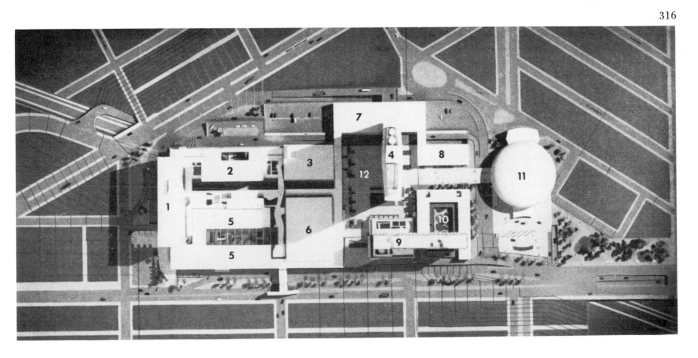

317. THE BOSTON CENTER, 1953.
Northwest view of model: in foreground hotel and motel. To the right, forty-story
office building. Convention hall entrance plaza, lower right hand corner.

234

Festival Theatre, New Rochelle, New York (Project) ☐ 1950

Medical Center, Mount Kisco, New York (Project) ☐ 1950

Lexington Park Building, Lexington, Massachusetts ☐ 1950

Residence Apthorp, Concord, Massachusetts ☐ 1950

Residence Hechinger, Washington, D.C. ☐ 1950

Residence England, Washington, D.C. ☐ 1950

Residence Napoli, Concord, Massachusetts ☐ ☐ 1950

Residence Barnes, Belmont, Massachusetts (Remodeling, project) ☐ 1950

Residence Payson, Portland, Maine (with Serge Chermayeff) ☐ 1950

New Hampshire University, Durham, New Hampshire Student Union Building, Competition, 2nd prize ☐ 1951

Trade School, Attleboro, Massachusetts ☐ 1951

Burncoat Junior and Senior High School, Worcester, Massachusetts. 30 classrooms, cafeteria, auditorium, gymnasium, special rooms, shops, etc. Associated with G. Adolph Johnson, Arch. ☐ 1951

Elementary School, Worcester, Massachusetts. 14 classrooms, library, gymnasium, cafeteria. Associated with Albert Roy, Arch. ☐ 1951

Amesbury Elementary and Junior High School, Amesbury, Massachusetts (Project) ☐ 1951

Costa Rica Mission (Survey) ☐ 1951

Housing Survey in the vicinity of San José, Costa Rica. In association with the Technical Cooperation Administration and Housing and Home Finance Agency ☐ 1951

Donnelly Office Remodeling, Boston, Massachusetts (Project) ☐ 1951

R.M. Bradley Twin House, (Project) ☐ 1951

Vischer Residential Furniture, West Indies ☐ 1951

Residence Pillsbury, Milton, Massachusetts ☐ 1951

Residence Vannah, Foxboro, Massachusetts ☐ 1951

Residence Stichweh, Hannover, Germany ☐ 1951

Five Fields, Lexington, Massachusetts, 20 residences, 6 Speculative Houses ☐ 1951–52

Lake Barcroft, Falls Church, Virginia, 3 residences ☐ 1951–52

American University Office Building, Washington, D.C. (Project) ☐ 1952

West Side Elementary School, Taunton, Massachusetts. 20 classrooms ☐ 1952

Two Elementary Schools, Warwick, Rhode Island. 13 classrooms each. Associated with Harkness and Geddes, Providence. Rhode Island ☐ 1952

Senior High School, Concord, New Hampshire. 32 classrooms ☐ 1952

Office Building for the American Association for Advancement in Science, Washington D.C. ☐ 1952

Hechinger Company Stores, Alexandria and Falls Church, Virginia ☐ 1952

Thonet Industries Inc., Furniture for Schools and Colleges (Design Research) ☐ 1952

Residence Caulfield, Washington, D.C. (Remodeling) ☐ 1952

Residence Cole, Cambridge, Massachusetts ☐ 1952

Residence Baruch, Newton, Massachusetts ☐ 1952

Residence Lang, Newton, Massachusetts ☐ 1952

Elementary School, Cambridge, Massachusetts. Associated with Carl Koch ☐ 1953

Elementary School, North Adams, Massachusetts. 32 classrooms ☐ 1953

Office Building for McCormick & Co., Inc., Chicago ☐ 1953

Building for Educational Television, National Education Association (Project) ☐ 1953

Wherry Housing, Quonset, Rhode Island. 350 units for the Navy ☐ 1953

Boston Back Bay Center, Boston Center Architects 1953

○ With Adolf Meyer
△ With Maxwell Fry
☐ With Marcel Breuer
☐ TAC/The Architects' Collaborative (Norman C. Fletcher, Jean B. Fletcher, Walter Gropius, John C. Harkness, Sarah P. Harkness, Robert S. McMillan, Louis A. McMillen, Benjamin C. Thompson).

ACKNOWLEDGEMENTS TO PHOTOGRAPHERS

BIBLIOGRAPHY

selected by Walter and Ise Gropius.

WALTER GROPIUS: BOOKS

Bauhaus Publications — 1922–25

Satzungen, Staatliches Bauhaus in Weimar: — 1922
I. Lehrordnung
II. Verwaltungsordnung
Anhang 1: Lehrkräfte und Plan der Lehrgebiete
» 2: Lehrgebiete der Werkstätten; Prüfungs-
ordnung
» 3: Verlag, Bühne
» 4: Küche, Siedlung

(with *L. Moholy-Nagy*)

Idee und Aufbau des Staatlichen Bauhauses, Weimar. *München, Bauhausverlag GmbH.*, 12 p. — 1923

Ein Versuchshaus des Bauhauses in Weimar. Herausgegeben von A. Meyer. 78 p. illustr. Beitrag von W. Gropius: Wohnhaus-Industrie. — 1923

Neue Arbeiten der Bauhauswerkstätten. 115 p. illustr. Beitrag von W. Gropius: Grundsätze der Bauhausproduktion. — 1925

Internationale Architektur. 111 p. illustr. — 1925
2. Ausgabe — 1927

Bauhausbauten Dessau. 221 p. illustr. — 1930

The new Architecture and the Bauhaus. Translated from the German by P. Morton Shand, with an introduction by Frank Pick. *London, Faber and Faber Ltd.* 80 p. plates. — 1935

The new Architecture and the Bauhaus. Translated from the German by P. Morton Shand, with a preface by Joseph Hudnut. *New York, Museum of Modern Art.* — 1936

Bauhaus 1919–1928; edited by Herbert Bayer, Walter Gropius, Ise Gropius. *New York, Museum of Modern Art;* 224 p. illustr. plans. See 2nd edition 1952. — 1938

Rebuilding our Communities (a lecture held in Chicago, February 23, 1945, under the joint auspices of the Institute of Design, the Chicago Association of Commerce and the Chicago Plan Commission), *Chicago, Paul Theobald.* 61 p. illustr. plans (ID book). — 1945

Architecture and Design in the Age of Science. *Spiral Press, New York.* — 1952

Bauhaus 1919–1928; edited by Herbert Bayer, Walter Gropius, Ise Gropius. *New York, Museum of Modern Art*, 1938. 224 p. illustr. plans. 2nd edition by *Ch. T. Branford Co., Boston, Mass.* — 1938, 1952

WALTER GROPIUS: ARTICLES IN BOOKS AND PERIODICALS

General

Sind beim Bau von Industriegebäuden künstlerische Gesichtspunkte mit praktischen und wirtschaftlichen vereinbar? *Verlag Poeschel und Trepte, Leipzig*, Nov. 1911. — 1911

Die Entwicklung moderner Industriebaukunst. Jahrbuch des Deutschen Werkbundes, 1913, p. 17–22, Abb. 18–20. — 1913

Der stilbildende Wert industrieller Bauformen. Jahrbuch des Deutschen Werkbundes, 1914, p. 29–32. — 1914

Ja-Stimmen des Arbeitsrats für Kunst, p. 26–29. — 1919

Baugeist oder Krämertum. Der Qualitätsmarkt, Leipzig, Jahrg. 2, Heft 1. — 1920

Baugeist der neuen Volksgemeinde. Glocke (Berlin), Vol. 10, p. 311, 1924. — 1924

Neue Bau-Gesinnung. Innendekoration (Darmstadt), Vol 36, p. 134, 1925. — 1925

Grundlinien für Neues Bauen. Bau- und Werkkunst, Wien, p. 13–47. — 1926

Geistige und technische Voraussetzung der neuen Baukunst. Umschau (Frankfurt a. M.), Vol. 31, p. 909. — 1927

Staffelung der Energien. Von der neuen Einstellung zur Arbeit. Innendekoration (Darmstadt), Vol. 39, p. 478. — 1928

Arquitectura Funcional. Arquitectura, Madrid, Heft 2. — 1931

Conferencia de Walter Gropius en la Residencia de Estudiantes de Madrid. Arquitectura, Vol. 13, p. 50–62, February. Ill. plans, perspectives, diagr. Lima, Perú. — 1931

Was erhoffen wir vom russ. Städtebau. Neues Rußland (Berlin), Vol. 8, Heft 6/7, p. 57–61. — 1931

Arquitectura funcional. Sur No. 3, Buenos Aires, Invierno. — 1931

Walter Gropius et la jeune école allemande. L'Architecture Vivante. 50 pl., 40 p. texte et plans, 1932, Paris, *Morancé.* — 1932

Formal and Technical Problems of Modern Architecture and Planning. Royal Institute of British Architects Journal, Ser. 3, Vol. 41, p. 679 ff. Transl. by P. M. Shand. — 1934

Bilanz des neuen Bauens. Technische Rundschau, Bern, Schweiz, Nov. 30, p. 1-3, 26-28, with illustrations. 1934

Background of the New Architecture. Civil Engineering, Vol. 7, p. 839–843, Dec. 1937

Education Toward Creative Design. Industrial Education Magazine (Peoria, Ill.), Vol. 40, p. 241–248, Nov. 1938

Living Architecture or International Style? Design, Vol. 47, p. 10–11, April. 1946

In search of a common denominator of design based on the biology of the human being. Princeton University. Bicentennial conference on planning man's physical environment, 1947. (Statements at the Conference) 1947, session VI. Princeton, N. J. 1947

Design Topics. Magazine of Art, Vol. 40, p. 298–304, December. 1947

Reconstruction: Germany. Task, No. 7/8, p. 35–36. 1948

Teaching the Arts of Design. College Art Journal, Vol. 7, no. 3, p. 160–164. 1948

In Search of a New Monumentality; a symposium. Gropius and others. Architectural Review, Vol. 104, p. 117–122, 127, September. 1948

In search of a common denominator. Building for Modern Man, T. H. Creighton, editor, Princeton University Press, p. 169–174.
Prefabrication: a Freedom from Limitations, p. 41–45. 1949

Not Gothic but Modern for our Colleges. New York Times Magazine, October 23, 1949, p. 16–18. 1949

Introduction. L. Moholy-Nagy, Experiment in Totality, by Sybil Moholy-Nagy, Harper & Brothers, New York. 1950

Design and Industry. One of three addresses at the Blackstone Hotel, Chicago, April 17, 1950, by Ludwig Mies van der Rohe, Serge Chermayeff and Walter Gropius on the occasion of the celebration of the addition of the Institute of Design to Illinois Institute of Technology. 14 p. 1950

Tradition and the Center. Harvard Alumni Bulletin, Vol. 53, p. 68–71, October 14. 1950

The Position of Architecture in the Century of Science. Architect and Building News, V. 200, p. 71–74, July 19. Lecture by Professor Gropius, arranged by the MARS group and held at the R. I. B. A. on 2nd July. Port., ext. of Grad. Center. 1951

Architecture in a Scientific Age. Listener, Vol. 46, p. 297–299, August 23. 1951

Not Gothic but Modern for our Colleges (Gropius awarded the Howard Myers memorial award for architectural writing, 1951). American Institute of Architects Journal, Vol. 17, p. 152–157, April. 1952

Gropius Appraises Today's Architect. Architectural Forum, Vol. 96, May, 1952, p. 111–112, 166, 170, 178, 182. Port. 1952

The Gropius Symposium held at the American Academy of Arts and Sciences, 28 Newbury St., Boston, Mass. Arts and Architecture, Vol. 69, May, 1952, p. 27–31, Ports. ill. 1952

Wie sollen wir bauen (Die Baukunst ist keine angewandte Archäologie). Die neue Zeitung, 16./17. Mai 1953. (Translation from «Not Gothic but Modern for our Colleges») 1953

Speech on the occasion of his seventieth birthday, celebrated at the Illinois Institute of Technology. Arts and Architecture, June. 1953

Bauhaus

Bauhaus. Vivos Voco, p. 11–16. 1924

Bauhauses, Grundziele des Staatlichen. Hilfe (Berlin), p. 226 1924

Idee und Aufbau des Staatlichen Bauhauses. Wohnkultur, p. 1–3. 1924

Grundsätze der Bauhausproduktion. Neue Erziehung (Berlin), Vol. 6, p. 656. 1925

Grundsätze der Bauhausproduktion. Vivos Voco, V, p. 265–267. 1926

Bauhaus in Dessau. Die Aufgabe. Velhagen und Klasings Monatshefte (Leipzig), Vol. 41, p. 86–90. 1926

Bauhaus-Heft. Sondernummer Offset-, Buch- und Werbekunst, Leipzig, No. 7, p. 356–410. Beitrag von Gropius, Breuer, Moholy-Nagy, Albers, Bayer, Stoelzl, Schlemmer; gesammelt von Moholy-Nagy. 1926

Education

Das Manifest der neuen Architektur. Stein, Holz, Eisen, Frankfurt am Main, August 5, 1926. 1926

Geistige und technische Grundlagen des Wohnhauses. Stein, Holz, Eisen, Frankfurt am Main, April 14, 1927. 1927

Architects in the Making. An exhibition by the Liverpool School of Architecture at the Building Centre... opening address. London. Typescript in the Royal Institute of British Architects Library. 1936

Art Education and State. Circle, p. 238–242. From the Yearbook of Education, 1936, Montagu House, London, W. C. 1, Faber and Faber Ltd. 1936

Education Toward Creative Design. American Architect, Vol. 150, p. 26–30, May. 1937

Essentials for Creative Design. Octagon, Vol. 9, p. 43–47, July. Address at the 69th Convention of the American Institute of Architects, Boston, June 2, 1937. 1937

Essentials for Architectural Education. PM, An Intimate Journal for Production Managers, etc., Vol. 4, No. 5, February-March, p. 3–16. Port., ill. 1938

Training the Architect. Twice a Year, No. 2, p. 142–151, Spring/Summer. 1939

Training the Architect for Contemporary Architecture. National Education Association, Dept. of Art Education Bulletin, Vol. 7, Record of the Convention at Atlantic City and Boston, 1941, p. 137–146. 1941

Practical Field Experience in Building to be an Integral Part of an Architect's Training. The Bay State Builder, July. 1945

Field Experience and the Making of an Architect. Excerpt. American Institute of Architects Journal, Vol. 4, p. 210–212, November. 1945

Frank letter to J. D. Leland. American Institute of Architects Journal, Vol. 7, p. 198–202, April. 1947

UNO and the Architects (comment by W. Gropius). Architect and Building News, Vol. 190, p. 232, June 20, 1947. 1947

Topics for the Discussion on Architectural Education. Metron, Nos. 33–34, p. 65–66. Un message de Walter Gropius au Congrès. 1949

Speech at the 36th Annual Convention of the Association of Collegiate Schools of Architecture. Association of Collegiate Schools of Architecture, Journal of Architectural Education, No. 6, Spring 1951, p. 78–87. Proceeding of the 36th annual convention. 1951

Architectural Education. In International Congress for Modern Architecture, Hoddesdon, England, 1951. CIAM 8, 1951 report of Hoddesdon conference, July 12, 6 p. mimeographed. — 1951

Blueprint for an Architect's Training. Kokusai Kentiku, Vol. XVIII, p. 61–67. — 1951

Letter to Mr. Kaukas on Architectural Education. Compass, London — 1952

Planning and Housing

Wie wollen wir in Zukunft bauen? Wohnungsfürsorge (Wien), Vol. 5, p. 152. — 1924

Wie wollen wir in Zukunft bauen? Wohnungswirtschaft. — 1924

Wie bauen wir billigere, bessere und schönere Wohnungen? Werkland (Vivos Voco, Leipzig), Vol. 4, p. 268, 1926. — 1926

Bauen und Wohnen. Baugilde (Berlin), Vol. 10, p. 1313. — 1928

Systematische Vorarbeit für rationellen Wohnungsbau. Bauwelt, Berlin, Heft 9, 1929. — 1929

Großsiedlungen. Zentralblatt der Bauverwaltung. Berlin, March 26, 1930. — 1930

Die soziologischen Grundlagen der Minimalwohnung für die städtische Industriebevölkerung. Die Justiz, Berlin, Heft 8, V. Bd., May. — 1930

Die Wohnung für das Existenzminimum. Internationale Kongresse für Neues Bauen (CIAM) und Städtisches Hochbauamt in Frankfurt am Main, 1930, p. 17–27. (Die soziologischen Grundlagen der Minimalwohnung für die städtische Industriebevölkerung).
do.; 3rd ed. *Stuttgart, Julius Hoffmann*, 1933, p. 13-23. — 1930

Flach-, Mittel- oder Hochbau? Neues Frankfurt (Frankfurt am Main), Nr. 2, p. 22–34, Februar. — 1931

Small House of Today. Architectural Forum, Vol. 54, p. 266–278, March. — 1931

Flach-, Mittel- oder Hochbau? Moderne Bauformen, Vol. 30, p. 321–328, July. — 1931

Die Wohnformen: Flach-, Mittel- oder Hochbau? Neues Berlin, p. 74–80. — 1931

Flach-, Mittel- oder Hochbau? International Congress for Modern Architecture (CIAM), 3d, Brussels, 1931. Rationelle Bebauungsweisen, *Stuttgart, Julius Hoffmann*, 1931, p. 26–47.
Karlsruhe. Dammerstock Housing, air view, p. 176–177.
Spandau-Haselhorst Housing, p. 186–187, plans, perspective, diagrams. — 1931

Flach-, Mittel- oder Hochbau? Schweizer Bauzeitung, Vol. 98, p. 95–101. — 1931

Wohnhochhäuser im Grünen. Eine großstädtische Wohnform der Zukunft. Zentralblatt der Bauverwaltung, Heft 49/50. — 1931

Wohnhochhäuser. Stein, Holz, Eisen (Frankfurt am Main), Vol. 45, p. 142. — 1931

Rehousing in Big Cities – Outwards or Upwards? Listener (London), Vol. 11, p. 814–816, May 16, 1934. — 1934

Minimum Dwellings and Tall Buildings. America can't have Housing, C. Aronovici, New York, Museum of Modern Art, p. 41–43. Diagrams. — 1934

Low, Medium or High Buildings? Housing Study Guild, editor. Abstract of papers... February. Ser. 1, No. 1, p. 3–7, with diagrams. — 1935

Verso un'Architettura vivente. Nuova Città, Vol. 1, No. 11–12, p. 48–52. Translated by V. Bini; from Amer. Arch., Jan., 1938. — 1938

Towards a Living Architecture. American Architect, Vol. 152, p. 21–22, January; p. 23–24, February. Portrait (January, p. 16). — 1938

Towards a Living Architecture. Kokusai Kentiku, Vol. 14, p. 105–107, December. Translated into Japanese. Port., ext. «A Way out of the Housing Confusion». — 1938

How to bring forth an ideal solution of the Defense Housing Problem. In collaboration with M. Wagner. U. S. Congress. 77th, 1st Session. House. Select committee investigating national defense migration. National Defense Migration, 1941, V. 17, p. 6949–6956. — 1941

Housing as a Townbuilding Problem. A postwar housing problem for the students of the Graduate School of Design, Harvard University, February-March, 60 p. mimeographed. — 1942

New Boston Center. A planning problem for the Harvard University's School of Design. Cambridge, Sept., 66 p. mimeographed. — 1942

Cities Renaissance. In collaboration with M. Wagner. Cambridge, The Authors. 15 p. mimeographed. — 1942

Conference on Urbanism, Cambridge, Mass., 1942. In collaboration with M. Wagner. The problem of the cities and towns; report, p. 95–116. The New City Pattern for the People and by the People. — 1942

Program for City Reconstruction. In collaboration with M. Wagner. Architectural Forum, Vol. 79, p. 75–86, July. — 1943

The Architect's Contribution to the Postwar Construction Program. Bay State Builder, Vol. 1, p. 27–30, 36–37, December. — 1943

Editorial on CIAM report at Bridgwater, England. Architects' Journal, Vol. 106, p. 246, 247, 248, Sept. 18, 1947. Port. — 1947

Urbanism. Architects' Journal, Vol. 106, Sept. 25, 1947 Lecture given at Bridgwater, England at International Congress for Modern Architecture. — 1947

Walter Gropius spricht über Städtebau. Excerpt from address before CIAM, Sept. 1947, Bridgwater, England, as reported by Eduard F. Sekler. Aufbau, Vol. 3, p. 83–84, April. — 1948

Organic Neighborhood Planning. Housing and Town and Country Planning. Bulletin U. N., No. 2, p. 2-5, April. Plans. — 1949

Faith in Planning «Planning, 1952», (Proceedings of the Annual National Planning Conference, held in Boston, Mass. Oct. 1952, American Society of Planning Officials, Chicago, Ill., p. 4–15. — 1952

Building methods and techniques

Glasbau. Die Bauzeitung, Mai. — 1926

Das flache Dach (Umfrage, veranstaltet von W. Gropius). Bauwelt (Berlin), Vol. 17, p. 162–168, 223–227, 361, 1926. — 1926

Spitzes und flaches Dach, Erwiderung auf O. Trinte. Bauwelt (Berlin), Vol. 17, p. 1038, 1926. — 1926

Normung und Wohnungsnot. Technik und Wirtschaft, Vol. 20, p. 7, 1927. — 1927

Wirtschaftlichkeit neuer Baumethoden. Bauamt und Gemeindebau (Hannover), p. 219. — 1927

Zum Streit um das flache Dach. Stein, Holz, Eisen (Frankfurt am Main), Vol. 41, p. 125, 129, 191. — 1927

Der Architekt als Organisator. Wohnungswirtschaft, 15. März 1928. — 1928

Der Architekt als Organisator der modernen Bauwirtschaft und seine Forderungen an die Industrie. F. Block, «Probleme des Bauens», *Potsdam, Müller & Kiepenheuer*, Vol. 1, Wohnbau, p. 202–214. Ill. — 1928

Der Architekt als Organisator der modernen Bauwirtschaft. Kreis (Hamburg), Vol. 4, p. 119–122, 1928. — 1928

Der Gedanke der Rationalisierung in der Bauwirtschaft. Reichsforschungsgesellschaft für Wirtschaftlichkeit im Bau- und Wohnungswesen. Technische Tagung in Berlin, 15–17 April, p. 14–26. — 1929

Der Gedanke der Rationalisierung in der Bauwirtschaft. Deutsche Kunst und Dekoration, Vol. 33, p. 231, 2 Abb., 1929. Technische Tagung, Berlin, Reichsforschungsgesellschaft für Wirtschaftlichkeit im Bau- und Wohnungswesen, *Beuth-Verlag, Berlin.* — 1929

Nichteisenmetall, der Baustoff der Zukunft. Metallwirtschaft (Berlin), Vol. 8, p. 88–91. — 1929

Stahlbau. Rundschau (Wien), Vol. 21, p. 60. — 1929

Byggnadsväsendets Rationalisiering. Stockholms Byggnadsförening, Okt. — 1931

Was erwartet der moderne Architekt von der Baustoffchemie? Zeitschrift für Angewandte Chemie (Berlin), Vol. 44, p. 765–768. — 1931

Was erwartet der moderne Architekt von der Baustoffchemie? Moderne Bauformen, Vol. 31, sup. 67–72, June. — 1932

The Role of Reinforced Concrete in the Development of Modern Construction. The Concrete Way, Nov./Dec., Vol. 7, No. 3, p. 119–133. Ill. — 1934

Prefabrication

Programm zur Gründung einer Allgemeinen Hausbaugesellschaft auf künstlerisch einheitlicher Grundlage mbH. (Ziel: Industrialisierung des Hausbaues). Manuskript. — 1910

Wohnhäuser (Prefabrikation). Berl. Tagblatt, Sept. 24 — 1924

Wege zur fabrikatorischen Hausherstellung (Haus 16 und 17) Bau und Wohnung; die Bauten der Weißenhofsiedlung in Stuttgart, errichtet 1927 nach Vorschlägen des deutschen Werkbundes im Auftrag der Stadt Stuttgart und im Rahmen der Werkbundausstellung «Die Wohnung»; herausgegeben vom Deutschen Werkbund. *Stuttgart, Wedekind & Co.*, p. 59–67. — 1927

Trockenbauweise. Baugilde (Berlin), Vol. 9, p. 1362. — 1927

Der große Baukasten. Neues Frankfurt (Frankfurt am Main), I/II, p. 25–30. — 1927/28

Siedlung in Stuttgart «Weißenhof». Reichsforschungsgesellschaft für Wirtschaftlichkeit im Wohnungsbau. Sonderheft 6, April, p. 104-106, 133, 136, 144, 147, 148. — 1929

Versuchssiedlung in Dessau. Reichsforschungsgesellschaft für Wirtschaftlichkeit im Wohnungsbau. Sonderheft 7, p. 1–136. — 1929

Kupferhaus. Bericht über das Kupferhaus der Hirsch Kupfer- und Messingwerke AG Finow (Mark). In Martin Wagner: «Das wachsende Haus», *Berlin, Bong & Co.* — 1932

General Panel System. Pencil Points, Vol. 24, p. 36–47, April. Ill., plans, diagrams. In collaboration with K. Wachsmann. Introduction by H. Herrey. — 1943

General Panel Corporation. (Prefabricated, demountable packaged building system.) New York. 3 pamphlets. In collaboration with K. Wachsmann. — 1944

General Panel Corporation. Arts and Architecture, Vol. 64, p. 28–37, November. House in Industry; a system for the manufacture of industrialized building elements by K. Wachsmann and W. Gropius for the General Panel Corporation. Ill., plan, diagram. — 1947

Progress in Housing (Prefabrication). New York Times, March 2, 1947. (Letters to the Times.) — 1947

Theater

Vom modernen Theaterbau, Berliner Tagblatt, 2. Nov. 1927. — 1927

Moderner Theaterbau unter Berücksichtigung des Piscator Theaterneubaus in Berlin. «Scene», Vol. 18, p. 4, 1928, Berlin. — 1928

Theaterbau. Reale Accademia d'Italia, Fondazione Alessandro Volta, Convegno di Lettere, Ottobre 1934, Roma, p. 154–177. — 1935

Le Théâtre total. L'Architecture d'aujourd'hui, Nr. 28, février, p. 12–13, (with English translation). — 1950

BOOKS ON THE WORK OF WALTER GROPIUS

Giedion, Sigfried. *Walter Gropius.* Paris: G. Crès & Cie, 1931. 15 p. 32 plates (Artistes nouveaux). — 1931

Argan, G. C. *Walter Gropius e La Bauhaus.* Torino, Italy: G. Einaudi. — 1951

Kurata, Chikatada. *Walter Gropius.* Tokio, Japan, 134 p. 100 plates. — 1953

REFERENCES TO THE WORK OF WALTER GROPIUS
IN BOOKS, PERIODICALS AND REPORTS

General

Behne, A. *Entwürfe und Bauten von W. Gropius*. Zentralblatt der Bauverwaltung, Vol. 42, p. 637–640. 1922

Wasmuth, Ernst. *Walter Gropius und Adolf Meyer, Bauten*. Berlin. 1923

Scheffauer, H. G. *The Work of Walter Gropius*. The Architectural Review. London, August, p. 50–54. 1924

Esprit Nouveau. *Développement de l'Esprit Architectural Moderne en Allemagne*. No 27, 6 pages, ill. 1924

Giedion, S. *Walter Gropius et l'Architecture en Allemagne*. Cahiers d'Art (Paris), Vol. 5, No. 2, p. 95–103. Ill. 1930

Platz, Gustav A. *Die Baukunst der neuesten Zeit*. Berlin. Ill., plans, p. 65, 78, 79, 81–83, 89, 90, 94, 118, 141, 178, 188, 368–374, 553, 578, 589, 600, 601. 1930

Pannagi, Ivo. *Walter Gropius*. Casabella (Milano), No 50, Ill. 1932

Hitchcock, H. R. *Modern Architecture*. New York: Museum of Modern Art, p. 156, 176, 183, 187ff., 193, 194, 195, 210, 219. 1932

Hitchcock, H. R. and Johnson, P. C. *International Style: Architecture since 1922*. New York: Museum of Modern Art, p. 141–147. 1932

Sartoris, A. *Gli Elementi dell'Architettura Funzionale*, p. 5, 13–15, 24, 27, 29–31, 36, 37, 39, 181–201, 501. 1932

Read, Herbert. *Art and Industry*. London: Faber and Faber, p. 32, 38–40, 101. 1934

Nelson, G. *Architects of Europe Today: Walter Gropius*. Pencil Points, Vol. 17, p. 422–432, August. Ill. drawings. 1936

Brock, H. I. *A Modernist scans our Skyline*. New York Times Magazine, April 11. 1937

Pevsner, Nikolaus. *Pioneers of the Modern Movement from William Morris to Walter Gropius*. New York: F. A. Stokes Co., p. 41–43, 179, 196, 197, 200, 202–206, 215, 216, 223, 229, 233. 1937
2nd ed. *Pioneers of Modern Design from William Morris to Walter Gropius*. New York: Museum of Modern Art, 1949, p. 18, 19, 113, 121, 129, 130, 131–135, 138.

Perkins, G. H. *Walter Gropius*. Shelter, April, Vol. 3, No. 2, p. 26–37, cover. With an introduction by H. R. Hitchcock. Ill. plan, complete list of works. 1938

The School of Design. Report of the President to the Board of Overseers, Harvard University, 1937/38, p. 24–25. 1937/38

Richards, J. Maude. *An Introduction to Modern Architecture*. Penguin Books Ltd., Harmondsworth, Middlesex, England, p. 69–73. 126 p., ill. plans. Revised ed. by J. M. Richards and E. B. Mock. New York: Penguin Books, 1947, p. 67–73. 1940

Giedion, Sigfried. *Space, Time and Architecture*. Harvard University Press, Cambridge, 1st–6th Edition p. 27, 84, 265, 266, 390–406, 560, 561. 1941

Sartoris, A. *Introduzione all'Architettura Moderna*. U. Hoepli, Milano, p. 26, 43, 62, 93, 96, 121, 161, 162, 167, 168, 190, 204, 299, 302. 1944

Zevi, Bruno. *Verso un'Architettura Organica*. Einaudi, Torino, Italy. 1945
Towards an Organic Architecture. Faber and Faber, London, p. 25, 26, 28, 30, 31, 32, 35, 49, 53, 54, 56, 57, 65, 71, 80, 104, 111, 115, 116, 119, 136, 137, 152, 153, 155, 161. 1950.

Dorner, Alexander. *The Way Beyond Art, the Work of Herbert Bayer*. Wittenborn, Schultz, Inc., New York, 245 p., ill. (Problems of Contemporary Art, No. 3) p. 123–125, 131, 202, 205. 1947

Hillebrecht, R. *Gespräch mit Gropius*. Baurundschau, Mai. 1948

Sartoris, A. *Encyclopédie de l'Architecture Nouvelle*. U. Hoepli, Milan, p. 9, 37, 46, 109. 1948

Architecture d'aujourd'hui, Vol. 20, Numéro spécial, Févr. 1950
Plan pour un enseignement de l'architecture, p. 69–75.
Haskell, D. *L'influence de Gropius en Amérique*, p. 45–47
Rudolph, P., sous la direction de W. Gropius. *Walter Gropius et son école*, p. 1–116.
Œuvres de Gropius et associés aux Etats Unis, p. 15–25.
Œuvres de W. Gropius et associés en Europe, p. 7–13.

Gropius in America. Harvard Alumni Bulletin, Vol. 53, October 14, p. 71-74, ill. 1950

Velarde, Hector. *Reminiscencias y Comentarios sobre Arquitectura Moderna*. El Arquitecto Peruano. Peru: Mayo-Junio. 1951

Kokusai Kentiku. Kurata, Chikatada. *Walter Gropius*, p. 2–9. *W. Gropius in America*, p. 14–60. Nosu, Yosiaki. *W. Gropius in Europe*, p. 68–77. 1951

Bush-Brown, A. *Cram and Gropius, Traditionalism and Progressivism*. New England Quarterly, March. 1952

Holford, William. *Gropius 1952*. The Architectural Review, July. 1952

Hoffmann, Hubert. *Walter Gropius 70 Jahre*. Werk und Zeit, Düsseldorf; May. 1953

Linder, Paul. *Homenaje a Walter Gropius*. El Arquitecto Peruano. Lima, Perú: Marzo-Abril, Nr. 188–189. (German translation added). 1953
Walter Gropius. El Comercio. Lima, Perú: May 17 (German translation added).

Schwarz, Rud. *Bilde Künstler, rede nicht*. Baukunst und Werkform, Heft 1, p. 9–24. 1953

Schwarz, Rud. *Debatte um Rudolf Schwarz*. Heft 2/3. Beiträge von: F. Meunier, H. Mäckler, H. Hoffmann, G. Remszhard, P. Klopfer, P. Röhl, L. Schoberth. (Beitrag von: Georg Muche in ,Werk und Zeit', April 1953.) 1953

Baukunst und Werkform. *Anmerkungen zur Zeit*. Heft 4, p. 163–165. 1953

Martin, J. L. *Walter Gropius, 70 Years*. The Architect's Yearbook, No. 5, London, p. 27–28. 1953

Weisman, Winston. *Group Practice*. The Architectural Review, September, London, p. 148–150. 1953

Kaufmann, Edgar, Jr. *What is modern interior design?* Museum of Modern Art, New York, p. 15–17, 24–25. 1953

The Back Bay Center. Forum, November, p. 103–115. 1953

L'Architecture d'Aujourd'hui, Dec. *Proposed Back Bay Center Development*, p. 4, 73–84 1953

Progressive Architecture, January, p. 73–84 1954

Giedion, Sigfried. *Space, Time and Architecture*. Cambridge, 10th Edition p. 27, 150, 341, 389, 391, 473, 509, 513, 543, 548, 549, 565, 604, 737, 738 1954

Bauhaus

De Fries, H. *Das Ende des Staatlichen Bauhauses.* Die 1925
Baugilde, Nr. 5, 7. Jahrgang.

Pevsner, N. *From William Morris to Walter Gropius.* Lis- 1949
tener (London), Vol. 41, p. 439–440, March 17. Ill.

Adler, Bruno. *The Bauhaus, 1919–1933.* Listener (Lon- 1949
don), Vol. 41, p. 485–486, March 24. Port., ill. of Bauhaus student work.

Martin, J. L. *The Bauhaus and its Influence.* Listener 1949
(London), Vol. 41, p. 527–529, March 31. Ill.

Taylor, Basil. *The Mission of an Art School.* The Listener, 1953
January 29, p. 172–174.

Bill, Max. *The Bauhaus Idea.* The Architect's Yearbook, 1953
No. 5, London, p. 29–32.

Shand, P. Morton. *The Bauhaus.* The Times Literary Sup- 1953
plement, London, May 29.

Baukunst und Werkform, Heft 1–4. Artikel v. R. Schwarz 1953
und Diskussionen.

Schools

Bauhaus Bauten, Dessau. Der Neubau, December 24, 1926
Heft 24, p. 277–282. Ill.

Bauhaus Bauten, Dessau. Cahiers d'Art, 9, p. 252–262. 1926

Ingenieurschule, Hagen. Zentralblatt der Bauverwal- 1929
tung, Heft 47.

School in Papworth, near Cambridge, England. Circle 1937
International Survey of Constructive Art, Faber and
Faber Ltd., p. 21, 22.

Wheaton College, Norton, Mass. Architectural Forum, 1938
August, Vol. 69, Ill.

Wheaton College, Norton, Mass. Pencil Points, Septem- 1938
ber, p. 144–149. Ill.

Village College, Impington, near Cambridge, England. 1939
Architectural Review, December, p. 227–234. Ill.

Harvard Graduate Center, Cambridge, Mass. Architecture 1950
d'aujourd'hui. Special Issue, February, p. 30–33. Ill.

Harvard Graduate Center, Cambridge, Mass. Architectu- 1950
ral Forum, December, p. 61–67. Ill.

Harvard Builds a Graduate Yard. Architectural Forum, 1950
Vol. 93, p. 61–71, December. Reprinted for Harvard
Foundation for Advanced Study and Research.

Centro per Universitari a Harvard di W. Gropius. Metron, 1951
Italy, Nr. 40, April.

Centre Universitaire. Architecture d'aujourd'hui, Nr. 38, 1951
Décembre, p. 41–48.

Harvard Graduate Center, Cambridge, Mass. Archi- 1951/52
tektur und Wohnform, Heft 2, p. 52–61. Ill.

Wohnviertel für Studenten der Harvard Universität. 1951/52
Architektur und Wohnform, Heft 2, 1952, Verlag
Alexander Koch, Stuttgart, p. 52–60.

Hua Tung Christian University, Shanghai. Interiors, 1952
Vol. III, January, p. 66–79. By the Architects' Collaborative and I. Ming Pei. Perspectives (part col.)
plans, sections.

Attleboro Jr. High School, Mass. Progressive Architec- 1952
ture, December, p. 63–76. Ill.

Harvard Graduate Center. Architect's Yearbook, No. 5, 1952
p. 146–151. Eleks Books Ltd., London.

Office Buildings

Die Faguswerke in Alfeld an der Leine. Der Industriebau. 1913

Die Eisenbauten auf der «Deutschen Werkbundausstel- 1914
lung» in Köln. Bautechnische Mitteilungen des Stahl-
werksverbandes, Düsseldorf, Nr. 1, Juni, p. 1–13.

Office Building and Machine Hall. Werkbund Exhibition, 1914
Cologne, Bautechnische Mitteilungen des Stahlwerks-
verbandes, July, p. 1–12. Ill.

Die Werkbundausstellung in Köln a. Rh. Jahrbuch des 1915
deutschen Werkbundes, Abb. p. 33–35, 49, 52, 54, 55,
99, 133, 138–141.

The International Competition for a New Administration 1922
Building for the Chicago Tribune. Chicago Tribune,
1922, copyright The Tribune Co., plate number 197, ill.

Municipal Employment Office, Dessau. Bauwelt, Heft 28, 1929
1929, ill.

Office Building for the «American Association for the Ad- 1953
vancement of Science». Progressive Architecture, Jan.,
p. 66 model and plan.

Office Building for the «American Association for the Ad- 1953
vancement of Science». Die neue Stadt, Nr. 3, p. 97–100.
Ill.

Planning and Housing

Bauhaussiedlung. Staatliches Bauhaus 1919–1923, Mün- 1923
chen: Bauhausverlag, p. 168. Ill.

Dernières Œuvres de Walter Gropius. Cahiers d'Art 1927
(Paris), Vol. 2, p. 118–120.

Großsiedlung bei Berlin. Wohnungswirtschaft, Heft 1929
10/11, Ill.

Großsiedlung bei Berlin. Soz. Bauwirtschaft, Heft 13, Ill. 1929

Siedlung Dammerstock bei Karlsruhe. Katalog der Aus- 1929
stellung Karlsruhe «Die Gebrauchswohnung». Ill.

Siedlung Dammerstock bei Karlsruhe. Zentralblatt der 1929
Bauverwaltung, November, Nr. 45, p. 725–731. Ill.

Siedlung Dammerstock bei Karlsruhe. Der Baumeister, 1929
Heft 2, p. 35–53. Ill.

Reichs-Wettbewerb für Versuchssiedlungen Spandau-Hasel- 1929
horst. Reichsforschungsgesellschaft für Wirtschaftlichkeit im Bau- und Wohnungswesen e. W. Sonderheft, No. 3, p. 24–34, February. Designed by Walter
Gropius and Stephan Fischer; with plans sections, diagrams, charts.

Spandau-Haselhorst, Berlin. Wettbewerb für die Reichs- 1929
forschungsgesellschaft. Zeitschrift für Bauwesen, April,
Heft 4, Ill.

Forschungssiedlung Spandau-Haselhorst. Zeitschrift für 1929
Bauwesen, Berlin, April, p. 79–89. Ill.

Siedlung Berlin-Siemensstadt. Bauwelt, Heft 46, 1930
p. 9–13. Ill.

Wohnhochhäuser am Wannsee, Berlin. Bauwelt, Heft 1931
35. Ill.

St. Leonard's Hill Apartment Hotel, near Windsor Castle, 1935
England. Cry Stop to Havoc; or, Preservation by Con-
centrated Development; scheme for a block of flats at
Windsor. Architectural Review, Vol. 77, May, p. 188–
192. Ill.

Recreation Center, Key West, Florida. Architectural Fo- 1942
rum, August, p. 83–85. Ill.

New Kensington Defense Housing, Pittsburgh, Pa. Archi- 1944
tectural Forum, July. Ill.

New Kensington Defense Housing, Pittsburgh, Pa. Architectural Review, London, September. Ill. — 1944

Michael Reese Hospital Development. A Hospital Plans: Seven Square Miles of Chicago Slums Schedules for Redevelopment. W. Gropius – Architectural Consultant. — 1946

Aluminum City, New Kensington. Journal of Housing, Self-Help Housing Issue, Oct., p. 330–332. — 1953

Theaters

Total Theater. Deutsches Reichspatent Nr. 470451, Klasse 37f., Dez. Ill. — 1928

Pannagi. *Teatro Totale.* Scenario, Nr. 6. Ill. — 1932

Halle, Stadthalle, Museum und Sportforum. Stein, Holz und Eisen, Woche 47, p. 832–838. Ill. — 1928

Theater Charkow. Bauwelt, Heft 35, p. 49–54. Ill. — 1931

Soviet Palace, Moscow. Die neue Stadt, Mai, Frankfurt am Main. Ill. — 1932

Single Family Houses

Platz, Gustav A. *Wohnräume der Gegenwart*, p. 54, 57–60, 75–78, 92, 94, 97, 173, 272, 316–318, 358, Tafel XII. Ill. — 1930

Gropius House, Lincoln, Mass. Architectural Forum, July, p. 28–31. Ill. — 1939

Gropius House, Lincoln, Mass. House and Garden, January. Ill. — 1949

Ford Residence. House Beautiful, December. Ill. — 1939

Ford, J. K. M. *The Modern House in America.* New York: Architectural Book Publishing Inc. Ill. — 1940

Chamberlain Residence, Wayland, Mass. Architectural Forum, Vol. 77, November, p. 76–77. Ill. — 1942

Frank Residence, Pittsburgh, Pa. Architectural Forum, Vol. 78, July, p. 160–170. Ill. — 1943

Abele Residence, Framingham, Mass. Architectural Forum, Vol. 78, p. 77–79. Ill. — 1943

Howlett Residence, Belmont, Mass. Architectural Forum, Vol. 107, May. Ill. — 1950

Kleines Wohnhaus in Hannover. Bauen und Wohnen, p. 450–452. — 1953

Prefabrication

Montage-Haus (Werkbund-Ausstellung Stuttgart). Deutscher Werkbund «Bau und Wohnung». Stuttgart: Verlag F. Wedekind & Co., p. 59–67. Ill. — 1927

Siedlung Dessau-Törten. Reichsforschungsgesellschaft, Mitteilungen Nr. 30, April, p. 17–21. — 1929

Wagner, M. *Copper House, Finnow, Germany* (Hirsch Kupfer- u. Messingwerke). Das wachsende Haus, p. 65–68. Ill. — 1932

Furniture

Werkbund-Ausstellung, Köln. Moderne Bauformen, W. Gropius: Möbel. Ill. — 1914

Anbaumöbel. Feder Katalog, Ausstellung Neues Wohnen. — 1930

Anbaumöbel (Serienmöbel – Unit Furniture). Form, Heft 2, Werkbundausstellung «Die Mietwohnung» Stuttgart. Ill. — 1931

Industrial Design

Schlafwagen. Jahrbuch des Deutschen Werkbundes, p. 133, Ill. — 1915

«Adler» (Carrosserie), Salon des Automobiles, Paris, octobre, 1930. «La Semaine à Paris», 10. octobre 1930. Ill. — 1930

«Adler» (Carrosserie), Salon des Automobiles, Paris, octobre, 1931. «La Semaine à Paris», 2 octobre, 1931. Ill. — 1931

«Adler» (Carrosserie). Club und Sport, Heft 9. — 1931

«Adler» (Carrosserie). Internationale Automobilausstellung, Berlin, März. Ill. — 1931

Exhibitions

Ausstellung Deutscher Werkbund, Paris. Bauwelt, Juni, p. 1–8. Ill. — 1930

Ausstellung Deutscher Werkbund, Paris. Die Form, Heft 11/12, Juni, p. 281–296. Ill. — 1930

Ausstellung Deutscher Werkbund, Paris. Der Cicerone, Heft 15/16, August, p. 429–434. Ill. — 1930

Exposition du Werkbund, Paris, Mobilier et Décoration, No 6, p. 270–275. Ill. — 1930

Deutsche Bauausstellung, Berlin. Soziale Bauwirtschaft, Heft 11/12, Juni, (Bauhüttenbewegung auf der Bauausstellung). Ill. — 1931

Deutsche Bauausstellung, Berlin. Innendekoration, Juli (Die Wohnung unserer Zeit). Ill. — 1931

Deutsche Bauausstellung, Berlin. Moderne Bauformen, Heft 7 (Die Wohnung unserer Zeit). Ill. — 1931

Ausstellung für Nichteisen-Metalle, Berlin, Circle international Survey of Constructive Art. London: Faber and Faber, Ltd., p. 19, 20. Ill. — 1937

Lohse, Richard. *Neue Ausstellungsgestaltung.* Zürich: Verlag für Architektur Erlenbach, p. 16, 17, 20, 52, 72, 142. — 1952

INDEX

47, 48, 65; – House Gropius, Lincoln, 71, 72.

Standardization, 18, 22, 50, 69, 74–78; – of component parts, 13, 74; – of houses, 50, 74.

Standardized units, 69, 75, 76.

Standards of performance, 45.

Steamship, 22.

Steel, 17, 23, 24, 46; – frame construction, 58, 67; – framework, light, 75; skeleton, 80, **187, 195, 202.**

Stevens Development Corporation of Cleveland, 89.

"De Stijl" Movement, 22, 70.

Stoelzl, Gunta, 28, 43, **108.**

Stove, Cast Iron, **106.**

Strawinsky, 31.

Streifenbau, 79, 83.

Structural nature of objects, 40.

Structure of the city, 13, 67, 79, 90, **226, 227;** – of the city, changing, 67, 79–83, –of the city, elements, 79–83; of the new city, looser, 80; – intellectual, 12; of reinforced concrete, 53; – of Universities, 12.

Stubbins, Hugh, Jr., **230.**

Studio-dormitory, 57.

Study for a city of 30,000 inhabitants, 13.

Sullivan, Louis, 68.

Superslums, 86.

Sweden, 43, 82.

Switzerland, 76.

Symbols, 84.

TAC, See Architects' Collaborative, The.

Taut, Bruno, 46, 47, 68.

Teachers, 35; – of architecture, 11, 89.

Teaching methods, Bauhaus, 11, 40.

Team, 14, 78.

Teamwork, 13, 30, 53; – of individuals, 14; – of the sections of the Bauhaus, 70.

Teapots, **110.**

Teatro Olympico (Palladio), 63.

Tecton Group, 82; see also Highpoint House.

Tessenow, Heinrich, 21.

Textile design, 35, 43.

Theater, 17, 48, 50; – at the Bauhaus, 30; –City, Jena, 35, 66, **152, 153;** – community, 65; – contemporary, 63, 66; – Design, Problems of Contemporary, 63, 65; – Greek, 62; – Hellerau, 21; illuminations, 50; – for Impington Village College, 56, 66; – in Kharkov, Project for a State, 64, 65, **158, 159;** light as an animating element in –, 64; – Limitless (Kiesler), 62; – Modern, 61–66, **151;** – of Renaissance and Ba-

roque, 61, 62; – total, 8, 50, 61, 62, 63, 64, **151, 154–157;** – Universal (Kiesler), 62; – van de Velde's with tripartite stage, 46; – Weimar, 31, 48.

Theatrical performances, Bauhaus Week 31; – space, 61.

Theatron, 62.

Thompson, Benjamin, C., 73, **243.**

Thonet, 50.

Thietze, Prof. Hans, 40.

Toerten Housing, 44, 70, 75, 86, 87, 88, **210, 211;** see Housing.

Torell, Eleanor, 89.

Total Theater, see Theater.

Tower apartments, 82.

Town with population limited to 30,000, 86, **226, 227;** – in the vicinity of Boston, 88; – planning, 11, 26, 79, 84; – – methods of, 85.

Townships, **226, 227;** see also Town, City.

Trade, free, 45.

Traffic System, 88.

Tragedies, Greek, 62.

Transparent staircase, 47, 48.

Transparency, 13, 48, 49, 55, 65.

Transport, 22.

Tray, Circular for Harvard Graduate Center, **106.**

Trellis, 71.

Triadic Ballet, 32, 33, 50, 66: see also Schlemmer, Oscar.

Tschudi, Hugo von, 20.

Tuberculosis Congress in Washington, International, 79.

Turntable, 64.

Tusschendiyken, Rotterdam, 79.

Typography, 29, 32, 43.

Tyrwhitt, Jaqueline, 2.

UNESCO, 1; – Building, Consulting Committee for, 14.

Unit, diversified residential, 85, 88; – furniture, **104;** – standardized component 74, 78.

Unité d'Habitation, Marseilles (Le Corbusier), 1947–52, 86.

United States, 2, 9, 12, 25, 43, 65, 76, 84, 89.

Universities, 16, 55; – American, 57; structure of, 12; – Caracas, Venezuela, 59; – Harvard, 11, 41, 89, **227;** – Hua Tung, 59, **138–140;** Yale, 41.

Urbanists, creative, 84.

Vaillat, 51.

Van Doesburg, Theo, 31, 70.

Van Eesteren, C., 70, 82.

Van de Velde, Henry, 20, 21, 25, 39, 45, 46, 63; – furniture, 20.

Van der Vlugt, 82.

Van Tijen, 82.

Vantongerloo, 52.

Villanueva, 59.

Vinci, Leonardo da, 41.

Wachsmann, Konrad, 76, **136, 137, 192, 193, 198.**

Wagenfeld, W., **108.**

Wagner, Martin, 86, 88.

Walk-ups, 80.

Wannsee, Slab Apartment Blocks on – shore, 81, 86; see also Slab Apartment Block.

Warchavchik, G., 1.

Washington, 12, 68, 79.

Way of life, new; see Exhibitions and new ways of life.

Weaving, 32, 43; – class, 42; see also Klee.

Week-end hotel for 10,000 people near Rio de Janeiro (Oscar Niemeyer), 82.

Weimar, 69, 75, 85; – Academy of Fine Arts, 39; see also Bauhaus; – period, 30, 31, 42.

Weise, Frank, 89.

Weissenhof Housing Project, Stuttgart, 1927, 21, 75, 81, 87, **195;** see also Housing.

Welch, Dr. Kenneth C., **230.**

Wells, H. G., 10.

Wells Coates, 10.

Werkbund, German, 21, 25, 46, 49, 51; Exhibition of the German, Cologne, 1914, 24, 46, 47, 48, 65, **94, 99–102;** – Exhibition, Paris, 1930, 49–52, **112– 114;** – Exhibition, Stuttgart, 1927, 75, 81; – Swiss, 36; – Yearbooks of the German, 22, 24.

Werkstätte, Viennese, 46.

Wheaton College Art Center, 1937, 12, 56, 57, **134, 135;** – Auditorium, 135.

Windsor Castle, **206;** see also Slab Apartment Block.

Woodcut by Feininger, see Feininger, 38.

Work, early, 20–24, **91–102.**

Workers, houses for agricultural, low-cost dwellings, Toerten, 70, **92.**

Working-class Apartment Houses, Tusschendiyken, 79.

Wright, Frank Lloyd, 47, 48, 67, 68; –, Johnson Wax Factory, Racine, U.S.A., 48.

Yale University, 41.

Yearbooks of the German Werkbund, see Werkbund.